Praise for

Storm in the Land of Rain

"A mesmerizing account of personal culpability told with brutal honesty, raw emotion, and meticulous recall. Foti's keen insight and elegant writing have the power to change the way we view family secrets and historic revisionism."

>   —**MARILYN E. KINGSTON,** former vice president of the International Network of Adult Children of Jewish Holocaust Survivors

"*Storm in the Land of Rain* is a remarkable true story about family and loyalty. Ms. Foti's exceptional courage in confronting a dark truth in the face of familial and nationalistic pressure is especially relevant in these turbulent times."

>   —**DAVE DAVIS,** former senior film executive at 20th Century Fox and Paramount Pictures

"Silvia Foti's book is an inspiring tale of civic courage, of a difficult struggle for historical truth. All the odds were stacked against her, but she bravely fought on, even though she found herself pitted against her family, her community, and practically an entire nation. A thrilling tale of personal redemption, I heartily recommend it."

>   —**EFRAIM ZUROFF,** Chief Nazi Hunter of the Simon Wiesenthal Center and director of the center's Israel office and Eastern European affairs

"*Storm in the Land of Rain* is a magnificent piece of investigative journalism. It reads as a fast-paced novel. I could not put this down."

>   —**STEVE LINDE,** former editor in chief of the *Jerusalem Post* and current editor in chief of the *Jerusalem Report*

"Silvia Foti has written a brave book at great personal cost that looks at how nationalism destroys historical truth, and personal truth as well."

   —**MICHAEL GOLDFARB,** host of the *First Rough Draft of History* podcast and author of *Emancipation: How Liberating Europe's Jews From the Ghetto Led to Revolution and Renaissance*

"I couldn't put this book down. *Storm in the Land of Rain* is part detective story, part family saga, part the morality tale we so desperately need to hear today, especially those of us unwilling to examine the past because it's emotionally easier to continue living in ignorance. It takes a courageous and deeply moral person to go to that frightening place: Silvia Foti is that person. She combines the research skills of a historian with the ethical concerns and instincts of the best investigative journalists to arrive at a very difficult truth, one that throughout her personally wrenching journey she does not want to believe. This is an important book: honest, brave, and superbly researched and written."

   —**DAIVA MARKELIS,** author *of White Field, Black Sheep: A Lithuanian-American Life* and professor emerita at Eastern Illinois University

"I think the book is a true revelation and a significant personal journey by a very brave, good person. What struck me the most is the complicity of silence by so many, including her mother and grandmother. The unanswered question is: Did her mother expect her to reveal the truth or continue with the cover-up? This book is much more than uncovering another 'Jew-killer.'"

   —**PATRICIA L. GLASER,** member of the board of governors for the Hebrew University of Jerusalem, a trial lawyer and chairwoman of her firm's litigation department who was described as a "Legal Legend" by the *Hollywood Reporter* and recognized by Lawdragon as one of the five hundred leading lawyers in America

"Silvia Foti grew up adoring the memory of her grandfather. Jonas Noreika was a national hero of Lithuania, a renowned resistance fighter who had battled both Nazis and Soviets and was executed for treason in 1947 in a Russian prison. Over time, his family had elevated him to near-saintly status, evoking his comforting presence at holidays and every family gathering. For decades, Silvia's mother had in fact devoted herself to gathering materials for what was to be a glowing paean to her father's memory. The book remained unwritten until, on her deathbed, she exacted a promise from Silvia to complete the work she had begun. The next 18 years of Silvia's life were consumed with fulfilling her promise, and would change her life irrevocably and in unexpected ways.

"As she embarked on her research, each answer seemed to yield a dozen more questions. Perhaps she wasn't asking the *right* questions? Perhaps her premise was not correct? But whispers of a dark side to Jonas began to arise. They were faint at first, and later harder to dispel. Cracks began to appear in her pristine portrait of Jonas. Doubts paralyzed her. What if he wasn't a perfect patriot after all? What if he wasn't the man that family lore had burnished to a brilliant sheen so long ago?

"In the end, Silvia's journalistic discipline won out over her cherished family history and love of Lithuania. She had discovered in herself a duty to the truth, no matter how painful. She had to find out definitively if Jonas Noreika, the Lithuanian hero, her beloved grandfather, was in fact a Nazi collaborator and responsible for the deaths of over fourteen thousand Jews in her ancestral home. While visiting a Holocaust site in Lithuania, she found herself unable to pray, but after accepting the reality of her grandfather's life, she instead wrote, 'I have no words. I do not know what to say. But I have come. Is it enough to bear witness? What else can I do? I cannot undo the past, or redress my grandfather's actions, but I am willing to face what was done. I am sorry, so sorry, for the unimaginable loss.'

"Silvia's search for the truth has finally ended. But her journey of atonement and giving witness has just begun."

—**NOEL M. IZON,** award-winning documentary filmmaker who has created some hundred programs for PBS, National Geographic, and the U.S. government and is best known for his film *An Untold Triumph* about Filipino American soldiers in World War II

"An amazing, moving, and meticulously researched work of far-reaching importance, particularly in our time when Holocaust denial is in the ascendant and the Shoah is being trivialized for political purposes. Foti's monumental work is a bulwark against Holocaust revisionism and demonstrates the uniqueness of the catastrophe that led to the decimation of Lithuanian Jewry."

—MARC ZELL, chairman of Republicans Overseas Israel and counsel in *Republic of Hungary v. Simon*, on the 2021 docket of the Supreme Court of the United States

"Every country has national heroes. For Lithuania these heroes are the partisans who defied two Soviet occupations at the start and the end of WWII. Many of these partisans lost their lives fighting for freedom, while their families were exiled to Siberia in desperate conditions for lengthy periods of incarceration. Silvia Foti had grown up in the shadow of the heroic stories of the struggle of her grandfather, Jonas Noreika, against the yoke of Soviet tyranny. Charged by the dying wish of her mother to author a memorial book about her grandfather, Foti set out on a journey of personal and national self-discovery, gradually learning that Noreika, while fighting the Soviets, had also been a convinced Nazi collaborator and had actively and willingly participated in the murder of thousands of his neighbors, the Jewish citizens of Lithuania. In thirty-six short chapters, *Storm in the Land of Rain* leads us through Foti's gradual exposure to the malicious actions of Noreika, and much to her own horror, her realization that she has been misled throughout her life, by both her own family and acquaintances of Noreika who were fully aware of his culpability in the Holocaust. Equally disturbing for Foti was the realization that Lithuania's continued national glorification of Noreika's heroism was an instrumental part of the obfuscation of the role and responsibility of some Lithuanians, including Noreika himself, in the events of the Holocaust. As Foti recognizes, anti-Soviet activism and Lithuanian patriotism cannot erase crimes of genocide. By continuing to celebrate some of the perpetrators as national heroes Lithuania actually sullies those who genuinely fought Soviet domination and the many righteous Lithuanians who valiantly attempted to save their neighbors from the murderous clutches of murderers such as Noreika. This is a brave book, for the easiest solution for Silvia Foti would have been to simply step away, and who could blame her? But, instead of letting it go, Foti describes the journey and brings honor to the true heroes of Lithuania."

—JON SELIGMAN, Director of External Relations and Archaeological Licensing for the Israel Antiquities Authority

"Silvia Foti has blown away the cobwebs of history to expose her own grandfather as a rabid antisemite, complicit in mass murder. This book should force Lithuanians to confront their self-serving mythology of resistance during World War II—a delusion which persists to this day."

—DINA GOLD, author of *Stolen Legacy: Nazi Theft and the Quest for Justice at Krausenstrasse 17/18, Berlin*

"In *Storm in the Land of Rain*, author Silvia Foti unravels her family's darkest secrets. In many ways this journalist's tale of intrigue, deception, and revelation reads more like a suspense novel than a Second World War documentary of her grandfather, Jonas Noreika, and his Nazi exploits directed against Lithuania's Jewish community. This detailed accounting of life in Eastern Europe, as Nazi and Soviet operatives seek to take advantage of nationalistic aspirations, antisemitic beliefs, and personal ambition, brings to light how 'villains' can be turned into heroes, even victims."

—DR. STEVEN WINDMUELLER, Rabbi Alfred Gottschalk Emeritus Professor of Jewish Communal Studies at the Jack H. Skirball Center of Hebrew Union College–Jewish Institute of Religion

"Silvia Foti's *Storm in the Land of Rain: A Mother's Dying Wish Becomes Her Daughter's Nightmare* is an anguished but honest book. Charged by her dying mother to write a biography of her adored, heroic, martyred grandfather, the patriotic Lithuanian leader Jonas Noreika, she comes to confront the truth of his wartime record and his role in the annihilation of Lithuanian Jews, two out of three of whom were murdered by Lithuanians, not Germans. Foti's research is meticulous, her writing is crisp, her journey searing, her quest for the truth uncompromising. This was not an easy book to write, but it is an essential book to read and it pulls back the curtain on Holocaust denial and self-exoneration in Lithuania and among Lithuanians who were told and retold a preferred narrative, which bears little resemblance to truth. One is left to wonder whether Lithuanian historians and the Lithuanian public are prepared to follow Foti's lead."

—**MICHAEL BERENBAUM,** professor of Jewish Studies and director of the Sigi Ziering Institute at the American Jewish University in Los Angeles, California

"In this meticulously researched and powerfully written book Silvia Foti unveils her search for the truth about her Lithuanian hero grandfather, General Jonas Noreika. What she discovers in the course of this coruscating personal journey are two profound evils. The first is that her iconic grandfather was a mass murderer. The second, even worse, is that the Lithuanian government, a member state of the EU and NATO, is deliberately whitewashing his crimes as part of their ongoing campaign of virulent Holocaust denial. Does the Holocaust matter anymore? This book is essential reading for anyone who believes that it does. Movingly, the book is dedicated to Lithuania, and rightly so."

—**MICHAEL KRETZMER,** producer and director of the documentary *The Lost Names of Birz*

"A phenomenal and haunting account of a nation trapped in the inferno of WWII, of the trauma and triumph of immigration, and of the search for truth and meaning beneath whitewash and lies that families and nations plaster over their past. Silvia Foti's story is both thriller and memoir. It's especially timely today, with antisemitism, including Holocaust denial, on the rise and media misinformation threatening the very concept of truth. A must-read."

—**LEV GOLINKIN,** author of *A Backpack, a Bear, and Eight Crates of Vodka*

Storm in the Land of Rain

STORM *in the* LAND *of* RAIN

A Mother's Dying Wish Becomes
Her Daughter's Nightmare

SILVIA FOTI

REGNERY
HISTORY
Washington, D.C.

Regnery History™ is a trademark of Salem Communications Holding Corporation
Regnery® is a registered trademark and its colophon is a trademark of Salem Communications Holding Corporation

ISBN: 978-1-68451-302-4

Originally published in hardcover with the title *The Nazi's Granddaughter*

Published in the United States by
Regnery History, an Imprint of
Regnery Publishing
A Division of Salem Media Group
Washington, D.C.
www.RegneryHistory.com

Manufactured in the United States of America

10 9 8 7 6 5 4 3 2 1

Books are available in quantity for promotional or premium use.
For information on discounts and terms, please visit our website:
www.Regnery.com.

To Lietuva, Land of Rain

God once said that when it rains it means He's crying over somebody. If a country calls itself Land of Rain it means God is crying over everybody.

—Močiutė

CONTENTS

Preface to the Lithuanian Edition

I promised my mother on her deathbed to write this book about her famous father, Jonas Noreika. If you are reading it in Lithuanian, I have surpassed my own expectations. I feared it would never appear in this country because emotions on this subject are still so raw, even more than eighty years later.

As I was working on this over the past twenty years, my father kept asking, Why does it have to be you? Why can't it be a historian? I answered, I don't know, Tėtė. All I know is that as his granddaughter, I'm in a position to tell this story in a way no one else can. Perhaps precisely because I am his granddaughter, the book will get more attention, and people can begin discussing what happened during the Holocaust in Lithuania more openly and deeply.

As a result, I have learned to embrace my role of being "just" his granddaughter. Unlike academics and historians, I am allowed to express my emotions and share my personal story. And so I do not shun my emotions in response to my grandfather's choices in participating in the country's cleansing of Jews. In fact, I explore them as deeply as possible—from denial, to depression, to bargaining, to anger, and finally to acceptance.

But I am also a journalist, trained in gathering facts and presenting them to the most powerful effect. I have included hundreds of footnotes taken from thousands of pages of documents written about Jonas Noreika and by Jonas

Noreika, about the Holocaust and World War II Lithuania. I have also inter-viewed family members and friends and colleagues who knew him, and I have drawn from my own conversations with my mother (his daughter), grand-mother (his wife), and Aunt Antanina (his sister).

As I struggled with this story, the journalist—a taskmaster driven to find-ing the truth no matter what—kept warring with the granddaughter—a scared little girl who wanted to protect her grandfather's and Lithuania's reputation. In the end, the journalist won.

But then my training as a journalist wasn't enough to do this story justice. I needed to be able to write "creative nonfiction," which applies all the literary techniques of fiction—characterization, setting scenes, narrative arc, plot, irony, metaphor, suspense, and tension—to a real story so that the reader feels more involved, and so that the story seeps into the heart. So I went back to school and got a second writing degree. I knew this story had to stir the heart to shift a Lithuanian's consciousness of what really happened during the Holocaust.

As Jonas Noreika's granddaughter raised in the United States, I can assure you that today in a free country it is possible to discover a horrible truth about your relative. Of course, nobody wants to admit that their relative was involved in killing Jews, so instead they typically go into denial. If their relative hap-pened to fight against the Communists, they might create a grand heroic story of a freedom fighter that might mask the dark truth. I was on this path with my own family.

However, it is one thing when a family does this, and quite another when an entire country does this. It manifests as a national problem, not only in Lithuania, but in other Eastern European countries that have been subjugated by the Soviet Union. And so this story on Jonas Noreika, declared a national hero by the government of Lithuania, has become a lightning rod for Holo-caust distortion across the world. If a Holocaust that took place more than half a century ago can be so distorted here, in Europe, what chance does the truth about genocides occurring today in Africa or the Middle East have?

When I started this story, I had no idea how much international attention it would get. Shortly after my story went public, the accusations from Lithu-anians started rolling in—that I work for the Russians, that I am a KGB agent, that I am an enemy of the state. It is true that Russian media were calling me, asking for interviews, promising an audience of millions, but I refused to talk to them. I didn't want them to use this story for their own propaganda. What I hoped for was that Lithuanians would own up to what had happened during the Holocaust of their own accord because it is the right thing to do. I hoped Lithuanians would accept responsibility for their own role in murdering Jews without any "help" from the Russians.

I grew up in Chicago as a patriotic Lithuanian, raised with the fervent idea that it is my sacred duty to help Lithuania in any way I can. To me, searching for the truth of what happened here during the Holocaust, no matter how painful, how embarrassing, how shameful, is patriotic. I dedicated this book to Lithuania out of love for this country. It is better to face the past in all its horror than to live a fairy-tale version of what happened. If we don't face the truth, we can never hope to be authentic, and we might repeat the past.

Many Lithuanians have asked me why I didn't focus more on the Soviet occupation. Why is it always about the Holocaust? Why do Jews have to get all the press? These questions miss the point, but reveal the pervasive victimhood mentality of Lithuanians. That is our identity—crushed by the Communists and the Nazis, and somehow still rising through the ashes. Every Lithuanian knows the repercussions of the Soviet Union's occupation. We grew up with that with our mother's milk, even in Chicago. That is not news. As a journalist, I'm trained to find what's new. The news is learning about Lithuanians' role in the Holocaust, and my hope is that this book will break open the discussion. This is a part of Lithuania's history that was hidden from me in Chicago and perhaps from you here in Lithuania, and I think the role my grandfather and other Lithuanians played in the Holocaust was left concealed, in part, because it was a convenient lie.

Even as I was sifting through my mother's archive, I noticed that nearly all of her material concerned the Communist occupations. There was almost nothing about the Nazi occupation. It's practically uncharted territory in Lithuania, and I anticipate that will change.

What struck me the most during my research is that there are two versions of what happened during the Holocaust—the Lithuanian version, which says it was all done by the Nazis, and the Jewish version, which says it was mostly done by the Lithuanians. How could the versions be so starkly different? In this book I tried to integrate the Lithuanian and Jewish versions into one account, which I believe is closer to the truth.

Although this book started as just a family story, anyone who reads it concludes quickly that Jonas Noreika stands for the spirit of Lithuania during World War II. He was part of all the major events—he led the five-day uprising against the Communists from Žemaitija in 1941, he was chairman of the Šiauliai District during the Nazi occupation from 1941 to 1943, he was sent to the Stutthof concentration camp from 1943 to 1945, he tried to lead a rebellion against the Communists in 1945 and 1946, he was captured by the KGB, and he was then imprisoned and tortured from 1946 to 1947 until his execution with two bullets.

His body was tossed in a mass grave, perhaps a form of poetic justice for a man who caused so many Jews to be tossed in muddy pits.

If you have decided to read this book, I leave you with a caution. Brace yourself. What you thought about the character of Lithuania might change profoundly, and it could be traumatic. It was for me. But at least you will not be alone, and the best thing to do is to discuss this as openly as possible. Today, for now, it's safe. You won't lose your life for talking and trying to understand the truth. At least that is what I tell myself every day.

I would like to thank Kitos Knygos, my bold Lithuanian publisher that took a courageous chance on this controversial book despite knowing the opposition it would face. Kitos Knygos is my hero, willing to defend the truth for Lithuania's psychological freedom from a big, fat lie.

Note: This preface, which originally appeared in the Lithuanian edition, has been edited for readers of the American paperback.

Long, Long, Long after the Beginning

Chicago 2019

My grandmother confessed that she fell in love with him because he looked like a Hollywood movie star—a swashbuckler battling the evil Communists who had subjugated and ravaged our tiny, proud country.

Over the years, she sang only his praises.

The details of his life that she crooned as I grew older only enhanced his image in my astounded eyes. He had been interrogated and beaten with a baton for two years in a crowded KGB prison. He had led a revolt against the Russians—not once, but twice. He had dared to clash with the mighty Germans, and for his impertinent insolence been sent to a concentration camp where the Nazis pounded him with their fists.

That story is all I knew for thirty-eight years. I had no hint of anything deranged about him.

So I was caught so implausibly uninformed that the shameful evidence flattened me. I had known nothing about his machinations in the genocide, nothing about his prowess in organizing the redistribution of the property of those marked for death with a yellow star, nothing about the sinister orders he signed to squash thousands of innocent civilians into a cheek-to-jowl-packed ghetto in advance of certain execution.

Apparently, and more surprisingly, neither did anyone else.

Or if they did know, they feigned ignorance. State-sanctioned ignorance, in my parents' homeland of Lithuania, where people wish I had done the same. My frank disclosure of my grandfather's deeds in a July 2018 *Salon* article—which led to front-page news stories in the *New York Times* and the *Chicago Tribune*—prompted not only cries of vindicated triumph from those who had been traumatized by the Holocaust, but also a clamor of outrage from Lithuanian patriots, who convinced themselves I must be a KGB agent working for Russia.

The Wroblewski Library in Vilnius, the site of the controversial plaque celebrating Jonas Noreika

The ensuing media explosion in Eastern Europe stirred an aspiring European Union Parliament candidate to swing a sledgehammer fourteen times against a bronze plaque commemorating my grandfather and to scatter its pieces all over the capital city of Vilnius.

Plaque attacks ensued. The local mayor glued my grandfather's plaque back together and defiantly displayed it again. Then, in an impressive political pirouette, he acquired a case of plaque remorse and impulsively removed the memorial in the middle of the night. The mayor's anti-plaque reaction

The original plaque honoring my grandfather, mounted on the exterior of the Wroblewski Library in 2000. It reads: "In This Building from 1945–1946 Worked a Noteworthy Resistor Lithuania's National Council and Lithuania's Armed Forces Organizer and Leader Jonas Noreika General Storm Shot February 26, 1947."

The new and improved plaque, hung in 2019. It reads: "In This Building from 1945–1946 Worked a Noteworthy Resistor, Stutthof Concentration Camp Prisoner, Lithuania's National Council and Lithuania's Armed Forces Organizer and Leader Jonas Noreika General Storm Shot February 26, 1947."

cued an incensed mob of patriots to pimp the plaque with a complete makeover and rehang it in broad daylight to the accompaniment of rousing folk music.

Plaque up: 3. Plaque down: 2.

It was flamboyant political opera.

Imagine Christopher Columbus's granddaughter revealing evidence that he had murdered indigenous peoples, publishing an article about his atrocities, calling for the removal of all his honors including the beloved national holiday, and causing a national scandal of daily press stories and protests in the United States. That is the equivalent of what has been happening in faraway Lithuania, where the real history of World War II has ambushed the newly nascent democracy with a vengeance.

My grandfather's plaque and the patriots who celebrate him may have polarized the Land of Rain like a Klan rally around a Confederate statue. But everybody can agree on at least one thing about him. My grandfather really did look like a Hollywood movie star.

PART I

DEATHBED PROMISE

Not Nearly as Long
after the Beginning

Chicago 1960s

The sacred Lithuanian warrior Vytis, depicted on our little country's coat of arms, occupied a big place of honor in our dining room. My mother had placed it there to ensure that his proud image would exert a constant influence upon our minds, if not upon our dinner table conversation. As a young girl, I gazed upon this white knight in full armor against a crimson ground and pondered the mystery of Vytis. He held his sword high, as if commanding me in his booming voice to love the old country forever, to never forget it, and always, always to fight for freedom.

My mother and grandmother had taught me all the magnificent legends of Vytis. His very name meant "the one who chases out our enemies." When I cried because I was scared of him, they shushed me. I didn't like hearing about how Vytis had hunted our encroachers in a bloody battle, killing and killing and killing. Nonetheless he entranced me, and I wanted to know everything about him: How he was thrown from his horse when our country fell under Russian, German, and Polish rule. (It remained subjugated for three hundred years.) And how on February 16, 1918—the most glorious day of our history—Vytis mounted his steed once again and led Lithuania to independence. My grandparents met and my parents were born during the twenty-two glorious years of liberty that followed.

3

Oh, how Vytis bewitched me! He conjured so many deep and mysterious feelings toward our hallowed homeland. Vee-TISS! I cried in agony about the Soviet Union's annexation of our land in June 1940. Vee-TISS! Vee-TISS! I wailed in horror at the story of the German invasion in 1941. I threw a tantrum of indignation when told how the Red Army reoccupied Lithuania and vanquished Vytis in 1944.

My mother and grandmother seemed like priestesses summoning Vytis as a lord luxuriating in a bloodbath as they wept over his gory sacrifice. I was horrified. And fascinated.

When I visited other Chicago families who had come from the fatherland, I noticed that they had hung their Vytis next to a crucifix. But my mother had positioned ours next to a photograph of her dashing father in his military uniform. Thus, in my mind—and perhaps in hers, too—Vytis became blended with my mother's father, Jonas Noreika. Although I had never known my grandfather, I had been taught to adore him as a hero who protected Lithuania. To me, it was Jonas Noreika riding that horse, brandishing that sword, bearing that shield, and dying valiantly as he battled our enemies.

CHAPTER ONE

A Daunting Legacy
Chicago 2000

B y some strange cosmic quirk, my mother and grandmother lay in the same hospital at the same time, both in danger of dying. Our family matriarchy threatened to collapse as I watched helplessly.

The schedule that I had arranged for my vigil allowed me to shuttle between their hospital rooms during those two harrowing weeks. Mom's room first.

Sitting at her bedside, holding her hand, rubbing it gently, I kept hearing in my mind the introduction to Beethoven's Fifth Symphony. The imaginary pianist pounded his chords—*dum!-da-da-dum!*—which sounded in my mind like jackhammers demolishing my life. Mom gripped the bed rail, causing it to rattle as she tried to pull herself up to a sitting position and failed, grimacing from bone-deep, soul-deep pain. She had been battling diabetes and debilitating back pain for years, had been admitted for routine tests and had somehow contracted a deadly infection. I tried to help her sit up, but she groaned in agony, shook her head, and wilted. She crashed back into the pillows, breathing violently.

Desperate to do something, anything—and still thinking I could fend off the inevitable—I asked, "Can I get you something?"

She graced me with a task. "Just a rubber band to pull back my hair," she whispered.

I took everything out of my purse—keys, wallet, pens—frantically searching for a rubber band. There had to be one in there. I found it and gently drew back her hair, which was damp with sweat and fear.

Then she complained of numbness in her left arm. "Maybe you can massage it?"

Welcoming the invitation to touch her, I slowly kneaded her arm, starting at her wrist and moving up to her elbow, as though working with clay. I desperately wanted to transform this shrunken wraith before me, this rag doll of her former self, to refashion her into the imperious opera diva who could belt out a high C.

"You know what this means, don't you?" she asked.

I continued massaging her arm. "What, Mom?"

"You have to write the book."

I studied her. "No, no, no, no. You're going to do it yourself."

She was past the denial that I was still clinging to. "You *have* to," she insisted. "Everybody expects it."

Still moving my hands up and down her arm, I looked out the window rather than at her pain-filled face. Outside on this end-of-January day, the temperature had plummeted below zero. The world had frozen. I wanted to sprint out of the room and run the way I used to, feet pounding the gravelly black track, sun scorching my shoulders, sweat dripping from my skin, feeling powerfully alive.

But Mom was waiting for me to answer. She had been working on a book about her father, the fabled hero, for as long as I could remember. She'd even earned a Ph.D. in literature five years ago in pursuit of improving her storytelling skills. I had always been in awe of this venture, observing all the sacrifices she'd made to collect material about my famous grandfather. I had waited eagerly for her to write his tale. Why she had never finished it, I didn't know. Now she expected me to chase the legend that she'd recounted to me all my life. I could see in her eyes that she was determined to impose her will.

No! You can't make me do this! My fingers caressed her hand, pleading. I didn't want her to die and leave me bereft. The book had been everything to her, a lifelong mission. I didn't want to think about why she was passing it on to me. Besides, I *couldn't* write the book. Despite being a journalist, I didn't believe I had the skills to write such a story. I had never attempted anything like it.

I heard her silent response: *It is your duty to continue where I left off.*

Obedient daughter that I was, I nodded, almost imperceptibly. And, almost imperceptibly, she acknowledged my promise. Then, smiling wanly with relief, she squeezed my hand with the last of her strength, sealing the contract. She closed her eyes and took a deep, satisfied breath. Soon her breathing became more even.

I unclasped my hand from hers and stood up to tend to the flowers sent by her friends—red roses mostly—that stood in vases on the windowsill facing the snow-blanketed park. Mom loved red roses. She had always had bunches thrown at her feet when she sang in the opera. I inhaled their fragrance. Noticing a dead one, I pulled it out, pricking my finger on a thorn.

As I gazed on my mother in her last hour of consciousness, wondering how I would fulfill this insane deathbed promise, I had no hint that our pact would rouse the dormant genocide genie in Lithuania, jolt the comatose country out of its stupor of guiltlessness, and force it into a reckoning that would scorch its conscience with lightning bolt after lightning bolt of blame. Sucking the drops of blood from my punctured finger, tasting their iron zip, I could not foresee the trajectory of my journey through the blood-sodden forests of Lithuania, or how my investigation would become linked with a court case against the country's great arbiter of history by a descendant of my grandfather's victims. This destiny of doom loomed far into the future; it would take twenty more years to reap. All I knew then was that my mother's impending death was much too much to bear, and my only guide was love.

My grandmother's room was two floors up, where she had been recovering from a heart attack. When I went to check on her, she was asleep. Wrenched by the twin disasters, I resumed my pacing of the hallways, dodging the nurses and convalescent patients with their portable IVs rolling along beside them. I wanted to pound my fists into the wall and leave two gaping holes.

The next day, Mom was unconscious, tangled in a web of tubes, her breathing a series of gurgles. I massaged her arm again, as she had requested the previous day. Her left hand, swollen like a water balloon, no longer responded to the pressure of my touch. *Squeeze.* Nothing. *Squeeze.* Nothing. Now, finally, I was forced to accept the fact that she wouldn't wake up—not for my father, not for my younger brother, and not for me.

I was thirty-eight years old with a husband and two children, and she had told me there was nothing more she could do for me. She'd been telling me what to do for so long that I'd learned to read her mind. She dominated mine. I felt as if I were an extension of her. She knew instinctively that she controlled me. Even now, her voice in my head counseled sternly, *Don't embarrass me or Lithuania by leaving your grandfather's story untold.* I was powerless to resist.

Her eyelids were open only a millimeter. I leaned over to search those tiny slits for someone I could recognize. There was nothing but a milky cloud hovering in the sky of eternity.

I needed comfort. I staggered out of my mother's room to go to my grandmother. Močiutė, as I had always called her, was recovering from her heart attack and would soon be sent home. When I entered her room, she was sitting up in bed, pillows stacked behind her, devouring a lunch of fried chicken and mashed potatoes oozing butter. The smell sickened me. The cooked white breast meat reminded me of rotting flesh. I couldn't imagine ever wanting to eat again.

"How's Dalytė?" she asked.

"Badly." I couldn't bring myself to describe the condition of her sixty-year-old daughter.

My grandmother dropped her fork onto her plate. It clattered loudly. She gazed out the window, her dulled blue eyes blinking at the relentlessly falling snow.

"Did she wake up yet?"

"No." That one word was all I could manage. I burst into tears.

She pushed away her food.

We gripped each other's hands, and in our unified sobs felt almost bonded into a single being. Eventually, not noticing that the nurse had taken away my grandmother's tray, or that the pink sun had set, we tried to compose ourselves. The room had gotten dark. I turned on the light.

"She asked me to write the book."

"What will you do?"

"I promised."

My grandmother covered her face and shook her head. She clearly did not approve of my mother's request. I took that to mean that Močiutė—unlike my mother—believed that I was inadequate to the task, that I couldn't possibly do the story justice.

Of course, she was right.

But I had no choice.

Vilnius
October 1, 2018

The Genocide Centre would like to call the court's attention to the fact that S. Foti, living in the United States, was not a participant in the historical events in question (she was not yet born), nor is she a professional historian. Her opinion about her grandfather is directly opposed to her mother's, J. Noreika's daughter. One can conclude from the published research of S. Foti that she is not familiar with the accepted methodology of historical research, such as that conducted by academic historians—which requires deep, critical analysis within a proper historical framework.

Vilnius Regional Administrative Court
File No. el-4215-281/2018
Response from the Genocide Resistance and Research [Centre] to the prosecution's claim against the Genocide Centre's refusal to change its historical conclusion on Jonas Noreika

CHAPTER TWO

Confronting the Shrine

Chicago 2000

S till dazed and enraged at her abrupt deterioration, I was ill-equipped to deal with the loss of my mother. I experienced it as desertion.

I was home, battling a headache from a rambling, anxiety-ridden, wine-filled night with my younger brother Ray, when he phoned at 6:00 a.m. to tell me that she had stopped breathing.

Rolling over in bed into my husband's arms, I wailed, "How could I have missed the moment?" My endless hours at the hospital seemed to have been an exercise in futility. I had planned to be there at the moment of her death, holding her hand and ushering her to the other side, but had failed.

When the phone had rung three hours earlier, it had been my father calling from the hospital to let me know that my mother had little time left. I had thanked him and said I would be right there. Why hadn't I rushed to the hospital then? I had tried to sit up, but my head felt leaden, as if it bore the weight of the world, and I had crashed back down, promising myself I would get up in five minutes. Instead, I had slept deeply for another three hours—and dreamt of a mudslide the size of a tsunami crashing through my parents' living room. The vivid dream vexed me not only for the rest of the day, but also for the next two decades as I labored on this book. What could it mean?

Thick brown muck flowed from the Marquette Park lagoon, oozing down Troy Street, gathering momentum, and advancing toward my parents' Chicago home.

It started as a thin trickle, then became a thick finger, then a rumbling stream, until it had gathered so much force that it rose like an angry tidal wave, submerging all the cars at the curb. Furiously, it mounted our front steps and crashed through the living room windows.

We were sitting around the glass cocktail table, drinking coffee that morning, and admiring a gray ceramic vase whose curled lips resembled rose petals.

We were startled by a rumbling, deafening sound like the roar of a freight train. As the mud hurtled through the window like a brown fist, we jumped from our seats to escape its punch. Mom and Dad looked shocked—whereas I had been expecting this.

"You see! I told you so!" I said.

Dad dove into his basement office to hide. Mom stood off to the side, trying to balance herself, knee-deep in mud that smelled like putrid fish. Just as the mud was about to reach me, I jumped into the hallway. Somehow, I was holding a mop in my right hand, a bucket in the left.

"What happened?" Mom asked, teetering in the muck.

"I don't know, but we'll have to clean it up."

"How? There's too much!"

When the sludge touched my ankles, oozing through my toes, it mysteriously came to rest. I felt a measure of relief.

"We can do it," I declared, having no idea where this false confidence came from.

Mom tried to extract one leg from the mire, then the other, but lurched and fell. Why? Why couldn't she help me? Did I have to clean everything myself?

Hour after hour, I filled the bucket with mud, which I hurled out the front door. I felt no fatigue, only a bulldozer's mechanical

resolve. The wind blew through the broken windows as I mopped.
Slowly, the mud receded, first by an inch, then a foot. The brown
goo retreated to the lagoon like a whimpering dog, leaving in its trail
a film of dirt and—oddly—soot. A rotten smell, as if the mud from
the lagoon had been laden with the stench of corpses, lingered.
　　By nightfall, the living room glistened.

I showered and downed a cup of coffee in the gloom of my kitchen, still trying to shake off that dream. Then I drove to my parents' house, about twenty minutes away, to discuss funeral arrangements with my brother and father. The front-door steps seemed to lead to a house of terror; it held a father, but no mother. In my dream, the mud had covered this entire street and these stairs before invading the living room. I didn't want to go in.

My brother arrived a few minutes later, and together we climbed those stairs. Ray was an engineer who, at our mother's urging, was pursuing a law degree—as our grandfather had done. Ray had been living in California for the last fifteen years, but had been flying frequently to Chicago on business, especially during this past year. Six inches taller than me, he had blond hair, blue eyes, and a black belt in karate.

"How are you?" he asked.

"Freaked out."

When Dad opened the door, he looked ashen. He was wearing the same black pants and shirt that he'd been wearing for days.

We stepped into the living room. Mom had decorated it, furnishing it with two chairs upholstered in gold velvet facing two wood-framed and elaborately carved loveseats. Paintings by exiled Lithuanian artists who were close friends of hers adorned the walls. She had particularly loved the Petras Petravičius woodcuts of old pagan rituals and the woodcuts of scenic farms by Magdalena Stankūnas. On the square glass table in the center of the room she had placed a gray petal-lipped vase by Maria Gaižūnas.

I recalled how, in my dream, the mud had swamped every crevice of this room.

As my father and brother sat down, I went to the kitchen to make coffee. Within a few minutes, I overheard arguing.

"She was so beautiful," Dad said. "I don't want to hide her beauty from everybody. We have to have an open coffin. She's too beautiful to cremate."

"What? Are you nuts?" my brother responded. "We have to follow Mom's wishes. She wanted to be cremated."

"I can override that," Dad retorted.

I was returning to the living room with our three coffees when I saw Ray stand up, looking like he was going to lunge at our father.

"There's no way I'll let you do that!" he shouted. "Mom's going to be cremated because that's what she wanted. I'll make sure of that. Do you understand?"

Dad—whom we called Tėtė—looked bewildered, like an overwhelmed little boy, then nodded and started to weep.

As Ray sat back down, he and I exchanged a look of relief. We were used to fighting about Mom's wishes with Tėtė. I handed out the mugs, and we busied ourselves with our coffee for a few moments. My chair was next to a small round table draped in a colorful shawl with a black fringe. The table held a Spanish-style lamp whose base was painted with swirls of gold-leafed flowers. Beside it, Mom had positioned a flamenco doll swishing her red dress. I hardly had any room to put down my cup of coffee.

"And the burial?" Tėtė asked.

"She wanted to be buried in Lithuania next to her father," I replied.

"It was always about her father," Tėtė said. "He's all she ever thought about."

"I know," I sighed.

"Maybe it's best that way," Tėtė said. "You know, we were talking about a divorce, at the end."

Ray and I exchanged glances. "We know," we said together.

We decided to have the wake and the funeral Mass in Chicago within the next few days, then to have the funeral home keep our mother's urn until we could go to Lithuania to bury her cremains.

"I've prepared the notice for the newspaper," Tėtė said, pulling out a slip of paper from his shirt pocket.

"When did you manage to write that?" I asked, bewildered, picturing him grieving yet dutifully hammering out the obituary at the typewriter keys after visiting Mom at the hospital.

"Last night. This morning I typed it." He proceeded to read it to us:

> Dalia Maria Kucenas died February 4, 2000, at 3 am at the age of 60. She lived in the Marquette Park neighborhood of Chicago. She was born in Kaunas.
>
> She is survived by her mother, Antanina Noreika; her husband, John Kucenas; her daughter, Silvia Foti; son-in law, Franco; son, Ray; daughter-in-law, Lori; grandchildren, Alessandra and Gabriel Foti, Andrew Kucenas; also her godmother and aunt, Antanina Misiun.
>
> Dalia was the daughter of Jonas Noreika, aka General Storm, a partisan leader.
>
> Dalia was a long-time soloist singer, and she participated in several Lithuanian theater productions. She was the Lithuanian Community's Cultural Council president and Korp! Giedra president. She was a member of the Lithuanian Foundation and other Lithuanian organizations. She received her PhD in Literature at the University of Illinois, Chicago.
>
> The wake is Sunday, February 6, from 3 pm to 8 pm at Marquette Park Funeral Home. The farewell greetings are at 6:30 pm.
>
> On Monday at 10 am, she will be in a funeral procession to Nativity BVM Church, and at 10:30 there will be a Mass for her soul. She will be buried in Lithuania. Please give your donations to the Lithuanian Foundation.

Welling up with emotion, I walked to the back of the house to the piano room, where my mother used to practice before performances. She had hung photographs of herself as Carmen, as Norma, and as Mimi from *La Boheme*. I would never hear her beautiful voice again. A primal howl rose up from the core of my being. I was so alone, so alone, without Mom. Even at thirty-eight years old, I felt like an orphaned child.

Shortly after her death, I returned to my old bedroom. Next to the piano room, it had become a repository of all Mom's research for her intended book. That project—writing my grandfather's story—had become for me a tangible connection to her, a means of bringing her back from the dead, a way for me to apologize for not having been with her at the moment of her death as I should have been.

In many ways, my old bedroom looked the same—the brick wall still a shiny fire-engine red, the wooden panels still gold and white, the floor still a little slanted down to the east. I looked out the window into my old backyard. Everything seemed so small, including my tiny childhood bedroom, where I had used a space heater to keep warm in the winter and a fan to keep cool in the summer, where I had written in a diary I named "Chris," where I had propped a pillow next to the wall and rocked myself back and forth, where I had sometimes cried myself to sleep.

My mother's research, memorabilia, and iconography filled three tall bookshelves. I pulled apart this shrine to her father, hauling it to my house piece by piece. Through all of that task her spirit was palpable. She appeared to me just as I wished, wearing her black stretch pants and her long-sleeved black turtleneck, her hands on her hips, tapping her right foot on the floor. She hovered as I sat there in my old bedroom and wondered where to start, looking around the room, engulfed by paper, books, letters, and folders about my grandfather. Both he and she continued to exert a presence.

The Cross of the Vytis, Lithuania's coat of arms, was displayed prominently—in the center of the largest bookshelf, which had been arranged like an altar. Mom had received this medal, the highest Lithuanian honor anyone could receive posthumously, from President Algirdas Brazauskas in 1997, for her father fifty years after his execution. I reached for it and held it in my palm, feeling the ribbon and the heft of the bronze medallion, almost sensing it pulse.

Next to the Cross of the Vytis, Mom had set the Order of the Great Duke Gediminas, given to her for her tremendous service to the country.

She had volunteered tirelessly—given fundraising concerts, written to newspapers, mentored younger artists—all for her devotion to freedom. On the top shelf, she kept her father's prayer book, the one he had used in the KGB prison. I sniffed its musty pages. So fragile, like a sick bird, it seemed about to crumble.

I felt overwhelmed with responsibility. Worse, my faith was rattled. I didn't understand God. He had allowed my grandfather to be executed by the Communists. He'd permitted Mom to die before she could fulfill her yearning to write her father's story. And he'd left this towering task to me.

I sorted through the jumble of relics and began to sift through the mass of documents: three thousand pages of transcripts from the KGB prison where my grandfather had been tortured and executed, seventy-seven letters written to my grandmother from a Nazi concentration camp, a fairy tale he'd penned for my mother when she was a young child, letters from relatives describing him, hundreds of newspaper clippings lauding his heroics, and nearly twenty photograph albums. Yet there was clearly so much more that I still needed to research.

I spoke to Mom in my mind and believed I could smell her floral perfume lingering in the air, caught at the back of my throat. *Mom, it's going to take a miracle to get this work done. Where am I supposed to start?* Silence. Maybe I was praying too. I felt like I was drowning in cement boots.

I could conjure her so easily because her presence clung to me like a silk scarf alive with electrostatic sparks. Her shadow standing in front of me seemed to whisper, *Then finish what I could not. Remember: you promised!*

The sheer volume of the material she had amassed made the challenge seem all but insurmountable. I knew almost nothing about Jonas Noreika. It was my mother who had known him. She was the one who was supposed to have written the book. Everything was secondhand to me, merely stories I'd been told of how he died a martyr in a KGB prison for leading a rebellion against the Communists. He had died fourteen years before I was born. Who exactly had my grandfather been?

Vilnius
October 1, 2018

In the file under review, the case originated over a dispute between the petitioner's [Grant Gochin's] and the [Genocide] Centre's assessment of J. Noreika's (General Storm's) activities in Nazi-occupied Lithuania. The petitioner demands that the Centre officially recognize that J. Noreika was directly responsible for the deaths of 1,800 Jews in Plungė and 800 Jews in Telšiai (which occurred July 12–13, 1941, and July 20–21, 1941). The Centre, however, has based its assessment on existing historical sources, and has therefore concluded that J. Noreika was not involved in the Jewish mass destruction operations in the counties of Telšiai or Šiauliai.

Vilnius Regional Administrative Court

File No. el-4215-281/2018

Response from the Genocide Resistance and Research Centre to the prosecution's claim against the Genocide Centre's refusal to change its historical conclusion on Jonas Noreika

CHAPTER THREE

The Imprisonment and Trial of Jonas Noreika

I, Jonas Noreika, son of Baltrus, born 1910 in the village of Šukioniai, Pasvalio district, Šiauliai region, Lithuanian SSR, living in Vilnius on Vivulskio street, number 31, not a party-member, finished high law studies, worked in the bourgeoisie Lithuanian Army from 1935–1940, wife Antanina Noreika, born 1911, with daughter living in Germany, in the British-occupied zone, not tried, imprisoned, was from March 16, 1946, declared guilty. I request to represent this group as their lawyer.

No, I demand it!

—KGB Transcripts, 1946[1]

A few months after Mom's death I hunkered in my home office, looking vacantly at a keyboard, trying to find the motivation to assemble the words. *My grandfather.* On my right towered three bookshelves packed with yellowing documents my mother had collected over forty years about her renowned father. *He died two score and thirteen years ago.* As a spring breeze blew in through my white curtains, I resolved to cast the story as a traditional biography, a third-person account that would include a sprinkling of secondhand memories and anecdotes told by my mother and grandmother. These might prove useful as footnotes for historians. *Larger-than-life legend.* The gold-sprayed bust of Jonas Noreika that I had lugged from my mother's studio now hung over my desk, his eyes glaring down at me. *Don't embarrass the fatherland.*

Growing up in Chicago's Marquette Park neighborhood, which boasted the largest population of Lithuanians outside the homeland, I had heard how at the age of thirty-six my grandfather had died at the hands of the KGB, a martyr for Lithuania's freedom. According to my family's account, he led an uprising against the Communists and won our country back from them, only to have it snatched by the Germans. He became district chief of the northwestern part of the country during the German occupation. Apparently, he fought the Nazis, who then sent him to a concentration camp. He escaped from that camp and returned to Vilnius, planning to start a new rebellion against the Communists—but was caught, taken to a KGB prison, and tortured.[2]

I recalled my last visit to Lithuania, three years earlier—in 1997—when my mother, brother and I had visited the Museum of Genocide Victims, the former KGB prison where Jonas Noreika's trial had taken place. My mother was on a concert tour and also conducting research for her book project, reconstructing the torture and trial so that she could chronicle the life of her celebrated father. He had been prosecuted with ten other rebels and then executed.

Inspired by my mother's keen interest, I was writing a long article about my grandfather for Chicago's *Southtown Economist*. It was published on April 18, 1997.

At the Museum of Genocide Victims, we were led to the basement to see the prison cells and interrogation rooms. My grandfather had stood for hours, waiting for his paperwork to be processed, in one of those two dark cells, the size of coffins, called "boxes." He was then dragged to a fifteen-by-ten-foot lime-green cell crammed with forty traitors. In the corner squatted a plastic pot (called a *parasha*) that served as a toilet. Lights glared round the clock. The whole system was designed to prevent sleep, to keep these bourgeois traitors from escaping this proletariat hell. That's why they conducted interrogations at night: to rob alleged conspirators of sleep and sanity. Prisoners were forced to stay awake from seven in the morning to ten at night and could be sent to solitary confinement if caught napping. My grandfather had dozed off after a long night of questionings and beatings; for that, he was sent to solitary confinement.[3]

Our guide showed us a series of chambers in which prisoners had endured torture inflicted for any of a number of reasons: falling asleep during the day, failing to confess, or tapping out a Morse-code message to a fellow prisoner in an adjoining cell. We viewed a "cold chamber," which looked like a large freezer with a thick refrigerator door. A KGB guard would have opened that door and forced a naked prisoner to crouch down on all fours to enter it. Our guide invited me to crawl into the refrigerator for the sake of my newspaper article, but I merely poked my head into the dark, musty interior. We were told that the prisoners who emerged from its confines usually contracted pneumonia.

Another torture room was apparently part of every prisoner's life. In the "water chamber" a tiny platform stood in the center of a small room filled with a foot of icy water. Prisoners were forced to stand at attention on the platform in their underwear. After hours of standing, they inevitably weakened and collapsed from fatigue into the water. Then they were made to stand in the frigid water until their knees buckled, after which they were beaten for their lapse. The punishment was circular, inescapable.

Down another hallway, we were directed to the "rubber chamber," a padded cubicle intended to muffle the cries of prisoners who had gone insane. Those who turned raving mad were wrapped in black straitjackets, some of which were displayed in a window, their extra-long sleeves and ties a testimony to the fact that ceaseless brutalizing of the body often leads to the unraveling of the mind—perhaps the worst agony of all.

The "death chamber" was where prisoners were shot in the back as they sat at a table in a kitchenette, unaware that they were about to be killed. That's how my grandfather was executed, the tour guide explained. We peered at an old, green wooden table and chair. I pictured my grandfather in that chair, drinking a cup of coffee, the guard sneaking up behind him and shooting him twice, my grandfather's body slumping over the table, his coffee spilling onto the floor.

My grandfather's *nom de guerre* was General Storm. A leader of the underground resistance movement, he was recognized as a hero and a martyr to the cause. I thought of all this as very romantic. These were my psychosocial

genetics: this glorious history whose telling always began with my grandfather's death, whether I was sitting on my grandmother's lap, in Lithuanian
school in Chicago on Saturday mornings, or in conversations with anyone
who had known him.

I felt like a princess, growing up as the granddaughter of a hero who had
bravely resisted the Communists and been tortured by the KGB. I basked in
the warm affection and approval of everyone in Chicago's Lithuanian community: at song and dance festivals, at summer camps, and at concerts in
which my mother sang. I was heir to Jonas Noreika's illustrious legacy: Jonas
Noreika the lionhearted. Growing up with this sense of family distinction, of
noble heritage, felt like having a trust fund. The aura of heroism seemed to
have been transferred magically to me, to inform my very essence. A diamond
tiara couldn't have made me feel more special.

From one of my bookshelves, I pulled out a biography of my grandfather
and studied the cover. It bore a photograph of my grandmother playfully
pulling my grandfather toward her by his necktie. The author was Viktoras
Ašmenskas—one of my grandfather's colleagues who, having taken part in
the rebellion, was imprisoned with him. I had been reading this volume for a
second time. Entitled *Generolas Vėtra* (General Storm), it was published in
1997 by the Genocide and Resistance Research Centre of Lithuania, which
runs the Museum of Genocide Victims, the one I had visited with my mother
and brother.[4] The museum was created in 1992, shortly after Lithuania's independence, to demonstrate to the world that, just as Jews had suffered and
perished during the Holocaust, Lithuanian nationalists had suffered under
Communism during World War II. Many of them had died in Siberia. My
grandfather's name is inscribed along with many others' on the gray marble
walls of the very building in which he was murdered in 1947.

During our 1997 trip to Lithuania, Ašmenskas had told me that death row
prisoners were held in isolation chambers in the basement near the coal bin.
In February 1947, while an inmate himself, he had gone up to a window there
to ask, "Hey, is Noreika there?" A voice replied from the darkness, "Yes, I'm
here." The voice belonged to my grandfather, who smiled as he grasped the
metal window bars.

I put down his book, which contained this account, and stared up at the gold-painted image of my grandfather. *How could you smile on death row? You were only thirty-six years old! Even when staring death in the face, you did not allow yourself to be overcome by man's natural terror. You never lost hope that your beloved country would be free.* Those traits of his—courage and optimism—I strung like pearls onto the necklace that was my family's legacy, my inheritance. I aspired to those same qualities; I wanted to be just like him.

In his book, Ašmenskas relates that shortly after he visited my grandfather on death row, the KGB drove my grandfather 176 miles northwest, to Telšiai, to testify against one of the men whom he had recruited to lead the rebellion. The KGB promised my grandfather his freedom in return for a damaging statement against Major Jonas Semaška.[5] My grandfather refused. He stood tall, defying the terrible Communists, and spoke of the Soviet occupation as the genocide of Lithuania. He must have known that such a declaration of loyalty could cost him his life.

Setting Ašmenskas's book down, I tried to absorb this part of the story into the very fiber of my being to strengthen my perseverance during adversity. I was delighted to claim such an outstanding pedigree.

I returned to my reading, feeling as if I had walked into a time capsule. It was heartening to realize that my mother's and grandmother's sacrifices had contributed to Lithuania's freedom. They'd had to continue their lives without their husband and father, knowing what torment he had endured during his last years. According to Ašmenskas, the KGB had thrown General Storm into an iron tank nicknamed the "Black Raven," which often was placed in the prison courtyard. Its sealed vertical compartments were like narrow coffins. A prisoner shut up inside one of them was forced to stand for hours. Occasionally prisoners crossing the yard walked past it. If no guard was patrolling, it was possible to have a brief conversation.

One prisoner hollered at the Black Raven, "Who's in there?"

"Jonas Noreika!"

The other prisoner shouted, "The Moscow Supreme Court agreed to abolish the death penalty! Write an appeal, to buy more time."

After a short silence, Noreika answered, "No, I won't write it. I categorically forbid you to write it in my name. My trial was not legal. I am a war prisoner. I followed my soldier's oath and duty. I have taken the highest responsibility in the war for freedom and will answer only to the National Council. By asking for a pardon, I would recognize the occupier's authority, thereby negating the authority of Lithuania's independent government. Let the Council know. Soldiers make decisions according to their conscience and the war's circumstances."[6]

At the Museum of Genocide Victims my mother, brother, and I stood at the front of an interrogation room in the basement and tried to picture the trial held on November 15, 1946. Jonas Noreika stood before a KGB prison judge, wearing gray prisoner's garb, his beard long and scruffy, his face and body bruised, his hands manacled. Was the judge wearing a military uniform? Was there a surly portrait of Vozhd (Leader) Joseph Stalin overlooking the proceedings? My grandfather declared himself to be the defense lawyer, representing the eleven men who had formed a rebellion against the Communists. The judge magnanimously agreed to this arrangement. He already knew the trial's inevitable outcome.

After the trial, my grandfather and a colleague were transferred to a nearby prison to await their execution. A fellow prisoner remembered seeing them in the courtyard near the gate; Ašmenskas described this scene in his book. One of the inmates exclaimed, "Men, look! Above Noreika's head shines a halo—and there's one over Zigmas!"[7]

I closed the book and patted its cover. This was the best part of the story, I always thought: the two heroes with halos glowing above their heads just before their execution. Surely it was a supernatural sign, signaling that they would be sent straight to heaven as a reward for their martyrdom.

Now, fifty-three years after those events, I perused the transcripts of the KGB trial and was able to read exactly what each man had said before being sentenced. The transcripts had been translated from Russian into Lithuanian, which I then translated into English. At the end of the trial, the eleven defendants gave their closing statements.

Stasys Gorodeckis, second-in-command to my grandfather, stated, "I'm on this bench because I dream of freedom, an independent Lithuania. I was responsible for pulling in human sacrifices. People are treasures and are necessary for the future. Yes, the defender was correct when he said the rest were brought to the bench because of my actions. Please do not sentence them severely. If the trial can focus on my past work, take into account my 'mistake.' I will reform."[8]

Gorodeckis was sentenced to ten years in Siberia and lived out the rest of his life with his family. He died a natural death in 2002.

Zigmas Šerkšnas-Laukaitis, groomed as the leader of the rebellion's death squad, professed, "Yes, I belonged to the partisans, but I also left them. Noreika involved me again with this matter, with organizing the youth, but I did not know they were called the death squad. Please take that into consideration to lessen my sentence."

Within three months he was executed—along with my grandfather.

All of the other prisoners' statements paled in comparison with my grandfather's; he went out in a blaze of glory. When it was his turn to speak, Jonas Noreika valiantly proclaimed, "I was born in Lithuania, prayed for the nation. Life under the Russians was difficult and dark. When I joined the Lithuanian Army I took an oath for freedom of religion, liberty, and independence. Because of my beliefs I joined the war against the Soviet government against the Bolsheviks. All the facts prove in this trial that my colleagues and I wanted an independent Lithuania. I could not just sit on my hands. I tried using all means available, but it did not succeed. I willingly worked for all of this."

Unlike the others, he did not beg for leniency. I admired his obstinacy in fighting for what was right. He kept his promises, no matter the consequences.

I'd heard all my life how my grandfather had asked that he be shot on February 16, the most glorious day in the country's history. On that date in 1918, Lithuania became free of Russia after three centuries of occupation. But intent upon exacting punishment until the last possible moment, the KGB refused Noreika's patriotic request. Instead, they executed him ten days later, having expressly brought in, from the Urals, a left-handed executioner known for his cold-blooded style. On the day of my grandfather's execution, the KGB—perhaps seeking to avoid drama—escorted him to the prison basement, asked him to sit at a table, and may even have given him a cup of coffee. When he least suspected it, the executioner crept up behind him and shot him twice in the head.

At the end of the tour of the former KGB prison my mother, brother, and I were met by a thin, elderly man named Rudolfas Jurgis Minajevas, who carried a guitar and sang a ballad that he had composed about my grandfather. It was Ašmenskas who had prepared this delightful surprise. He took us to the window on death row through which my grandfather had answered him all those years ago. There Minajevas sang a ballad that allowed us to visualize my grandfather's last days.

> One cloudy February morning,
> Suddenly everyone wakes up.
> The Soviet guards are lively again!
> The fierce judge
> Smiles with calm:
> As he sentences Jonas Noreika to death.
> Death by bullets is reasonable!
> A song erupts in blood.
> They stilled our soldier too soon!
> The Fatherland is quiet,
> Remembering at least for a while
> How the dull-witted Soviets tortured him.
> The mind doesn't rest.
> Be free, homeland,
> As you belong to Holy Mary.
> The brother's blood is pure
> And will not dry in our memory!
> We will rise passionately and fight.[9]

After his execution, my grandfather's body was tossed into a pit on the grounds of Tuskulėnai Manor, about five miles away, and covered with limestone.

It lay entombed there for more than fifty years, while his spirit both sustained and haunted our family.

Vilnius
October 1, 2018

The petitioner [Grant Gochin] relies on the theories of J. Noreika's activities based on research conducted by Andrius Jonas Kulikauskas, a lecturer at the Vilnius Gediminas Technical University, Department of Philosophy and Cultural Studies, as well as Evaldas Balčiūnas. They have concluded that:

1. J. Noreika led the criminal gang, the Lithuanian Activist Front in Telšiai, which acted in the name of the Republic of Lithuania, the Lithuanian nation, and the Žemaičių Land. In that capacity, he killed more than 3,000 Jews in one month. He also arrested, humiliated, tortured, and condemned more than 300 Lithuanians.

2. J. Noreika was chosen to serve the Lithuanian Provisional Government and the Nazi occupiers as chairman of the Šiauliai District because he was particularly suited to managing crimes against humanity.

> **Vilnius Regional Administrative Court**
> **File No. eI-4215-281/2018**
> **Response from the Genocide Resistance and Research Centre to the prosecution's claim against the Genocide Centre's refusal to change its historical conclusion on Jonas Noreika**

CHAPTER FOUR

The Last Letter

The last communication from my grandfather to my mother was sent from the KGB prison on December 25, 1946, two months before his execution. It was a letter from a loving father to his seven-year-old daughter. In my parents' home this letter was often read aloud on Christmas Eve. My mother had encased it in a velvet-trimmed frame and hung it in the dining room. It now rested in my office, displayed on top of volumes of Lithuania's history during World War II, as a librarian might showcase a rare or precious item.

My mother and grandmother had fled Lithuania eighteen months before the date of this letter. They left when the Soviet Union occupied the country for the second time, in July 1944. They were living in Switzerland when the letter arrived. They would not learn for years that my grandfather had died two months after writing it; the Communists did not disclose his death until 1956. The complete lack of information about his fate during those twelve years kindled in my mother and grandmother a mixture of hope and fear that effectively paralyzed them. What should they do? Where should they stay? How would Jonas find them? Their frequent recounting of this situation as I was growing up created a sense in me that time had stopped when my grandfather was taken prisoner, that he would be held interminably, and that I had to get him out.

By 1956, my mother and grandmother had moved to Chicago. My mother met my father at Loyola University. They married in 1960 and welcomed my arrival a year later. In 1964, my brother was born.

The letter of December 25, 1946, was a family treasure, a talisman that my mother would touch when she spoke of her father. One Christmas Eve, perhaps in 1975, our family gathered around the dining room table and squeezed into our places one by one in that small room. Mom set out a plate for my grandfather, a tradition to honor the departed. His plate and his glass of wine remained in place throughout the meal. As always, Mom began with a prayer. "We are gathered here to remember your birth, Jesus Christ, for which we are grateful, and also our relatives who are still suffering under the Communist occupation, as well as those who have passed away, like my father." The mention of him made her cry. Močiutė squeezed my hand for comfort, as always. But Mom, with her flair for the dramatic, removed the framed Christmas letter from the wall and read it.

> Dalia! To my one and only child,
>   You don't know cruelty, why birds made of lead reflect the sun's rays while dropping destructive bombs on large cities. You still don't know deceit. Your heart is like the white dove on my windowsill. Yet you will mature and comprehend everything, that life is an eternal struggle. Only the strong win. Power rules. But power is two-sided: creative and destructive. Creative power is love, while destructive power is hate. I want to see you strong, firm, and filled with creative power. May God help you, my child of love.[1]

When she finally hung the letter back in its place, she lifted a silver tray of *plotkelės*, unconsecrated Communion wafers, and offered one to each of us. Tradition required us to share this wafer with everyone present, wishing each person good health, good luck, good grades in school, good fortune in work, or anything else he or she particularly wanted. When it came to the wafer that she had placed on my grandfather's plate, we each broke off a piece of it and wished him happiness and success in heaven, or asked for his help in life—as if he'd been beatified.

On other occasions, I asked his help in establishing a writing career, something I had set my heart on by eighth grade. Mom often told me that her father had been a very good writer; he'd worked as a journalist for newspapers and military magazines, had written short stories, even a novel, and had won literary prizes. I would break off a piece of his wafer and chew it slowly, entreating him: *Grandfather, you know I've already chosen a career in writing. I know it's not practical. Močiutė wants me to be a lawyer, like you, but I'd rather be a writer, also like you. If you have any influence, please look over my shoulder and help me.*

Then we would sit down to eat twelve cold dishes representing Christ's twelve disciples. These included black bread, potato salad, red beet vinaigrette, a green salad, fried cod, herring with onions, herring with tomatoes, herring with green peppers, herring with carrots, herring with mushrooms in sour cream, poppy-seed milk, and cranberry pudding. As we nibbled and sipped, I would check my grandfather's glass of wine every few minutes to see if he had drunk any of it. When we weren't looking, my father would gulp down its contents and set the wine glass back in its place. He then would draw our attention to the evidence that my grandfather had just joined us for dinner. We always laughed. Nonetheless, the presence of our heroic grandfather was made palpable—as was our loss, and the injustice of his absence from our lives.

It was not easy to live with the constant shadow of his memory. We commemorated his birthday, October 8. We also marked the date on which he had requested to be executed (even though the Communists killed him on February 26). Their cynical and callous attempt to consign Jonas Noreika to oblivion served, as intended, to sharpen our grief.

This perpetual sense of bereavement, this shroud of grief, caused division in our family. As Mom and Močiutė groomed me and Ray to identify with our courageous ancestor, my father often must have felt like an outsider. Dad almost certainly resented the fact that he never seemed to measure up against his phantom father-in-law. "Your mother's father was a general; mine was a janitor," he remarked.

Every room in the house declared that our family was Lithuanian—forced by the Communists to live, against our will, in another country. We often acted as if we comprised a country unto ourselves here—as if the backdrop of a free America were purely incidental, of little consequence to us. Our true goal was to obtain freedom for Lithuania.

"Someday, Lithuania will be free," Mom told us. "It's up to us to help save the country from the Communists. My father died fighting for our country's freedom, and we must do everything we can to live up to his honor."

On Saturdays Ray and I attended Lithuanian school, where we'd have to write essays about how we could help the fatherland achieve its freedom. In one essay, written when I was about eight years old, I asserted, "I have to get a good education and get involved with the American government to convince this country's leaders to save the Baltic country. They'll send American soldiers to Lithuania to kill the Communist monsters."

When I showed the essay to my mother, she beamed and read it over the phone to my grandmother, who (I was told) also glowed with pride. Then I showed it to my father. He smiled blandly, saying, "That's good, Silvia," and went back to reading the Lithuanian daily newspaper *Draugas* (Friend).

"Don't bother your father now," Mom said. "He's busy." She noticed my frown. "Why are you crying? You should feel lucky you even *have* a father. The last time I saw mine, I was four years old."

She went into the piano room that housed the Lithuanian encyclopedia set, pulled out the volume labelled *N*, and opened it to the entry "Jonas Noreika." In forty lines, it provided a thumbnail sketch of the man whom she constantly compared to Dad.

"Do you see?" she said. "Your grandfather was a hero. He died for his country. That's why I grew up without a father. You need to feel grateful that you have a father."

I looked at Dad. He shrugged and walked into his basement office, saying, "I need to work on *Lituanus*." He was the publication's volunteer business administrator by night; by day he worked for Chicago City Hall as a bookkeeper in the comptroller's office. "I have two jobs," he liked to say.

Mom saw my crushed expression. "Your father's very busy, that's all. He goes to work during the day to pay our bills. At night, he works for the Lithuanian cause, just like my father used to. You understand, don't you?"

"I suppose so," I mumbled.

Dad was a quiet man who managed to stay out of everyone's way. Because he seemed emotionally distant, my mother invoked the spirit of her father as the other adult male role model for Ray and me. Her father's sentences, encased in red velvet, hung with his photograph next to the Vytis.

I envied my mother for having had a father who could write her a letter like that. Although I had never met my grandfather, I'd learned to love him the way a daughter loved a father.

All exiles have their private griefs. My family's tragedy, I thought, was grander, more epic than most.

My grandfather's legend and my promise to my mother obliged and encouraged me to write. While raising my son, then three years old, and my daughter, aged seven, I ran a freelance writing business. Neither my young children nor my husband of fourteen years could understand my obsession with my grandfather. I seemed to spend more time with his ghost than with them. They, too, felt the sacrifice of his martyrdom; it was a multi-generational cost.

Vilnius
October 1, 2018

The petitioner [Grant Gochin] claims that J. Noreika was one of the most prominent antisemites in Lithuania who desired and relished the idea of killing Jews, who drew others into killing Jews, who justified their actions, and who personally ordered the

shooting of Jews in Plungė. The petitioner requests that the
[Genocide] Centre accept his version.

Vilnius Regional Administrative Court
File No. el-4215-281/2018
Response from the Genocide Resistance and Research Cen-
tre to the prosecution's claim against the Genocide Centre's
refusal to change its historical conclusion on Jonas Noreika

CHAPTER FIVE

The Blue Danube

F ive months after my mother's death, my grandmother was again critically ill. I faced another unfulfilled promise: I had not yet learned to play "The Blue Danube" waltz on the piano that Močiutė had bought for me ten years earlier. Her gift had been accompanied with that one request: "Please learn how to play 'The Blue Danube.' I want to remember my wedding day, the happiest day of my life." Even her gift to me was a means of paying tribute to my grandfather.

I estimated that it would take a few weeks to learn to play the waltz to Močiutė's satisfaction. She hated mistakes.

I got a copy of the score, set it on the brown upright piano, and tentatively began to practice. I had taken lessons for eleven years as a child and occasionally accompanied my mother as she sang, but it had been at least a decade since I had played the piano. And "The Blue Danube" is a difficult piece, with four-note chords that require spanning an octave with one hand. My fingers were slow at first, but I gradually gained confidence—first with the right hand, then with the left, then with both together. But everything sounded sour. I needed to call a piano tuner.

"You haven't tuned your piano in ten years?" he asked incredulously.

"I barely touched it," I said, defensive.

"It's a crime to ignore a piano for this long."

"I know. Can you hurry?"

As I continued to practice in those early days of summer 2000, nothing seemed to be in harmony. How could I possibly fulfill my promises? How could I go on without Mom or Močiutė? I spent hours going over the notes of my grandmother's wedding song, until I felt the patriotic music in my bones and heard the rustle of long dresses swirling around a glittering ballroom.

I became so accustomed to playing the song that my mind wandered as I stroked the keys. Everything from my mother and grandmother had always come with a condition. And those conditions had framed my entire life. My grandmother's gift of a piano had come with the condition that I learn to play a complicated waltz reminiscent of the Noreika mythology; I learned the piece because she expected it of me. My mother had claimed on her deathbed that she wouldn't die in peace unless I agreed to write a book about her hero. Because I wanted their love and approval, I agreed to all their demands: do everything you can to help Lithuania by learning the language, understanding the country's complex history, and passing down to your children the stories of our heritage. I didn't question these requirements, but I had delayed acting upon them.

Wanting to let my grandmother know that I was working to fulfill my promise and practicing "The Blue Danube," I visited her at her apartment a few blocks from my home. I sat on her bed while her caretaker Nijolė clanged pans in the kitchen, preparing dinner.

"How's the book going?" Močiutė asked.

"Slowly, but I'll finish it; don't worry." I thought this would give her great comfort.

"Don't write it," she said flatly, with more energy in her voice than I had heard in months. "Just leave it alone."

"What do you mean 'leave it alone'?" This was hardly the response I'd expected.

"It's best to just let history lie. There's no need to dig around."

I assumed that her grief over her daughter's death a few months earlier had made my grandmother delirious. Perhaps she didn't want the enormous task that I'd inherited to burden me the way it had my mother. Or maybe, facing her own death, she wanted to free me from my obligation as a parting gift. I searched Močiutė's face but could not read it.

I had been sorting through my mother's research notes for the past five months, trying to make sense of my grandfather's life. The Lithuanian community's expectation that she produce a definitive account must have weighed heavily upon her. Marquette Park was composed chiefly of exiled Lithuanians and their children, all still grieving over the loss of their country and intent upon reclaiming it. Seething over their ancient enemy with a new name—the Communists were now Russians again—our community spoke and acted as if of one mind, like a chorus. It told my mother that a hero like her father could enhance the prestige of their relatively unknown nation on the world stage. Jonas Noreika's glorious deeds, once publicized, would earn notice and acclaim for the fatherland.

I was still thinking, naively, that it was my mother's perfectionism that had caused her such mental, emotional, and spiritual stress over the project. I didn't ask my grandmother why she wanted me to drop the story. It was generous of her to want to spare me an onerous job that might consume my life. Instead, I tried to placate her. "Don't worry," I repeated. "I'm young and strong. I have lots of time. Besides, I promised Mom."

Močiutė shook her head and rolled over in bed to face the wall.

I didn't take her appeal seriously. Instead, I devoted myself to practicing "The Blue Danube" on the piano again and again. I wanted to keep my promise to her. Maybe I believed it would stop her from dying.

Days later she was rushed to the hospital. Her condition became so critical that the only way I could perform a piano recital for her was over the phone. I implored a nurse to hold the receiver to my grandmother's ear, while my husband held the receiver on my end. I played with all my heart, pounding the chords, swaying back and forth, finally fulfilling my promise. I pictured Močiutė gliding around the dance floor with my grandfather on their wedding day, setting our family history in motion: my mother's birth, her father's disappearance, the emergence of General Storm, my grandmother's flight from the homeland, and her agonizing longing for it ever since. As I played, I imagined Močiutė transported back to the happiest day of her life.

When I finished, I asked over the phone, "Did you like it?"

"Yes," she whispered. Nothing more.

I wanted her to praise my effort the way she had cooed over my school essays. I wanted her to recover. But the only sound I heard was her laborious breathing. The nurse informed me that she needed to rest.

The next day, I visited her in the hospital. "How did you like 'The Blue Danube'?"

"It wasn't worth it," she said, looking straight through me.

"What wasn't worth it?"

"Everything."

We were interrupted by a Eucharistic minister, who asked her if she would like to take Communion. She waved her hand dismissively.

She seemed like a stranger. She had been going to Mass regularly, cherished the rosary that she carried in her purse, and sang a song to the Virgin Mary every time we drove somewhere on vacation. Now she was refusing Communion?

Confused by her strangeness, I sat on the edge of her bed and held her hand. I was immobilized by an invisible web; we two were the ones left, and soon I would be alone. Whom would I turn to for answers? How was she dealing with the knowledge of what would happen next?

The minister left, shrugging his shoulders.

I couldn't help but wonder why Močiutė hadn't taken Communion. I asked her, "Do you believe in God?" I wanted her to still have faith, to believe in heaven so that she'd have solace during her last breath.

She replied, "Christ was just a clever Jew who tricked the world."

I looked at her as if for the first time. Then I made excuses for her: the contemplation of death must have rattled her mind. I held on to my image of Močiutė on her wedding day, waltzing with her handsome husband, my beloved grandfather, to the popular Viennese tune—one-two-three, one-two-three. I let my heart soar to its legendary cadence.

After my grandmother's death on July 6, 2000, my father, brother, and I made arrangements to take my mother's and grandmother's cremated remains to Vilnius and bury them in the fatherland according to their wishes. Viktoras Ašmenskas, the colleague of my grandfather's who had written the book about him and was somehow closely connected to the Lithuanian government, had been in touch with us several times before our trip. Three years earlier he had helped my mother to secure a gravesite for my grandfather at Antakalniai, the cemetery in Vilnius where Lithuania's military heroes and cultural luminaries were buried. He had also helped to coordinate a DNA analysis of the remains, at the government's expense, to ensure that they were those of Jonas Noreika. Unfortunately, because the bones had been buried in limestone for so long, all genetic markers had deteriorated beyond recognition.

In a phone conversation with Ašmenskas about coordinating my mother's and my grandmother's burial arrangements, we asked if he could help to arrange another attempt at a DNA test of our grandfather's bones, so that we could bury all three family members together. Perhaps forensic technology had improved, we reasoned. He told us that he would contact the Lithuanian government and respond to us in writing.

A few weeks later, we received a letter from Ašmenskas informing us that the government had agreed to analyze our grandfather's remains but that this time we would have to pay for the investigation ourselves. My father, reading the letter aloud to me and my brother, asked, "Who's going to pay for this?"

"It was Mom's wish," I said. "You have more than enough to pay for it." He had been bragging about how he'd earned a million dollars on the stock market.

"He wasn't my father," Tėtė countered. "Why should *I* pay for it?"

My brother and I exchanged a glance, a silent conversation passing between us. In fairness, our father had paid the household bills and helped to fund our college educations, but he had never been known for spending beyond the basics. While we were growing up, he frequently lectured us about the importance of saving money. The amount of his savings reflected his self-worth.

"We'll pay for it," said Ray.

"Good." Tėtė resumed reading the letter.

Ašmenskas suggested that we time the burial of our mother and grandmother to coincide with my grandfather's ninetieth birthday on October 8. We liked the idea. What's more, it would give us time to hire a DNA-analysis company to confirm the identity of our grandfather's remains. Ašmenskas asked if we would allow him to speak to the director of the school named after our grandfather. Perhaps the director would invite us to a ceremony to mark the occasion. We agreed.

Ašmenskas's letter ended by querying my father as to whether he wanted to be buried next to my mother.

"How should I respond?" Tėtė asked quietly.

"That's up to you," I said.

He shook his head. "I don't think she wanted me next to her. Did she ever mention that to you?"

My heart sank for him. "No. She only mentioned that she wanted to be buried next to her father."

"You know, this is the first time I'm beginning to realize how strange our marriage was."

In the ensuing months, Ray coordinated the DNA analysis with Rimas Jankauskas, a scientist at the University of Vilnius who had been involved in the excavation of my grandfather's bones in 1994.

My grandfather was one of many Lithuanians executed by the KGB and buried in the park of Tuskulėnai Manor. "The place was convenient: It was strictly guarded and not far from downtown, where the KGB was headquartered. KGB officials were afraid of guerrilla activities in the outskirts of Vilnius," wrote Dr. Jankauskas in a personal letter to my brother.

Nearly one thousand bodies were buried in that park between 1944 and 1947. Fifty years later, on July 4, 1994, exhumations by a team of archeologists and anthropologists began. Seeking to identify Jonas Noreika's remains, Dr. Jankauskas had narrowed down the possibilities to two skeletons, numbers 550 and 551, both found in hole number 29. Now he sent samples of their thigh bones, along with the hair and blood samples that my mother had provided, to a company in Canada that my brother had chosen for DNA analysis. After several attempts, that company responded with the same result that the Lithuanian government's inquiry had yielded years earlier: because the bones had been buried in limestone for so long, it was impossible to identify the DNA.

We would bury our mother and grandmother at the gravesite earmarked by the government for our grandfather, but his remains would not join theirs.

Weeks before our trip to Lithuania, my father had a heart attack—his second—and decided to stay home under the care of his new wife, Nijolė. She had been my grandmother's caretaker during the five months from my mother's death until my grandmother died.

My brother and I would make the emotional pilgrimage by ourselves.

PART II

A TROUBLING RUMOR

CHAPTER SIX

Ghosts

The sad, quiet duties that fall to families as they prepare their dead for burial were unexpectedly lent an official, ceremonious air. Ray and I arrived in Vilnius on a cool, overcast day in early October that smelled of rain. We were the last passengers to disembark after the long flight. We slowly descended the steep steps onto the tarmac, carrying in thick cardboard boxes the funerary urns that we had taken as carry-on luggage. Ray held Mom's ashes, while I clutched Močiutė's. They were heavy—about twenty pounds each—and I was afraid I would lose my balance. Gripping the handrail to steady myself, I caught Ray's eye. He gave me a reassuring smile. Our relationship had deepened with the one-two loss of our mother and grandmother, followed by our father's swift remarriage.

About fifteen relatives and a few friends awaited us at the foot of the stairs, each with a dewy flower and a dry kiss. I failed to recognize many of them. Most, I assumed, were relatives of my grandparents, since my mother had been an only child. Others were colleagues of my grandfather. All were dressed in somber gray coats. A black hearse idled behind them.

I knew that many of those here had written letters to my mother. We had met briefly on previous trips, but they addressed me as if we had known each other for years. Bewildered, I tried to remember from conversations I'd had with Mom exactly who was who. My grandfather's nephew Stasys Grunskis, whose hair was as wild as Einstein's, shook my hand vigorously. My mother's friend Zita Kelmickaitė, who had choreographed everything for our arrival, was a celebrity in Lithuania. She was short, with an intense gaze and an electrifying smile. She directed everyone as if we were on a movie set, ordering the videographer, photographer, and journalist to follow us, instructing our relatives to surround us for the photo ops, and continually whispering to an attendant. All the while she kept telling us how happy she was to see us, how much our mother meant to her, and how proud she was of all that our grandfather had done for our country. Her boundless energy buoyed us during this distressing moment. One could see why she would soon be hosting her own morning TV show.

When I had contacted Zita to tell her that my mother and grandmother had died and that I didn't know how to fulfill their shared wish to be buried in their homeland, she'd said simply, "I'll help you."

An attendant dressed in black took the urns from us and placed them in the hearse. After holding them on our laps during the long flight from Chicago, it felt strange to be relieved of this sacred duty. *You're finally here, Mom and Močiutė!*

The attendant arranged long-stemmed white lilies and ferns artfully around the urns as the photographer snapped pictures and the videographer recorded. I turned to survey the small airport, my head flooding with thoughts. Now that my mother's and grandmother's burials in Vilnius were imminent, I felt that I was being further separated from them—by this place with its bloody history that so fiercely called them home.

Ray and I sat in the back of a relative's car following the hearse through the city streets, many of them narrow and cobblestoned. An October wind swept past, carrying gold, green, and red leaves that crackled and somersaulted over each other until a strong gust scattered them.

This was not merely a five-thousand-mile trip from Chicago: it was a sixty-year trek back into our family's history, a journey to a time when our grandfather was still alive, when our mother's side of the family was still intact, and when the country was being gutted by the Communists and the Nazis. The twenty-two years of independence between the two world wars had been snuffed out. It was a time when Lithuanians were sent to Siberia by the Communists, and Jews were beaten to death by the Nazis or driven out by the truckload to ghettos and then to the woods to be shot.

The wake for my mother and grandmother was held at Vilnius Cathedral. My brother and I stayed at an apartment lent to us by a friend of our mother, and Zita picked us up in a chauffer-driven black limousine. "Everything has been arranged," she assured us. "Don't worry about a thing. Of the photographs you gave me, I chose two in which your mother and grandmother look like they're facing each other. I thought that would be best."

Ray and I nodded, thanking her again for attending to all the details.

"I placed your mother's urn on a higher pedestal than your grandmother's. What do you think about that?"

I smiled. "Even though she was younger, Mom was always in charge of our family, so I think that's appropriate."

"Good. That's what I thought too."

When we arrived at the cathedral, Zita ushered me and Ray inside, where several hundred guests dressed in black were waiting. More visitors arrived in a steady stream throughout the afternoon. Photographers, videographers, and journalists mingled with the crowd. Zita positioned us at the end of a receiving line in a side area near the urns. My mother's bronze urn was sculpted in the shape of a lotus flower. Its turquoise color with speckles of gold reminded me of the sea. My grandmother's yellow marble urn was simpler in style. Both urns stood on white pedestals surrounded by pale lilies and roses.

As the guests stood in line to offer their condolences, several I did not recognize asked, "What about the book on your grandfather that your mother was working on? Did she finish it?"

I answered, "No, she didn't—but before she died, she asked me to complete it for her. She left me all the material on him."

Each of them squeezed my hand, patted me on the shoulder, and gave me words of encouragement. "He was such a hero. We need stories about our heroes. Thank God you're doing this! You're a good daughter to take this on."

Although there was no physical trace of my grandfather in the room, we all felt the presence of his spirit. I sensed him standing behind us, inches away, breathing on my neck, wearing his army uniform with the captain's insignia, observing the ceremony, and greeting everyone who came. He shook their hands through ours. I kept turning around, half-looking for him.

One of my grandfather's colleagues, Damijonas Riauka, approached. He had shoulder-length gray hair and a beard hanging down to his chest. "I haven't shaved since your mother died eight months ago," he informed me. "I plan to let it grow forever, even if it stretches to my belly."

"Thank you. How kind of you," I murmured. Was that the right thing to say to someone who grew a beard to commemorate your mother's death? I found it odd but heartening.

He pointed to a man dressed in an air force uniform and asked under his breath, "Do you know who that is?"

"Yes." On this third trip to Lithuania, I easily recognized Viktoras Ašmenskas, who had been in the KGB prison with my grandfather and recently had been of such assistance to my family. "What about him?"

Damijonas shook his head, his beard swaying. He lifted his forefinger and jabbed it into my arm. "He betrayed your grandfather," he hissed. We were out of everyone's earshot. "He's the one who informed the KGB. The double agent."

My brother and I stared at each other, dumbfounded.

"It's all in the transcripts," Damijonas affirmed. "The ones your mother asked me to translate from Russian. You have them, don't you?"

"Yes, of course." They lay in my home in five white binders, all three thousand pages.

"It's all there. You'll see. You'll need them for the book."

I glanced at my mother's urn. *What do you think about that, Mom?*

She had never spoken of this.

The next morning seemed unnaturally bright for a burial. Ašmenskas turned to my brother and me, his eyes gleaming, and pronounced, "You both are like my children. I loved your grandfather." Before the procession to the cemetery, he led us two blocks to the Library of the Lithuanian Academy of Sciences. He wanted to show us a bronze plaque. This was the building in which Jonas Noreika had worked as a lawyer by day, while serving as an underground resistance leader by night. As Generolas Vėtra, he had issued secret directives to partisans.

Even though I was in mourning, I was taking notes for the book. The most critical part of the story, I believed, concerned my grandfather's attempt to lead his country to freedom during the second Communist takeover. Ašmenskas gave us a wreath to place at the foot of a bronze likeness whose inscription read:

> In This Building
> from 1945–1946
> Worked a Noteworthy Resistor
> Lithuania's National Council
> and Lithuania's Armed
> Forces Organizer
> and Leader
> Jonas Noreika
> General Storm
> Shot February 26, 1947

Shaking his head, Ašmenskas told us, "He wanted to be shot on the most celebrated day of our history, February 16. But the Communists postponed his killing for ten days."

I had heard this lament many times from many quarters, this odd complaint about my grandfather's execution date. The refusal of his stated choice of date—in an apparent effort to consign him to obscurity—seemed to resonate deeply among patriots. Caught up in the moment, I felt an impulse to raise my fist to the sky in indignation.

The October 2000 funeral of my mother and grandmother at Vilnius Cathedral. The attendants pictured include Lithuanian chairman of the Supreme Council Vytautas Lansbergis (center) and my brother and me (far right, front)

I was sorry that my grandfather had had to endure so much. This execution story—which ironically served to lionize him—had strongly influenced my life, inspiring my decision, by the time I was in high school in the 1970s, to become a journalist, fantasizing that I would write about Lithuania and help free it of Communist tyranny.

Upon returning to the cathedral, my brother and I were astonished to find not only old-guard partisans in attendance, but current dignitaries. Even Vytautas Landsbergis, the country's chairman of the Supreme Council, and his wife appeared to pay their respects to the widow and daughter of General Storm. The crowd hushed and parted while photographers and videographers strove to capture the event. Landsbergis, formerly a music professor, had been the country's first head of state after it regained its independence on March 11, 1990. His conservative party—the Homeland Union—was running in the upcoming parliamentary elections. I had met the chairman of the Supreme Council on previous trips with my mother, who was a friend of his.

He shook our hands. "I'm so sorry about the loss of your mother and grandmother, but so happy that you brought them here to be laid to rest in

Lithuania. They are like national treasures to us. Your grandfather was a great hero."

His wife hugged me, and I thanked them both for coming. "We're so honored you're here," I responded.

From the cathedral we proceeded to the cemetery, where we watched attendants lower our mother's and grandmother's ashes into the sandy ground while a young woman played a sad song on a violin.

Zita cleared her throat. "We're gathered here today to honor Dalia Kučėnas and Antanina Noreika. Dalia's children have brought them both back to the country where they were born. They chose this day, October 8, because it would have been their grandfather's ninetieth birthday. Although they have done so much for us, I still have one request of them."

She turned to my brother and me. "Don't forget Lithuania."

I felt very patriotic. Despite having grown up on the other side of the world, Ray and I could never forget the fatherland, even if we tried. It was always in our thoughts; that was how our mother and grandmother had raised us.

And we were about to learn how profoundly our grandfather had shaped Lithuanian history.

Vilnius
October 1, 2018

The [Genocide] Centre does not consider the petitioner's [Grant Gochin's] investigation as soundly academic due to the following reasons:

- he has failed to implement proper historiographic principles;
- he has failed to follow the methodology accepted by historical research experts;
- his researchers, Andrius Kulikauskas and Evaldas Balčiūnas, are not known as professional historians;

- several of the petitioner's conclusions are not based on reality,
  but rather on the time period's disinformation propaganda.

> **Vilnius Regional Administrative Court**
> **File No. el-4215-281/2018**
> **Response from the Genocide Resistance and Research Centre to the prosecution's claim against the Genocide Centre's refusal to change its historical conclusion on Jonas Noreika**

CHAPTER SEVEN

Fatherless

*I, Jonas Noreika, without reservation, promise to faithfully
serve the Lithuanian Republic, to defend with my might and life
the Lithuanian nation, its freedom and independence without
regrets, to conscientiously follow the Constitution of the Republic
of Lithuania, its statutes, and the orders of my superior officers,
and to protect all the secrets entrusted to me; I pledge to be a vir-
tuous and honorable Lithuanian soldier, so help me God.*
—Soldier's Oath, November 13, 1930[1]

Ray and I had been invited to visit our grandfather's birthplace and the
school that was named after him, located about an hour's drive from the
nation's capital. I'd been looking forward to this part of our journey ever since
Viktoras Ašmenskas first suggested it. Now eighty-eight years old with snowy
white hair, he no longer felt comfortable behind the wheel and had asked his
son to drive us. My brother and I sat in the back seat of an old but reliable blue
Falcon; Viktoras sat in front with his son.

We headed north out of Vilnius. As our car swerved into the next lane to
pass a slow-moving truck, I gazed out the window, recalling the descriptions
I had read of my grandfather's childhood. In 1976, Antanas Čiakas, a maternal
cousin of my grandfather, had written my mother a number of letters. One of
these stated that my grandfather, the youngest of ten children, had grown up
on a tenant farm in Šukioniai, a small town on the outskirts of Šiauliai, with
four surviving siblings: Stasys, Pranas, Ona, and Antanina.[2]

We drove past acres of rye, wheat, corn, and flax, and endless evergreen and birch forests. The roads were free of traffic, and we enjoyed the view of fall foliage and small blue lakes. I thought of Antanina, my grandfather's favorite sister, who had served as both godmother and nanny to my mother. Antanina escaped Lithuania with my mother and grandmother in July 1944 and went with them to Germany, Switzerland, and then Argentina. In Buenos Aires she fell in love, at the age of forty, with Kostas Misiūn. Consequently, she remained in Argentina when my mother and grandmother received their long-awaited visas to the United States.[3]

After I graduated from journalism school at Northwestern University in 1984, I visited my great-aunt Antanina in Buenos Aires and lived with her for two years. During my stay, I was entertained with countless stories of my famous grandfather's childhood. I also learned Spanish, freelanced for a few publications, and met Franco Foti, whom I would eventually marry.

It seemed that everywhere we looked in Lithuania, there were indications of how much Jonas Noreika was revered. A kilometer away from his homestead we spotted a blue guidepost with white lettering: *J. Noreika's Birthplace* 1 →. We stopped to take a photograph of the sign. I scanned the field with its few pear trees and could almost envision my grandfather as a child.

I had reconstructed my grandfather's early life until the age of twenty from the stories of my grandfather's cousin and my great-aunt. He was born to Baltrus Noreika and his wife Anelija Čekaitė, who was seventeen years younger than her husband. She married in 1890 without a dowry. Perhaps it was thought that she was young enough to bear her considerably older husband so many children that the prospect of all those hands on the farm was even more valuable than a dowry.

Baltrus owned a horse and a cow and had good business sense. Shortly after getting married he bought a wagon and hired a friend who knew the way to the Baltic Sea. In June the two travelled to the place where Latvian fishermen netted and sold herring. These fish were prized for their rich taste, which required no seasoning. Baltrus poked the herring through the eyes with a stick, smoked them, and brought his wagonload home just as the town's people were celebrating the feast of the Holy Trinity. After selling out his entire stock, he resolved to make the same trip every year thereafter. Soon he added eel to the menu. Within a few summers, he had amassed two thousand rubles—the equivalent of about thirty thousand dollars today. He put the money in a savings account.

By the age of fifty he had five children working on the farm and was very busy tending to his livestock and rye fields. Young Jonas followed him everywhere. The fields had to be sown, harvested, threshed, and winnowed before the rye was brought to the mill to be ground into flour. Or it might be sold to a distillery to make whiskey. The family's existence was a tenuous one, always at the mercy of the weather.

In the late fall of 1913, the golden rye was six feet tall, swaying gently in the wind. A killing frost was predicted, and Baltrus worked frantically on a cold, rainy day to cut as much rye as possible and gather it into bushels before the temperature plummeted. He did not stop when his feet froze.

The next day, he had frostbite, pneumonia, and a raging fever.

As he lay dying, he held the hand of three-year-old Jonas and gave his older children his last instructions: "I will be leaving your mother with five children, so the older ones must help take care of the two youngest. Somehow you must also find a way to provide an education for Jonas. He's so clever, even at this age."

Antanas wrote that while Baltrus was on his deathbed, surrounded by family and friends, he was encircled by a radiant white light and saw a vision. "I see her! Oh, Lord, how happy I am to see Mary, Mother of God, and all the saints!" My great-aunt, too, had told me about this white light; several witnesses had seen it. It was regarded as proof that Baltrus frequently prayed to Mary, that he died in a state of grace under her protection, and that he most likely would go straight to heaven.[4]

Stasys—who, at twenty-three, was the eldest of the children—was thrust into the role of head of the family. From then on, everyone called him "Broleli" (Brother Dear) or "Tėtuši" (Little Father). Jonas, an athletic youngster with a mischievous streak, looked up to his big brother as his new father.

Life was harsher after their father's death. Their mother had resolved never to remarry. She and Stasys became strict, even brutal, disciplinarians. Both whipped Jonas on his bare buttocks for the smallest infraction. After being punished, the boy usually sought out his sister for comfort. Although only five herself, it was she who was primarily responsible for his care.[5]

The next year, in 1914, war broke out. Germans bombed Šiauliai. Gray smoke rose only a few kilometers from Jonas's home in Šukioniai. The invaders helped themselves to residents' food supplies and stole their chickens. Rumors circulated that the Germans were murdering children and forcing adults into labor camps.

Stasys was conscripted into the Russian army—a fate viewed as a death sentence. No Lithuanian wanted to fight for the Russian Empire, and Russian soldiers were often seen barefoot, haggard, and hungry.

Jonas, bewildered, did not understand where Stasys had gone.

To everyone's surprise, Stasys returned a few weeks later. At the same time, the two thousand rubles that had been deposited into the family's savings account disappeared. Perhaps Stasys had used it to buy his freedom—although the official story, Antanas wrote, was that the Russians had released him because he was the head of the family.

Yearning for male companionship, Jonas began following his brother Pranas around. One crisp fall day he begged Pranas to take him riding. His mother forbade him to go, but he was so insistent that she finally relented. He mounted the saddle, holding tightly to his dog, Taksiukas (diminutive for the breed "Taksas," or dachshund), and promised his mother that he would stay close to his older brother.[6]

After riding for some time, the brothers released their horses in a pasture and built a fire to bake potatoes. Jonas offered his dog a steaming hot morsel, but the dog spat it out and danced like a stiff rabbit, much to the brothers' amusement. As the sun cast a red glow on the forest, Jonas convinced Pranas—who may, by then, have been slightly drunk—to allow him to check the horses by himself.

By nightfall, Jonas had not returned. Pranas became frantic. When the night sky had deepened into purple, he dashed home in dread, hoping that his little brother might have been found. Seeing Pranas come back alone, their mother flew into a fury and beat him. Shamed, Pranas leapt on his horse and galloped back into the forest to resume his search. Their mother enlisted women from the village to help. Finally, the boys' sister Ona heard a dog barking and followed Taksiukas straight to Jonas, who was sleeping fitfully under a tree. When Jonas awoke, he ran into his mother's arms. "Mother, I couldn't find Pranas or the fire! I started crying because I didn't know where to go, so I decided to lie down."[7]

They brought him home. By the next morning, several inches of snow had fallen, blanketing the forest. It was remarked that little Jonas had been lucky to escape his father's fate.

In April 1916, the family's lease on the farm in Šukioniai expired, and they moved to a cattle farm in Joniškiai. There was a primary school two kilometers from the village. Jonas did well in his studies and skipped a grade. His family expected that he would grow up to run a large farm or become a politician. Perhaps one day he would own a business like the Jews did. Jews, whom the peasants referred to as "Litvaks"—to distinguish them from the "true" Lithuanians—owned many of the country's small businesses. They were envied and fiercely resented.

Two years later, a miraculous event transpired: on February 16, 1918, Lithuania became an independent nation for the first time in over a century. The Germans, however, still maintained a strong presence in the country, so no celebrations were held.

Life was much the same for eight-year-old Jonas. His mother continued to find cause to whip him; only the obedient Antanina was exempt from her wrath. When Jonas failed his end-of-the-year school examination, his mother belted him energetically, exclaiming, "You're a disgrace and an embarrassment to the entire family!" Antanina stood outside the barn, listening. After the beating, Stasys took a contrite Jonas back to school and begged the teacher to reinstate him. She agreed, and Jonas worked diligently from then on, achieving first rank in his classes.[8]

After the family had moved again—to a farm outside Kaunas—Stasys decided to immigrate to Argentina. Whether he had tired of being the head of the family, wished to escape his mother, or fantasized about travelling to an exotic country to earn a fortune, my aunt did not know. Land and opportunity were plentiful in Argentina in 1924.

But Jonas must have been crushed by this second abandonment by someone he had regarded as a father. He threw all his energy into his studies.

A year after Stasys's departure, Jonas wrote a four-page letter to his brother on behalf of their mother, who was illiterate. She had learned that Stasys was corresponding with a Lutheran girl from their village and that he planned to send for her and marry her as soon as she arrived in Argentina. Their mother dictated:

> Dear son,
>
> I, your loving mother, write you my first letter through my son Jonas. I greet you in the far-off land with God's words, "Praised be Jesus Christ," and await your pleasant response, "For ever and ever."
>
> Hey, son! You have been raised by me. It is as if my treasure has been sent to a distant land beyond the seashore. I don't see you at home harvesting crops on a patch of field, working to earn bread for me. Fall has begun for us. The summer flowers are fading, just as my days on earth will end. Will I see you at least on my deathbed?
>
> Oh, how I thirst that you should have luck and wealth! And honor! Even though you are searching for this in a distant, distant land. I hope that you can soothe my aching heart by taking my advice. Don't fall in the mud, don't anger my heart or the heart of God, and remember your family.
>
> I ask that you not heed your young heart, that you not take that young maiden not of our faith. Marry a young girl who still has the wreath of rue, a pretty, true Lithuanian who is of your faith.
>
> You will enrage my heart and ruin my last days if you marry that girl who is not of our faith. I will not give you my blessing if you marry her.
>
> Your loving mother[9]

Stasys never married the Lutheran girl, and he never returned to Lithuania. He remained alone on his Argentinian farm, becoming a sad and bitter man.

Three years after penning that letter, Jonas graduated from high school and was planning to go to college. But so much rain fell that spring that all of his family's crops were destroyed, leaving them financially ruined. Dejected, Jonas had no choice but to join the army.[10] He enrolled in the military school in Kaunas, and within months was transferred to Klaipėda, where he was sworn in to the army on November 13, 1930, at the age of twenty. His head shaven, he stood in a long line of soldiers, held his cap at his waist, and raised his right arm to take the soldier's oath. A priest may have walked down the row, holding a cross to bless the new recruits. In effect, the army became Jonas's new father: one he would love, obey, honor, and defend until death. It would instill in him discipline and confidence, and it would never leave him helpless as his father and brother had.

The accounts of Antanas and my great-aunt left me wondering how profoundly my grandfather's life had been affected by his growing up without a father. To what extent did the army shape his identity?

Preoccupied with my deathbed promise to my mother, I believed that if I could portray my grandfather's true character I would fulfill my sacred obligation.

Vilnius
October 1, 2018

The petitioner [Grant Gochin] depends on the judgment of Noreika's granddaughter, S. Foti, claiming, "She believes that Jonas Noreika was...a perpetrator of the Holocaust, and that this has been one of Lithuania's greatest cover-ups of the last century."

Vilnius Regional Administrative Court

File No. eI-4215-281/2018

Response from the Genocide Resistance and Research Centre to the prosecution's claim against the Genocide Centre's refusal to change its historical conclusion on Jonas Noreika

CHAPTER EIGHT

A Tarnished Halo

My brother and I were delighted to arrive at the Jonas Noreika Grammar School. It was a modest, white-brick building with oak trim. Hundreds of children must have run through its halls and sat in its classrooms, learning about my grandfather's World War II exploits, as we had done at our grandmother's feet. Viktoras Ašmenskas, imposing in his decorated Lithuanian Air Force uniform, had arranged for our welcome as honorary guests. We had been asked to distribute prizes to the winners of the student races held to mark our grandfather's ninetieth birthday.

The school director, Boleslovas Tallat-Kelpša, a stout man with disheveled white hair, grasped our hands energetically, saying how pleased he was that we had come to host the ceremony. At his direction the students, holding flowers, lined the halls to greet us as we entered the building.

Tallat-Kelpša offered us frothy mugs of beer. We could hardly refuse, though it was not yet noon. Ray and I were led to his office, where he proudly showed us a thick scrapbook filled with articles about our illustrious ancestor. Many of the clippings included the familiar photograph of Jonas Noreika arrayed in his military uniform. We had seen this picture every day of our childhoods. I set down my beer to flip through the album's pages. The headlines were repetitive: "Generolas Vėtra: 'I want to die on February six-teenth'"; "In memory of Generolas Vėtra"; "A monument will stand in Šukioniai." The director, secretaries, teachers, and children all looked on as Ray and I perused the book.

"Our mother had similar scrapbooks of our grandfather," I told the director in our native tongue.

He patted me on the back. "I can imagine. I heard you are writing a book on Jonas Noreika, that you have taken over the task from your mother. How wonderful!"

"How did you decide to name the school after him?" I asked.

He stroked his chin and answered, "It was during a meeting of the county board. We wanted to pick a new name, to replace the Russian one. Your grand-father's name surfaced immediately." Then, abruptly, he pulled me and my brother aside. Lowering his voice, he confided, "I got a lot of grief at first, when we picked his name."

The comment perplexed me. But all eyes were still upon me, as if I were a great celebrity. I struggled to conceal my confusion.

"He was accused of being a Jew-killer," whispered the director.

My eyes met Ray's. He, too, was aghast. *Accused of being a Jew-killer? What could the director mean? Had we heard correctly?* I studied his face for a moment, feeling off-balance, then looked around the room at the teachers and others assembled. Who were all these people? And who was I? Or my mother? Or my grandmother? Or my grandfather? My mind whirled in disbelief. *There must be some mistake. It can't be true.*

The school director was still talking to me, but I couldn't hear him. I felt as if he were speaking from the other side of a long and winding tunnel. He clearly expected a response from me, but I was at a loss for words—or even for thought. I didn't want to have a conversation about the possibility that my grandfather was a Jew-killer. It felt as if my brain were doing somersaults. As my legs seemed about to buckle, I grabbed a chair and plopped down heavily, breathing deeply to stop my heart from sprinting, every nerve in my body at military attention.

The director stroked my arm reassuringly. "I'm getting more support now than ever from the Lithuanians for choosing your grandfather's name. Everything is fine now. All of that is in the past, just Communist propaganda. We're so happy you and your brother have come to help celebrate the Olympiad."

I stammered an inane reply. I wanted him to stop talking, to take back what he had said. I wanted never to have heard it. *Why would he say such a thing?* My mother and grandmother had never mentioned any such accusation. Nor had anyone else I knew. My legendary grandfather was part of my identity, my DNA. I felt such shame at hearing him accused of being a Jew-killer, shame I didn't want to face. *My grandfather was a hero. He was.* Feeling lost, I couldn't wait for the ceremony to end.

Still stunned, I went through the motions expected of a guest of honor. I took my place with my brother in a clearing in the woods where several chairs had been placed so that we could watch the races. The school director formally introduced us to the crowd, and we waved to the children who would race along the marked trails. I felt as if I were straddling two identities: one the granddaughter of a national hero, smiling and accepting the crowd's affection and accolades; the other a glassy-eyed, distracted journalist. The schoolchildren looked thinner than their American counterparts, I noted. The director handed us cookie-sized, ceramic medallions depicting a runner and bearing the words: "Race—In Honor of J. Noreika—Storm's 90th birthday, Šukionių Grammar School, 2000."

Each winner rushed up to us, panting heavily and holding out a hand for the medal. "Are you really his granddaughter?" they asked me.

"Yes, I am."

Throughout the awards ceremony that followed, my mind was darting. I noticed the bark peeling from a birch tree and was reminded of a hike at a Lithuanian scout camp in Michigan when I hadn't been able to resist stripping the silver-white bark from a birch tree. The leader had rushed over. "Don't do that! These are all over the native land, and they're considered sacred. The souls of the dead rest on birch-tree branches." Now I looked up at the silver leaves softly rustling—*a Jew-killer, a Jew-killer.* Did my grandfather's soul repose here, in the Lithuanian forest? *What am I supposed to believe?* I asked him. *Who are you? The rumor's not true, right?*

When the ceremony had ended, we visited my grandfather's birthplace once again—this time accompanied by a crowd. A black granite plaque embedded in a five-foot-tall rock marked the spot where his home had once stood. I looked out over the green field he must have surveyed as a boy. Walking across it, I reached a crumbling, white stable with a small grocery store in the corner.

The school's staff and students then assembled around the black monument. General Storm's nephew, Stasys, gave a speech. "I tried to visit him at the KGB prison in 1947, before he sacrificed his life," he intoned. Like many others, Stasys used the language of martyrdom rather than acknowledging that my grandfather had been executed. "He was a holy man, for a friend who was there saw a halo around his head before he was murdered. All of you are standing here today because of men like Jonas Noreika, who fought for our country's freedom. Never forget that!"

A halo around his head. A holy man. This account reflected the glorious stories that I had heard and cherished all my life. I didn't want to give them up; indeed, there seemed to be no reason that I should. If General Storm was a Jew-killer, why would he be so revered, with a school and monuments dedicated to his memory? It wasn't possible. The school director must be wrong.

I clung to the notion of my grandfather's halo.

After a few more speeches, I was startled when the director requested that I address a few words to the audience. The children, with their windblown hair and open faces, looked up at me so expectantly that I couldn't decline. Struggling against my misgivings and my resentment over the rumor, I began: "I never met my grandfather, but all my life I heard about the wonderful things he had done. I always wished that I could have met him. Looking at you, the students of his school, I feel that I've met him, because I see that his spirit lives on in you. And I'm sure he considers you to be his grandchildren too."

Upon our return that evening, Viktoras Ašmenskas regaled me and my brother with tales of our grandfather's deeds. He described how they had worked together in the underground resistance movement, been arrested by the Communists, and been taken to the KGB prison. From there, Viktoras was sent to Siberia—and our grandfather was executed.

I asked bluntly, "Have you ever heard a rumor about him killing Jews?" Viktoras fixed me with his penetrating blue eyes, as if measuring me. Then he nodded. "The Nazis appointed him to the position of district chief in 1941. He felt conflicted about taking it, but he thought he could help our country more by accepting it than rejecting it. He was good at diplomacy, at playing both sides of the fence. So he took the job."

Before I could stop myself, I asked, "Do you think he made the right decision?"

Again his blue eyes cut through me. "Definitely. But many others don't."

I had always known that my grandfather was the district chief; this post was considered the height of his political career. But I had never considered that he might have been a Nazi collaborator. Yet Viktoras didn't seem at all surprised by my question; it was as if he had known about the rumor for years. How many others knew? Why hadn't my brother and I known?

As Ray and I readied ourselves to leave the apartment in downtown Vilnius, the phone rang. A male voice I didn't recognize said, "I was at your grandfather's funeral. I'm the one with the beard."

"I'm sorry, I don't seem to remember you," I replied. *Who was this?* I knew it wasn't Damijonas, the colleague of my grandfather's who hadn't shaved since my mother's death. And I doubted it was Chief Council Chairman Landsbergis.

He laughed. "I can understand why. There were so many there. How could you possibly keep track of everyone? Anyway, I called to apologize that more of the country's leaders didn't come."

"What do you mean?"

"They were afraid of what the Jews would say."

"Excuse me?" I had the sensation of falling through a trapdoor. *How common is this knowledge? How is it that everyone seems to have heard the rumor but me?*

He let out a long sigh. I waited for him to continue. *What did he mean by saying that more leaders would have come? What did he mean by "what the*

Jews would say"? What could they possibly say? I wanted to ask him these questions, but I hesitated. A tangle of confusion, shame, and denial left me ill-prepared to confront him. *Is this what it feels like to be in the slipstream of an alternate universe?* Time had slowed, but I could do nothing to avoid what was to come.

The caller cleared his throat. "I also wanted to tell you that the country was going to build a statue of him, but we just can't do it because of the controversy. I'm so sorry."

"What?"

The taste of bile crept into my throat. My mother had spoken of a statue that she expected the government to build to her father's memory; she had told me that its completion was just a matter of time. *So there would be no statue, after all? Can you please explain why?* I couldn't voice the questions; they froze before reaching my lips. Also, I was afraid of the answers.

Unwilling to betray my hurt and sudden panic, I allowed seconds to elapse. After an awkward silence, the caller wished me a pleasant trip home and said, "Goodbye."

I hung up slowly. I recalled what the school's director had said about its name being controversial, about the rumors that my grandfather was a "Jew-killer." I replayed the mystery caller's words. I felt betrayed that my grandfather wouldn't get the statue promised by the state. I pictured him powerfully rendered in bronze, his boots planted firmly on the ground, his sword raised, and me kneeling at his feet. I wanted that statue, a symbol of his true heroism.

I turned to Ray. "I can't believe this. This is too much." I related the caller's words.

My brother was stunned and indignant.

I began pacing the room. "I thought *he* was the victim," I said.

"This certainly is an unexpected twist," replied Ray, after a pause. "Although it would be just like Mom and Močiutė to neglect telling us."

"You think they knew?"

"They must have heard the rumor."

"Why wouldn't they have told us?" I was sure he was wrong, but thankful to have him there nonetheless; my brother was the only other living soul who could understand exactly what I felt. Our childhoods had been infused with the worship of our grandfather.

I rubbed my temples, remembering my mother's and grandmother's whisperings about the Communists' smear campaign to sully Jonas Noreika's name. But that was the Communists. No one had said anything about the Jews.

A gust of wind blew through the open kitchen window, rattling the gray metallic shades. Rain slanted in. We closed the window and switched from tea to wine. We talked late into the night, trying to piece our memories into a whole story. I was unwilling to surrender my status as the granddaughter of a hero. Would I be compelled to break my promise to my mother?

Vilnius
October 1, 2018

The true Jewish massacre designers were not the Lithuanians, but the Third Reich government. There is no reliable data to prove that J. Noreika gave orders to kill Jews, or that he himself participated in the operations to annihilate Jews.

Vilnius Regional Administrative Court

File No. eI-4215-281/2018

Response from the Genocide Resistance and Research Centre to the prosecution's claim against the Genocide Centre's refusal to change its historical conclusion on Jonas Noreika

CHAPTER NINE

The Arrest of Jonas Noreika

Back home in Chicago, I resumed my life as a wife, mother, and free-lance writer. While catching up on the assignments that had been postponed until my return, I deliberated over how to approach Jonas Noreika's story. Everyone in Marquette Park whom I told about the disturbing rumor—including my father, my uncles, my mother's closest friends, and my own—thought that it was most likely Communist propaganda designed to wound Lithuania's national pride. They advised me to proceed with caution. The only person who told me directly to drop the project was my father's new wife. She said it would "make Lithuania look bad." Meanwhile, the journalist in me recognized that the unexpected complication could result in a far better story.

So I equivocated. I delayed investigating the rumor about Jewish deaths. Instead I decided to wade through the mountain of information left to me by my mother. During my spare time I attempted to record the memories and impressions of my grandfather passed down to me by various family members. I reasoned that this undertaking would occupy me for quite a while, allowing me time to process and to assess the unwelcome new angle. And over the next few years, my familial and professional obligations left me very little spare time. I lamented the irony that my writing career didn't leave me time to write the story that so preoccupied me. Finally, after years of agonizing over a solution to this conundrum, I decided to pursue a secondary school English teaching certificate; a teaching job would free up my summers. Seven years after my mother's death, upon obtaining a second master's degree and fulfilling the requirements of a student teacher, I landed a position at a selective-enrollment urban high school where I taught literature and journalism—and eventually creative writing. I would finally have ten uninterrupted weeks each year to write the story.

I could not have known that this odyssey would last another decade. Nor could I have foreseen how it would precipitate an acute personal crisis.

Over the years, I sifted through my memories. The most vivid moment in my grandfather's life—recounted to me the most often by my mother, grandmother, and great-aunt—was the last day that the three of them had seen him, in Šiauliai. It was at nine on Wednesday morning, March 17, 1943, a date that gradually acquired mythical proportions in my mind. The events of that date had shattered their lives; everything thereafter was measured as having happened before or after that day. March 17, 1943—a date shared with St. Patrick—symbolized the Trinity's very antithesis: unholy disunity, horror, and distrust between Lithuania, Germany, and Russia, the three countries vying for control of their native land.

As my mother had told me, she was playing with one of her dolls when two Gestapo agents dressed in gray wool coats banged on the front door of the family apartment. Because her father was chief of the district, their two-story, yellow-stone, government-owned home at 265 Vilnius Avenue was spacious in comparison to those of the neighbors. The family's second-floor suite had six rooms. She remembered a walnut buffet filled with expensive German tea sets, a chess table, and her father's pistol and sword hanging on the wall. Next to a three-foot crucifix before which the family prayed was the image of Vytis, Lithuania's national emblem.[1]

My grandmother peeked through the lace curtains and shuddered when she saw the agents stamping snow from their cleated boots. "Oh, my

God. Oh, my God!" she cried, and crossed herself. "It's them! What can we do?"

She whispered to her daughter, "Dalytė, go and open the front door."

My mother was too frightened to obey.

The agents knocked more loudly and then kicked the door, bellowing, "Open up!"

"Just do as I say!" my grandmother ordered. She reasoned that the men might have pity upon her husband when they saw that he had a four-year-old child.

Even when I was a child myself, I could imagine my mother as a young girl on the day she lost her father. It was only a week after her fourth birthday. Moments before the Nazis had stormed into the room, she had been picking lint off her doll's red velvet dress. She recounted the tale so vividly that my spirit became more strongly bound up with hers with each retelling.

A month before, the civilian German government had issued a proclamation inviting all Lithuanians between the ages of seventeen and forty-five to join the SS. It declared that the Führer was conferring a high honor upon the local population in permitting them to participate in this unit. Posters had appeared throughout the country on February 24, 1943:

> Lithuanians:
>
> When the German soldiers, by order of the Führer, Adolf Hitler, in 1941 liberated your home country from Bolshevism, they saved you from the fate of national extermination. Since then, you have contributed your share in the fight against Bolshevism by your work on the farms and in the towns, but also by your service in the security organs of the country and through active participation at the fronts. This struggle has now reached its culmination point. Bolshevism is threatening to engulf Europe. In the first place your home country is endangered.... Victory will save you, your life and that of your children, your property, your culture, the continued existence of your people on your native soil, your place of work and your collaboration

in the European community. To arms! To work! With Adolf
Hitler to victory![2]

At the appointed registration time, no one appeared. In order to avoid
being drafted, men of the ages stipulated neither attended school nor reported
to work. The German government pressured its designated local leaders,
including my grandfather, to urge the youth to join. But all resisted, as if of
one mind.

"This was one of Lithuania's proudest moments," my grandmother told
me. "Lithuania was the only country to resist creating an SS Legion."[3]

On the same day on which my grandfather was arrested, the German-
controlled government closed all universities and destroyed cultural treasures
at the Lithuanian Academy of Sciences. It declared that no Lithuanians would
be allowed to join the German Army, as they were unworthy of becoming German soldiers. Instead they would be given menial jobs to assist the armed forces.
This was an act of vengeance for their refusal to join the SS.

My grandfather was reading the newspaper *Tėviškė* in the living room
when the Gestapo officers came to arrest him. Forty-five other leaders of the
community also were taken hostage that day, to demoralize the populace and
to terrify it into complying with German demands.

Even a few years before she died, my mother still shivered when she
repeated the story of her father's arrest. She had always struggled with guilt for
being the one who opened the door to the men who took him away. Irrationally,
she blamed herself for his arrest and for the shattering of her family.

"But Močiutė *made* you open the door," I pointed out.

"I've been replaying that moment ever since," she replied. "I just wish I
weren't the one who opened the door."

"You're under arrest," one of the agents had informed her father. "Under
the orders of the Kaunas Security Police. You have one hour and thirty minutes to gather your things. Eat a big breakfast, pack warm clothes, and take
some food for your trip."

None of them—Jonas, Močiutė, or my mother—knew that he was on his
way to Stutthof, a Nazi concentration camp.

Vilnius
October 1, 2018

We would like to draw your attention to the fact that on February 23, 1943, J. Noreika was arrested and imprisoned at the Stutthof concentration camp for inciting Lithuanians against the Reich Commissar's attempts to mobilize Lithuanians [to join the SS]. Karl Jäger, Commander of the SD [Einsatzkommando] in Lithuania, wrote the accusation [against J. Noreika] himself.

Vilnius Regional Administrative Court
File No. el-4215-281/2018
Response from the Genocide Resistance and Research Centre to the prosecution's claim against the Genocide Centre's refusal to change its historical conclusion on Jonas Noreika

CHAPTER TEN

Tender Letters and a Dark Fairy Tale

My native land calls and pulls my heart. The feeling is unbear-
ably strong, as if it were a storm brewing within me, saying, "You
will return, you will return to your fatherland." But when? For
St. John's Festival? I doubt it. Or maybe, maybe you know better.
A couple of days ago, I dreamt of our wedding day filled with
flowers. It was just before entering the church while everyone
waited for us. I was in one room, while you were in another. I
didn't see you, but I knew that you were there. I wait.

—Jonas Noreika, June 13, 1943[1]

When my grandfather arrived at the Stutthof prison, in present-day Gdansk, Poland, he was permitted to write letters. I was told that he sent a letter to my grandmother every week without fail—which surely proved his love for her. I spent years reading, translating, and scrutinizing these seventy-seven letters to my grandmother, in addition to the fairy tale that he wrote to my mother in 1943 and 1944 from Stutthof, and the three thousand pages of KGB transcripts detailing his rebellion.

I was still unwilling to confront the allegation that he had played a role in murdering Jews.

Struggling to be an objective journalist, I asked myself: How could he be a Jew-killer if he had been in a Nazi concentration camp? Didn't that alone prove his innocence?

I opened the white binder holding the letters and flipped through its pages. I wasn't sure what I was looking for. Would I stumble upon evidence that he had played a role in the murders with which the rumors charged him? Would I find any expressions of remorse for his having taken part in the Lithuanian Holocaust? It seemed odd that he had been allowed to write letters from a Nazi concentration camp at all. Did Jews also write letters home from this camp?

The Nazis had required that he write in German so his messages could be censored. My mother had asked my grandmother to translate my grandfather's German correspondence into Lithuanian. Thus I was reading the letters that my grandfather had written in the Stutthof prison to my grandmother in her own handwriting. In 1943 the camp held twenty thousand prisoners. That number swelled to nearly sixty thousand by December 1944— just before the Soviet invasion. Most of the prisoners were Jews.[2]

On August 1, 1943, my grandfather wrote to my grandmother in an inexplicably playful mood: "I received your last package on July 29, just a couple of days ago. Chocolate and vitamins. A big thank you. Don't send luxurious things because at this time it's so difficult to get such luxuries. I am healthy and in good shape—as if in my youth I had won a 100-meter dash. You don't believe it?! Believe it!"[3]

The Nazis had let him receive luxuries in a concentration camp? Surely such goods were generally confiscated. What could account for this special treatment? I flipped through the letters, trying to get a better sense of who this man was. In a letter dated August 29, 1943, he sounded frustrated by the infrequency of his wife's correspondence: "You still don't understand what your letters mean to me. Your letters are a tender breath of the fragrance of the fatherland's flowers."[4]

My grandfather's letters were suffused with a Lithuanian nationalism very familiar to me. Reading them conjured images from my childhood. My brother and I had visited our grandmother every Saturday after our Lithuanian classes to have lunch with her, to receive tutoring and help with our homework, and to listen to her stories about her famous husband. At 5:00 p.m. each Saturday we followed her from the kitchen to the living room and seated ourselves next to an oak table with a photograph of our grandfather in his military uniform on it. He was movie-star handsome, with a strong chin. It was her custom to reach for the picture and hold it in her lap, staring at it wistfully. She wore her widowhood so proudly. We had been blessed with an impossibly romantic grandfather.

On September 29, 1943, in a passionate mood, he penned these lines: "Meilė, meilė, meilė. Whether we utter that one word in German or English or French or Russian, it always sounds the most tender in Lithuanian—To love, to love, to love! Oh, how pure is that emotion. Liebe!... Love!... Amor!... Meilė! Yes, yes!... Now the world is stepping backwards, sighing, sobbing, crying, bleeding from hatred to love. To love! And we will understand each other better if, in this life, the Lord will allow us to be together forever."[5]

His hope that he and his wife would be reunited demonstrated that he had not resigned himself to dying by German hands.

My grandfather's last letters were sacred to our family, serving as testament to his love for his family and his noble sacrifice for his country, as well as a touchstone to our identity as persons tragically displaced from our fatherland.

Yet I was disappointed by how little the correspondence disclosed. Subject to German scrutiny, its content was deliberately vague and mundane. In a letter dated October 3, 1943, my grandfather wrote, "It's not possible, my love, during war to foresee everything so perfectly. Sometimes you have to make decisions listening to the voice in your heart.

"I'd like to know what is going on with my colleague Eisalinis, how he feels and how his family is faring.

"About your decision to remain as the elementary school teacher, I can't advise. I trust that you chose according to your desires. You can get closer to the children's souls in grammar school than in high school teaching a foreign language."[6]

The mention of Eisalinis was a reference to Gebietskommissar Hans Gewecke, my grandfather's superior when he was the head of the Šiauliai District during the Nazi occupation.

On December 26, 1943, my grandfather wrote, "In today's dramatic situation, hopeful rays shine—one day we will live freely in a free land.

"…Do you still get 50 percent from the regional leadership?…Who is working in my office, the salon?

"P.S. Yla sends you his greetings."[7]

I remembered meeting Father Yla in my parents' living room when I was a teenager. He pressed his memoir into my hands, saying that he and my grandfather had been great friends. My grandmother and mother stood, weeping, both of them overcome with pride and sorrow—emotions that had become so fused in my family, I couldn't distinguish between them.

Father Yla, struck by my grandfather's devotion during Mass, had asked him to write a prayer, which he included in his published account, *A Priest in Stutthof: Human Experiences in the World of [the] Subhuman.* My mother copied out this prayer in her own distinctive handwriting, framed it in a border of orange tulips, and hung it on the dining room wall: "In the prison basement, the fading man's bony hand reaches out to You. In the bloody war, within the grenade-bombed ditch, a suffocating soldier's last sigh calls for You. Upon hearing terrible news, he leans against the window, kneels and calls Your name, Beloved."[8]

Part of this text was inscribed on my grandfather's tombstone. How could someone as devout as the author of these lines possibly be guilty of killing Jews?

The torch of faith and patriotism that had been passed from my grandfather to my mother to me linked us inextricably. If she had planned to write a book about him and had died before realizing this goal, clearly it was my obligation to continue where she had left off.

Yet I was surprised by how little she actually had written. I had expected to find a manuscript; instead, I encountered only preliminary research: an archive of documents, and perhaps twenty handwritten pages describing her last day with her father. There also were a few poems in Lithuanian, expressing her longing for the homeland. Could she have heard the rumor about her father? She and my grandmother must have believed him innocent and the rumor to be a fabrication by the Communists, intended to ruin his good name. Nonetheless, the accusation would have shocked and hurt her. Is that why she had not made more progress with her book? What, then, could be expected of me?

I was greatly relieved that nowhere in the seventy-seven letters was there any mention of Jews. Nevertheless, at some point, I would have to confront the rumor head-on.

I contemplated Jonas Noreika's bust, now hanging above my desk. I had not surrendered my dream of completing a book about a man whose patriotism and bravery would reflect honor upon my family. To delay the research I dreaded, I decided to reread the fairy tale that he had composed for my mother when she was six years old.

I pulled a copy of his tale from her binder. The main characters were a princess named Elytė, also six years old, and her father, a duke fighting evil usurpers. But the story of the struggle for a lost kingdom ended abruptly; because of his evacuation from the Nazi concentration camp, my grandfather had never had time to finish the story.

The bleak tale had been sent in the mail from German-occupied Poland to German-occupied Lithuania in 1944 in eleven installments. My grandmother read each new episode to my mother, who sat in her lap in their large government-owned apartment in Šiauliai, which had been granted to my grandfather while he served as chief of the district, a post he held for eighteen months—until his arrest.

I wondered what his duties had entailed. My research had disclosed that he'd held the highest position available to a Lithuanian under the Nazis' thumb. Šiauliai, founded at the junction of two roads where ancient hunters and warriors met, was the fourth-largest city in Lithuania, after Vilnius, Kaunas, and Klaipėda. By the time my grandfather assumed office, it boasted thirty-two thousand inhabitants, including eight thousand Jews: 25 percent of the population.[9]

My grandfather's jurisdiction, however extended much farther than the city limits; he was chief of the entire Šiauliai District, a region encompassing three thousand square miles: about one-eighth of the country.[10] His sphere of influence included Gruzdžiai, Joniškis, Kriukai, Kruopiai, Kuršėnai, Linkuva,

Lygumai, Meškuičiai, Padubysis, Pakruojis, Papilė, Pašvitinys, Radviliškis, Skaistgiris, Stačiūnai, Šaukėnai, Šiauliai, Šiaulėnai, Tryškiai, Užventis, Vaiguva, Žagarė, and Žeimelis.

While my grandfather was in charge there, as I would soon learn, the Jews in these hamlets, villages, and county parishes were checked, transferred to a ghetto, and shot. In addition, all the property that the Jews left behind was counted, inventoried, registered, and transferred to new owners. I would soon find out that my grandfather's signature appeared at the bottom of several documents ordering the transfer of Jews to ghettos and the redistribution of their property.

At present, however, I was engrossed in his fairy tale.

It was evidently an allegory, with frogs symbolizing the enemy and a witch representing their leader. The valiant duke, of course, stood for my grandfather. The story, first read to my mother by her mother, was later shared by my mother and grandmother with me and my brother: "The duke had to go off to war. He had to meet the enemy, defeat the enemy, and free the country.

"What would life be without their country?"

Unlike most fairy tales, this one did not have a happy ending. The duke had to stay in his kingdom to fight the evil giant frogs who had overtaken the land. He could not rescue his captive daughter.

It was clear to me as an adult that the fairy tale alluded to the wrenching decision that Jonas Noreika faced, torn between his love and duty to Lithuania and his love and duty to his wife and young daughter. Should he advise his family to remain in Lithuania to await his potential return, or to flee to safety? Perhaps my grandfather anticipated that he would forfeit his life and was signaling to his wife that he had to desert them in order to give their daughter a chance.

The tale ended with: "I can't remain as half a man. I must die."

This forecast of doom was my grandfather's last communication to his young daughter before he was taken by the Germans from Stutthof in anticipation of the Soviets' arrival. Possibly he intended to finish the story at a later date.

Shortly after Lithuania regained its independence in 1990, I reworked the fairy tale and created an ending. Not only did I translate and rewrite the original, changing the duke and duchess to a king and queen, but I published the new version in *Lituanus*, a Lithuanian American quarterly then managed by my father.[11] I wanted to demonstrate what a great hero Lithuania had produced. To me, my grandfather epitomized the soul of Lithuania during World War II: romanticism, nationalism, and the valiant fight against the Communists and the Nazis. His imprisonment and execution only served to burnish the chronicle of his life. A newly independent Lithuania had resurrected him as a celebrity, and I had gotten caught up in magnifying the myth of Jonas Noreika's legacy.

And now I cast the doubts prompted by the horrifying rumor that he had killed Jews to the back of my mind.

Vilnius
October 1, 2018

The petitioner claims that in the Centre's 2016 edition of its newsletter, Alfred Rukšėnas wrote a 26-page article depicting Noreika as a protector of the Jews, as someone who had no genocidal tendencies. Rukšėnas focused exclusively on Noreika's actions concerning the expropriation of Jewish property, using the euphemism "economic genocide," thereby reducing the crimes of Noreika. The "economic genocide" conducted by Jonas Noreika should be understood as the obliteration of an ethnic group through its economic destruction; however, the Centre paints an incredibly rosier picture.

Vilnius Regional Administrative Court

File No. el-4215-281/2018

Response from the Genocide Resistance and Research Centre to the prosecution's claim against the Genocide Centre's refusal to change its historical conclusion on Jonas Noreika (summarizing claims by petitioner Grant Gochin)

CHAPTER ELEVEN

The KGB Transcripts

I contemplated the three thousand pages of KGB transcripts sitting in front of me. My hope was that they would yield details of my grandfather's rebellion against the Communists during the second Soviet occupation—and that this task would serve as a welcome delay in my investigation of the rumor.

Somehow my mother had managed to obtain these Russian documents shortly after Lithuania's independence in 1990. It seems that she had bribed someone to make copies, asked a friend to smuggle them from Vilnius to Chicago, and then mailed the transcript copies to Damijonas Riauka—her father's colleague during the five-day uprising against the first Soviet occupation—to be translated into Lithuanian. She had paid him thousands of dollars for this service.

Damijonas was also my mother's volunteer clipping-service agent. He had taken it upon himself to cut out articles about her father and to send them to her, accompanied by lengthy letters. I remember her occasionally, over the course of nearly a decade, mentioning the arrival of these packets to me. "Last week it was three; this week, another two," she had remarked. "He just never stops! It's been like this for years. I can't even bear to open his envelopes anymore."

I now understood how overwhelmed she must have felt. Damijonas continued zealously in his role as a provider of both old and recent clippings even after my mother's death. My grandfather remained a subject of interest in the fatherland, and the articles concerning Jonas Noreika were accompanied by letters of detailed instructions as to how I should write my book. I winced at the arrival of each new package.

My mother had organized the three-hole-punched KGB transcript pages into five thick white binders. I had hoped that their contents would follow a chronological order, beginning with my grandfather's first interrogation after his capture by the KGB in March 1946 and ending with the last, shortly before his execution on February 26, 1947. But the transcripts weren't so easily organized. Jonas Noreika was one of eleven rebels who stood trial together; their testimony, too, was included. Attempting to follow the threads of the various accounts was like trying to analyze a spiderweb. Nearly every page of the typed Lithuanian translation bore Damijonas's handwritten commentary in the margins or between the lines. I found myself having to read each page two or three times: first the translation itself, then Damijonas's commentary, then both together in order to understand his view of the interrogations. Only then could I begin to render the transcripts into English. The massive amount of information in the seven files regarding the eleven accused individuals forced the realization that I couldn't possibly decode all of it; I would have to select the passages I wanted to translate for the book.

On the first page of his translation, Damijonas had drawn a color-coded diagram, with commentary, of individuals and groups he believed to have been spying on my grandfather.[1] The KGB's Security Service, led by Lithuania's Communist Party leader Antanas Šniečkus and high-ranking KGB officer Aleksandras Guzevičius, had recruited Juozas Markulis, a doctor who convinced the partisans that he was the head of an underground intelligence group.[2] The partisans unwittingly chose this undercover agent as one of the main leaders of their new Joint Democratic Resistance Movement (BDPS). (He was nicknamed "Erelis," or "Eagle.") In addition to these "false partisans," as Damijonas called them, there was a network of KGB secret agents named "Falanga," or "Phalanx," specifically assigned to spy on my grandfather. His co-accused, Viktoras Tamulis, was apparently another KGB agent. Tamulis had sent "AŠ" to "steal" a plane. "AŠ" was Viktoras Ašmenskas, whom Damijonas evidently believed also to be a KGB agent.

Ašmenskas asserted—both in his book, which was based in part on transcripts of these same KGB documents, and to me in person—that he had intended to fly the plane to Sweden to distribute my grandfather's "Proclamation to the World's Nations."[3] Damijonas, however, had placed the word "steal" in quotation marks to indicate his suspicion that this was a fake plan, designed by the KGB to entrap Jonas Noreika. But then Damijonas saw conspiracies everywhere. He was regarded as an eccentric by some in Chicago's Lithuanian community; I had been warned to take everything that he said with the proverbial grain of salt. So Viktoras Ašmenskas was either Jonas Noreika's best friend or his worst betrayer. That was another mystery I didn't know if I could untangle. But it paled in comparison with the accusation that my grandfather had been a Jew-killer.

These KGB transcripts were supposed to be proof that Jonas Noreika had been a hero who had deserved the Vytis Cross, the highest honor that Lithuania could bestow posthumously, and the public streets and the school named after him. The Museum of Genocide Victims, whose assessment was officially recognized by the Lithuanian government, relied heavily upon these transcripts. I needed to find out for myself whether these same transcripts contained proof that this celebrated man was involved in the killing of Jews.

As I combed through the transcripts, I made notes of details from each of the prisoners' accounts, then ordered the events chronologically so as to trace the rebellion and its strangulation by the KGB. Then I integrated the accounts that I found in books, newspapers, and radio transcripts. To these I added descriptions by Noreika's colleague Damijonas Riauka, the translator of these documents, and Viktoras Ašmenskas. Finally, I included stories from my mother and grandmother. This process yielded seventy-eight single-spaced pages of notes.

In the end, two years of reading and translating compelled me to conclude that my grandfather's purported rebellion against the Communists was little more than a quixotic suicide mission; it was never a serious challenge to

the Soviets' iron grip on Lithuania. Nonetheless, it was clear that he had suffered enormously for the attempt. His martyrdom by the KGB for Lithuania's
freedom captured the government's and media's attention, and that attention
made him a hero.

The Soviets had invaded and occupied Lithuania, "liberating" it from the
Germans, in July 1944. While the remaining Jews, the few who had survived
the Nazis' extermination campaign, were relieved at this development, Lithuanian nationals were horrified. The Soviets terrorized Lithuanians, forcing
them into the Red Army and deporting thousands to Siberia and the gulags.
Thousands sought refuge in the forests; many became partisans. These "bandits"—Damijonas had stricken out every KGB reference in the transcripts to
"bandits," replacing each with "partisans!!!!"—attempted to reclaim villages
and succeeded in at least one case, although at a terrible cost. Between the
years 1944 and 1953, approximately thirty thousand partisans fought Soviet
soldiers, and about twenty thousand lost their lives.[4]

Jonas Noreika was evacuated from Stutthof by the Nazis in early 1945 and
then promptly conscripted into the Red Army. Upon his demobilization later
that year he returned to Vilnius, where he arrived on November 27, 1945. He
went directly to the home of Vladas Jurgutis, a sixty-year-old professor who
had become a father figure to him while they both were detained at Stutthof.
There my grandfather befriended Vladas's niece, Elena Jurgutytė.

My mother later suspected that Elena had fallen in love with him. She had
visited him in the KGB prison, and she kept his prayer book and handkerchief
for nearly five decades before returning them to my mother in 1990, when
Lithuania regained its freedom. In my mother's archives was a letter from
Elena, in which she described her admiration of my grandfather:

> He came to Uncle's often, and every Sunday we ate a better-than-
> usual lunch. After lunch, Uncle would let Jonas and me take a
> walk. I admit I looked forward to those walks. Like Stasys Yla
> wrote in his book *Men and Monsters*, Noreika wanted to expand
> his knowledge by helping Prof. Jurgutis in the camp. I wanted to
> enrich my spirit by keeping company with Noreika. We talked

about everything: art, music, religion. We imagined we were on top of a hill, looking out upon the wide space and stars. He was like my older brother. I was like his sister. I remember how he once explained rather lengthily that a person's spiritual world could be meager or very rich, and that no one else knows this inner world, nor our thoughts. That is why we must always try to enrich our spiritual world in every way possible. With his inspiration, I, with my youthful zest, tried to work, study, and improve myself. I was studying at the Vilnius University Business Faculty in the second course, and from early 1946, I worked in the Vilnius Conservatory accounting office.

I remember well how we celebrated Christmas Eve in 1945. He broke off two pieces of the Christmas wafer, placed them on the table and said they're for his wife and daughter. Later he ate them himself.[5]

My grandmother had once said, with some bitterness, that women swarmed around her husband wherever he went and that his receiving so much female attention often made it difficult to be his wife.

Soon after my grandfather arrived in Vilnius, he obtained a job as a lawyer for the Library of the Lithuanian Academy of Sciences. A bronze plaque honoring him now adorns its wall. It was there that he met librarian and writer Ona Lukauskaitė-Poškienė again. She had been the manager of the Šiauliai library during the Nazi occupation, when he had been the chief of Šiauliai District. The two immediately forged a bond of trust. Ona's sister Sofia had married Domas Jasaitis, a physician who lived a few doors down from the Noreikas' address. Ona told her new colleague that her brother-in-law and sister had fled to Germany on July 26, 1944. (My grandmother, mother, and great-aunt had fled two days later.)

The Soviets had intensified their deportations of Lithuanians to Siberia to demoralize the populace. Their campaign against the families of "bandits" included the exile of six thousand people in a two-month period. Typically, Russian soldiers surrounded a targeted house in the middle of the night, when their targets were all likely to be home and the operation could be conducted quietly. Anyone who resisted or attempted to flee was beaten or shot. Families were often deliberately separated as they were herded into cattle cars that took up to two months to reach Siberia.

Ona invited Noreika to her home on Giedraitis Street, House No. 10, Apartment 1. In the transcripts, her apartment was described as having a desk, a small round table, a worn sofa, a bookshelf, a wall clock, seven chairs, and a violin. According to her testimony, her guest requested that she try to obtain a large quantity of white paper. She promised to get it without asking the reason. She did not yet know that Noreika had been approached by Zigmas Šerkšnas-Laukaitis on behalf of partisans in the forest who needed to print their newsletter. Instantly, she thought of Stasys Gorodeckis, chairman of the Vilnius printing house with whom she was acquainted through the Writer's Union, located a few blocks from the Academy of Sciences.

When she approached Gorodeckis at the Writer's Union the next day, he understood right away that the paper she claimed to want was to be used by the underground. When he questioned her, she told him about Noreika. Gorodeckis demanded a meeting.

The two men met the next afternoon in Noreika's office, on the second floor of the Library of the Lithuanian Academy of Sciences. They recognized each other at once. In 1937, during my grandfather's stint as a lawyer for the Lithuanian army, he had prosecuted Gorodeckis—then the leader of the Lithuanian Scouts—for refusing to join the military. The Scouts were pacifists, and Gorodeckis was seen as setting a terrible example for the country's youth. Consequently, he was sent to jail—but evidently was released almost immediately. I learned these facts from his son, Sakalas. Astonishingly, Gorodeckis forgave my grandfather, perhaps in recognition of the vastly changed situation.

Gorodeckis recounted his meeting with my grandfather to the KGB:

At about 14:00, [Ona] Poškienė and I came to his station at work. Since he stood and talked to me openly, I understood Poškienė had told him about me. After we were introduced, we spoke about the paper. I told him about the possibility of stealing it from the storage area [of the printing shop I ran]. He told Poškienė to fulfill this assignment, and she agreed.

We then spoke about political matters. We agreed how necessary it was to have a center for the partisans to unite. I understood no center yet existed. It was just being formed. I told him about my attempts to do the same and we both agreed to join forces.

Some people came near and we couldn't talk freely, so we decided to meet at the apartment of Poškienė.[6]

Noreika, Gorodeckis, and Poškiene met at her apartment up to three times a week, often arriving at eight in the evening and staying until ten the next morning. They resolved to steal supplies for the partisans' *Freedom's Bell* from the government-run newspaper *Žaibas* (Lightning); these were kept—unguarded—at a Bernardine monastery. The bell after which the clandestine publication was named had been donated in 1920 by Lithuanian Americans, primarily from Chicago, shortly after the homeland gained independence in 1918. The words engraved on the bell became the homeland's national slogan, embraced by the partisans fighting the Soviets: "Ring through eternity for Lithuania's children. Freedom is unworthy for those unwilling to defend it."[7]

In January 1946, Gorodeckis accompanied my grandfather to the government storehouse. After inspecting the premises, which were usually open until 11:00 p.m., they realized that they would need a car with a reliable driver to steal the paper and deliver it to the partisans. This proved problematic, and the plan never came to fruition. In truth, few of their plans did.

Undaunted, they decided to launch an anti-Soviet rebellion, calling themselves Lietuvos Tautinė Taryba, the Lithuanian National Council. Poškiene explained their roles:

Ona Poškienė: It was Noreika's idea to create the Lithuanian National Council with our support. The three of us were its members.

KGB: What were your responsibilities?

Ona Poškienė: Since Noreika was a captain in the army, it was agreed he would lead the partisans. Gorodeckis would bring more members into the council. I would edit the documents.[8]

The rebellion that they envisioned depended for its success upon an invasion of Russia by England and the United States to save Lithuania from the Communists. Apparently, most Lithuanians were convinced that those powers would intervene to restore their democracy. After all, just a few years earlier, in 1941, Germany had invaded the country and freed it from the Soviet Union.

As the KGB interrogations revealed, the planned rebellion would have entailed the bombing of bridges, highways, and roads to paralyze the Soviet army, rendering it unable to act against English and American soldiers. The leaders of the uprising planned to issue Noreika's proclamation to the world announcing Lithuania's freedom. The declaration was to be translated into English and French and flown out by plane from Klaipėda to Sweden, with Viktoras Ašmenskas piloting. Viktoras Tamulis, the leader of Klaipėda's underground, had assisted in procuring a plane.

This was the rebels' vision: once the armed uprising was launched simultaneously with the invasion by the United States and England, a so-called death squad composed of young men led by Zigmas Šerkšnas-Laukaitis would seize Vilnius's radio and electrical stations and terrorize the Soviets in retaliation for the repression and deportations. They would supply paper to print announcements and food and medicine to partisans newly armed with American and English weapons. Lithuanians would mount a parade and dance in the streets, crying "Valio!" ("Hurray!") as a new government was formed. They had even devised a list of leaders for the new government once the country was free.

But their hopes for an American invasion were in vain. In February 1945, when Germany's defeat seemed imminent, British prime minister Winston Churchill, American president Franklin Delano Roosevelt, and Soviet premier Josef Stalin met in Yalta, Crimea, to draw up plans for Germany's division into Allied occupation zones. By then the Soviets had occupied Lithuania, and neither Roosevelt nor Churchill was willing to challenge Stalin's control of

Eastern Europe. Although the Yalta Conference inadvertently set the stage for the Cold War, the United States had no interest in military engagement with the Soviet Union.

In July 1945, the Soviets announced an "amnesty" and "legalization" campaign directed at partisans in hiding. A Soviet report dated 1957 stated that of the 38,838 partisans who consequently declared themselves, 8,350 were regarded as "armed nationalist bandits"; the other 30,488 were classified as "deserters avoiding conscription."[9]

But not all the partisans turned themselves in. Resistance to the Soviets continued, though confrontations with the NKVD (the Soviet Union's interior ministry, tasked with police work, prisons, and labor camps) and the MGB (Ministry for State Security) were replaced by more clandestine activities.

The partisans built bunkers in the forests. Thirteen thousand Soviet collaborators died at the hands of the partisans.[10] One of the partisans' most beloved leaders was Colonel Juozas Vitkus, code-named "Kazimieraitis." In the KGB transcripts, my grandfather referred to him as the "Old Man":

> In Nov. 1945, I left the Red Army and returned to Lithuania to help the country. I decided to join all of the bandit-formed groups under one leadership. In Jan. 1946, on a Vilnius Street, I met Zigmas Šerkšnas-Laukaitis, who knew me when I was captain of the former Lithuanian army. I asked him what he knew of the bandits [partisans] in Lithuania. He answered that in the Dzukija territory there were 300–400 people belonging to these groups. It was led by the colonel of the former Lithuanian army with the code name "Old Man"... Colonel Vitkus. I told him of my desire to meet him, to speak of centralizing leadership among all the armed forces in Lithuania.[11]

Noreika, Ona Poškienė, and Gorodeckis had hoped that Colonel Vitkus would agree to lead the partisan groups against the Communists. To their great disappointment, he declined without explanation. The three members of the fledgling Lithuanian National Council decided that Noreika, who was a captain in the army, would provisionally be appointed as leader. He devised a *nom de guerre* for himself: Generolas Vėtra (General Storm). As Viktoras Ašmenskas noted in his book, some thought that Noreika had chosen the name deliberately so as to be confused with the NKVD division leader General Vetrovas. To my mind "General Storm" was just a strong, romantic name. Gorodeckis assumed the code name "General Secretary Radžiūnas."[12]

The two men wrote flyers and directives aimed at uniting the armed partisan groups scattered throughout the country. Ona was the typist. In order to convey the impression that the Lithuanian National Council was an established body with its own history, they entitled their first decree "Number Five." They reasoned that readers would assume that an organization distributing its fifth edict must be thriving. The directive, whose release was timed to coincide with elections in January 1946, urged Lithuanians employed by the Soviet Union in administrative and political posts to resign their positions and cut all ties with Bolsheviks. Under the proud letterhead of the Lithuanian National Council, it proclaimed:

All nation's workers—Join the general war against the Bolshevik dictatorship.
To the fighters—Eternal honor
To the traitors—Dishonorable death

The page was signed by "Generolas Vėtra, the Supreme Chief-of-Staff Leader of the Lithuanian Armed Forces."[13]

Half of the Lithuanian population dutifully boycotted the Soviet elections.[14] This gesture of rebellion, however, cost the patriots dearly; thousands were deported to Siberia. The number of persons registered as "anti-Soviet elements"—including teachers and professors, school and college students, farmers, industry workers and craftsmen—totaled 320,000.[15]

Later directives from the council ordered Lithuanians to apply for Soviet government jobs so they could act as double agents who would secretly protect Lithuanian interests. The council also instructed civilians to join an armed uprising. In all, the Lithuanian National Council issued fourteen documents, which my grandfather listed during one of his interrogations:

1. Directive #5: I told you about this
2. Directive #6: How to organize partisans into regional groups
3. Directive #7: Protesting the deportations of anti-Soviet elements to distant regions of the Soviet Union, and regarding the creation of the death squad
4. Order #1: Announcing that Generolas Vėtra has assumed his duties
5. Order #2: Organizing the partisans into groups
6. Order #3: Forming four regional partisan groups, and establishing military command [posts] in cities, districts, and towns
7. Order #4: Concerning safety and security of partisan headquarters, to create the strongest anti-Soviet conspiracy
8. Instructions for keeping secrets
9. Decree regarding Soviet workers
10. Directing attention to world countries (message to be sent abroad)
11. February 1946 political review
12. March 1946 political review
13. Decree regarding the duties of Generolas Vėtra and General Secretary Radžiūnas
14. Proclamation of an armed uprising against the Soviet Union in Lithuania[16]

As my grandfather affirmed:

> The orders, directives and proclamation were written by me personally, but several changes and edits were made by Gorodeckis and Poškienė. Gorodeckis wrote the political reviews.[17]

The group had organized a network of messengers and spies to distribute these documents to the partisans. At one point Noreika gave Poškiene money to make copies that were to be taken to a messenger code-named "Elytė." This was Elena Kakariekaitė, a history student at the University of Vilnius, who

lived on Gediminas Street, House No. 35, Apartment 2, and was described in
the transcript as: "normal weight, blonde, blue eyes, and a straight nose."
Zigmas, the leader of the death squad, had introduced her to my grandfather,
telling him that she had access to the partisans in Alytus, Panevėžys, and
Telšiai, who were led by Colonel Vitkus.

When the council determined that it needed to establish a base for the uprising in Kaunas, Gorodeckis suggested enlisting the help of his old high school
friend Viktoras Ašmenskas, who lived on Kestučio Street, House No. 43. As a
representative of the State Literature Publishing House and the deputy director
of the Fine Art Fund, Gorodeckis drove to Kaunas two or three times a month
and frequently visited Ašmenskas. According to the stained pages of Gorodeckis's
testimony, "For various work reasons, we kept visiting each other and spending
nights at each other's apartments. We talked openly about politics from the anti-
Soviet position, and from this I came to know Ašmenskas as an anti-Soviet. In
January 1946, I decided to include Ašmenskas in our anti-Soviet group."[18]

Ašmenskas, though, was apparently already working for the Soviets—and
actually admitted as much to Gorodeckis. Ašmenskas's own statement to his
KGB interrogators read:

> I did not agree with [Gorodeckis's] suggestion because I was an
> agent of VSLK (NKGB) [the Soviet secret police, intelligence and
> counter-intelligence force, before being renamed the MGB] and I
> couldn't join in a war against the Soviet government.
>
> I did not relay this conversation with Gorodeckis to the oper-
> atives in VSLK. I met with him more than once after this, but the
> subject of anti-Soviet activity only arose in January 1946 in his
> home in Vilnius, where he told me about an anti-Soviet national-
> ist underground center, leading workers to unite anti-Soviet
> Lithuanians in a war in Kaunas and the surrounding area, start-
> ing to the left of Nemunas River. All the scattered bandits [par-
> tisans!!!] would be united from Marijampolė, Vilkaviškis, Šakiai,
> Lazdija, Alytus, and Kaunas, and he requested that I find people
> in Kaunas, whom I would personally verify, to help organize the

bandit groups in a nationalistic organization. He did not personally name any individuals. As to my anti-Soviet activity, I personally obliged myself to inform on him, as I had given my agreement, and I began to follow him.

Later, I unavoidably fell under his influence and entered his Vilnius anti-Soviet organization.[19]

Apparently Damijonas was right about Ašmenskas—or at least partly right. Viktoras Ašmenskas did work for the Soviets at one point. And while Ašmenskas seems to have been a reluctant recruit, a conflicted Lithuanian patriot, he may have supplied the Russians with the information that precipitated the February 12, 1946, arrest of partisan organizer and death squad leader Zigmas Šerkšnas-Laukaitis. This arrest was a terrible blow to the council.

Zigmas may have been betrayed by Ašmenskas. Or he may simply have been caught up in the mass arrests of young men that the Communists were carrying out to thwart any rebellion against their nascent totalitarian regime—charging them with counterrevolutionary activity and sentencing them to up to fifteen years in Siberian work camps. At the same time, tens of thousands of Russian civilians were sent to colonize Lithuania. All political parties other than the Communist Party were forbidden.

At this critical juncture, the Lithuanian National Council issued a directive informing the partisans that the leader of the armed uprising would be Generolas Vėtra (General Storm, that is, Jonas Noreika) of the Armed Forces, and that four army districts would unite in this effort. Included were mobilization instructions in preparation for armed conflict. A further proclamation addressed civilians:

> Attention! Attention! We invite Lithuania's people to participate in the armed uprising. More will be announced through the radio at the beginning of the war.
>
> Lithuania is starting a large uprising. Whoever wants peace, raise your white flags, and there will be no danger. Whoever does not listen to this order will die.

The uprising will be led by Generolas Vėtra. All whites, rise
up to war against the reds. Come out with white and national flags.
Raise your weapons.[20]

On March 5, 1946, former British prime minister Winston Churchill
delivered his "Iron Curtain" speech at Westminster College in Fulton, Missouri. "From Stettin in the Baltic to Trieste in the Adriatic, an iron curtain has
descended across the Continent," Churchill intoned. Noreika, Gorodeckis,
and Poškienė concluded that an armed invasion by America or England was
imminent.

As Ona Lukauskaitė-Poškienė would explain under KGB interrogation,
"We thought, when the uprising was near, that we would take steps to fight
against the Red Army. We relied on the local people having arms. Noreika set
the example in the summer of 1941, when, a few hours after the German invasion of the USSR, most Lithuanians were armed with weapons they kept for
safekeeping. Noreika knew that among the partisans were two soldiers with
experience in the former army. They counted on help from abroad, and
planned to use the radio station in Vilnius during the uprising."[21]

And as my grandfather himself would declare, "My entire underground
activity was based on my deep belief that war between the Soviet Union and
the English–American bloc was unavoidable, and that the moment of war was
fast approaching, and this would change Lithuania's status to a free state.

"I felt it imperative to do all possible at this moment in Vilnius, to take
control of the government in my own hands in the name of the Lithuanian
National Council, and as chief of the Armed Forces of Lithuania, to proclaim
this to all the country's residents."[22]

Ten days after Churchill's "Iron Curtain" speech, on March 16, 1946, Jonas
Noreika was arrested by the KGB, along with Ona Lukauskaitė-Poškienė and
Stasys Gorodeckis, at Poškienė's apartment. The KGB handcuffed them and
conducted a detailed search. They found a typewriter and several Lithuanian
National Council documents.

My grandfather and the other two leaders of the council may have been
betrayed by Ašmenskas, as Damijonas believed, or by Zigmas after his arrest

a month earlier. The informer could equally well have been one of the several KGB agents assigned to spy on my grandfather.

At the time of Jonas Noreika's arrest, the KGB meticulously recorded his possessions. He owned a watch with a chain, 389 rubles, two neckties, a number 5 gray belt, a scarf, a key, and a receipt with his name written on it in Russian. At his home, the KGB found his identification No. 2716 card, other photo cards, and 120 pages of letters in Lithuanian and German. Perhaps most of these were letters my grandmother wrote to him when he was a prisoner of the Nazis.

I stared at his face in the KGB prisoner-identification photo. He looked so unlike his younger self—bearded, features heavier and worn, his stare sterner, more menacing than in his famous military portrait.

The first interrogation of Jonas Noreika began on March 16, 1946, at 11:50 p.m., and continued until the next morning.

That same night, Poškienė was interrogated for eighteen hours and Gorodeckis for nineteen. They were returned to their cells during the day and forbidden to sleep.

Noreika's second interrogation began at 8:00 p.m. the next day and ended ten and a half hours later, at 6:30 a.m. There were often three interrogators in the room: one facing the prisoner and one standing on each side. In his book, Ašmenskas described a common interrogation method. The prisoner was told to lie on a chair on his stomach, his head hanging over one side, his legs over the other. The guard used a rubber baton, called a "banana," to loosen the inmate's tongue. The prisoner was smacked on the head without warning and had the chair pulled out from under him, after which he was again forced to lie facedown on the chair and endure another blow with the baton. Finally he was permitted to sit. After a few hours of this treatment, he was taken to another room and subjected to interrogation by a different guard.[23]

According to Ašmenskas's book, my grandfather was officially interrogated 113 times. At first, he sought to avoid giving too much information. He posed as a loyal Communist, a conscript in the Red Army and a member of SMERSH, its counterintelligence agency. Later I would learn that this claim had prompted a couple of Lithuanian historians to suspect that my grandfather was a spy for the Communists. I gave this theory little credence. The KGB transcripts clearly showed that he was "the creator and leader" of a group fostering a rebellion against the Communists, as he eventually admitted:

> Being an anti-Soviet, I stood on the path of a war actively organized against the Soviet government, and met on my path those who are like-minded. I created in Vilnius an anti-Soviet center.
>
> Gorodeckis and Poškienė agreed with this outlook. We planned to schedule a date for the uprising. We counted on removing the Soviet government as the uprising unfolded, especially where there were few Russian soldiers.
>
> We would start the uprising in Vilnius, then broadcast it publicly through the radio station to the rest of the nation.[24]

Despite being a KGB agent, Ašmenskas was also arrested, last of all the rebels. On March 17, 1946, a KGB agent named Muravjov went to Ašmenskas's home but did not find him. The agent instructed Ašmenskas's wife that her husband must go to Trakai Street. When Ašmenskas returned to Kaunas, he burned all documents associated with the Lithuanian National Council, including the political reviews and Directives #6 and #7. On March 19 he drove to Vilnius to warn Gorodeckis that he was being followed by the KGB. But he was too late; Gorodeckis had been arrested three days earlier. When Ašmenskas arrived at Gorodeckis's apartment, he was met by the KGB and arrested.

On April 5, Jonas Noreika admitted his guilt to the KGB. On that date, Ašmenskas recalled seeing guards pull my grandfather by his legs down a long flight of stairs, the back of his head thumping on the edge of each stair.[25]

From April 30 to May 5, Noreika was subjected to five days of solitary confinement as punishment for having communicated with prisoners in the next cell by means of Morse code.

J. Verseckas, also a KGB prisoner during the spring of 1946, recalled my grandfather's being brought to the cell that he shared with about ten others. Noreika declared, "When I'm free again, I'm going to write two books whose titles will depend on the political climate in Lithuania." The inmates urged him to recite a few passages from his proposed manuscript. He responded: "Dear reader, upon finishing the last page of my memoir, please visit Vilnius, no matter where you live. Stop by the KGB building, look at the barred windows, and remember that here were imprisoned, tried, tortured, and killed the sons and daughters of Lithuania, among them, this book's author: Jonas Noreika."[26]

My grandfather was executed for having worked with the Germans during the Nazi occupation and for heading the rebellion at the start of the second Soviet occupation. But nothing in the KGB transcripts indicated, or even suggested, that he had been responsible for the murder of Jews. Perhaps ironically, I had my wish; my dreaded search thus far had yielded no proof of the monstrous rumor. Nevertheless, I couldn't help but note that the KGB had never questioned Noreika directly about his possible involvement in the Holocaust. They were concerned only with his anti-Soviet activity, and specifically with his efforts to form an anti-Communist rebellion. They seemed utterly indifferent to the fate of the Jews.

Having chosen to regard the KGB transcripts as a reliable account of Noreika's career, the Genocide Centre had issued a document to my mother stating that no evidence existed of her father's having taken part in Jew-killing. How could both the Genocide Centre and the Lithuanian government express complete confidence in the KGB records? Knowing about my grandfather's association with the Nazis, why did the Lithuanian government make no further attempt to investigate any role he may have played in the Holocaust? Evidently, the limited account suited their desired narrative.

I must admit that I understood their position. By 2009, nine years after I had first heard the "Jew-killer" rumor in the school named after my grandfather, I still had not investigated his potential role in the murder of the nation's two hundred thousand Jews during World War II. Ninety-five percent of Lithuanian Jews had perished; this was the highest percentage in any European nation under Nazi occupation.[27] As my father's new wife remarked, any inquiry "would make Lithuania look bad." This implied I would be deemed a bad Lithuanian and most likely shunned by the community if I somehow managed to prove the rumor true. The prospect terrified me.

Vilnius
April 7, 2019

Stanislovas Tomas, a human rights lawyer running for election to the European Parliament, was filmed smashing the plaque honoring Jonas Noreika on Sunday and streamed it on Facebook. He reported his actions to police and waited to be arrested next to the plaque with a sledgehammer.

Last month, a Vilnius court dismissed an American Jew's lawsuit against a state museum's glorification of Noreika, citing the complainant's "ill-based" intentions. He sued the state-funded Centre for the Study of the Genocide and Resistance of the Residents of Lithuania for erecting a plaque honoring Noreika, a local anti-Communist hero who died while in Soviet custody.

The case is thought to be the first in which civil servants publicly defended in court the actions and good name of an alleged collaborator with the Nazis.

Times of Israel, **April 8, 2019**

CHAPTER TWELVE

Beginning the Dreaded Search

Whether the book that I was preparing to write would serve as a tribute to my grandfather and the homeland or would, in my quest for truth, inescapably become an exposé, clearly it demanded my concerted effort. To hone my skills, I resolved to pursue a master of fine arts degree in creative nonfiction.

My obligations to my family and my teaching career precluded my enrolling as a full-time graduate student. Since Murray State University was the closest institution to Chicago that offered a low-residency program, I undertook the six-hour drive to Murray, Kentucky, each summer from 2009 to 2012 to attend an intensive ten-day session. The coursework required for the degree was to be completed on a part-time basis, online. I was delighted to learn that all my professors were graduates of highly regarded MFA programs. My father would be proud of me for obtaining a stellar education at a quarter of the usual price.

As I drove south on I-57 in the summer of 2009, I catalogued my losses: Mom gone; Močiutė gone; $40,000 in student loans to enable me to rearrange my life so as to accommodate the writing of this book; nine years of my life already lavished on the manuscript—with nothing to show but an equal number of unsatisfactory drafts. In addition, I felt bound by a solemn promise that might be impossible to keep. If my grandfather proved to be not a hero, but a Jew-killer, the story I would be compelled to tell was not the one my mother had demanded I write.

My professors convinced me that my nagging doubts and determination to establish the facts were as important to the story as my grandfather's wartime deeds. The narrative, they urged, should be framed by my own emotional journey as I grappled with his hidden history. I had planned to produce an objective biography; now I would write from a personal perspective to create a memoir chronicling my inquiry. The adoption of this new, subjective mode felt like a reprogramming—almost like surrendering a saint. As a journalist, I had always written in third person; it felt strange to insert myself as a protagonist on a quest. My professors and fellow students assured me that if my grandfather *was* a Nazi collaborator, this in no way reflected any guilt or responsibility upon me. Remorse applies only to one's own actions. They urged me to investigate the rumor immediately.

I was grateful that none of my mentors or university peers were Lithuanian. The voice of my community whispering in my head, "Don't make Lithuania look bad" became muted in Murray. The academic support gave me the courage to delve into the evidence about my grandfather and the Jews at last. Wracked with dread anticipation, I hoped that I would view the appalling disclosures as evidence for a journalist to bring to light rather than as a scandal for an ashamed granddaughter to bury.

Sifting through the voluminous material amassed by my mother, I came across a yellowed booklet measuring seven by five inches. Had it been misplaced inadvertently? Had it been slipped between these stacks of soft newspaper articles lauding Noreika's valor to prevent its fragile leaves from crumbling? Or had this document been purposely hidden? The rest of the file was in meticulous order.

Could the pamphlet be of any consequence? On the front it bore the title *Hold Your Head High, Lithuanian!!!* I turned it over to study its back cover:

Vytauto Didžiojo [Vytautas the Great] descendants!
Farmers, Students,
Businessmen, Priests,
Managers, Employees
And Lithuanians of all trades!

Enough sleeping and gnawing of the crust of dried bread.
We can have the best horses and most delicious food!
Everyone to work then, from youngest to oldest!
Let's look at what we can do!!!!!

Inside, the text consisted of a thirty-two-page rant against Jews.

In the land of Klaipėda, Lithuanians are being overthrown by the Germans, and in Greater Lithuania, the Jews are buying up all the farms on auction. What are we going to do if all the capital and land will be in the hands of Jews?!
Hold Your Head High, Lithuanian!
We must make a solemn oath in our hearts: Don't buy products from a non-Lithuanian! Jews drive through the countryside and buy up the cattle, flax, and crops. Let us make our holy vows: Don't sell to them! Once and for all: We won't buy from Jews! We can sell them only butter, eggs, and cheese. And only when they won't make a profit from them.[1]

What was this booklet doing in my mother's archives? How many Lithuanians in 1933 held these views? As I read through this antisemitic screed, my hands trembled as if a snake were slithering among my fingers and wrapping itself around my wrist, my forearm, my elbow. The hatred was so raw, so virulent. *This is what makes Lithuania look bad,* I thought: *the author of this work, and all those like him.*

Journalist!
All Lithuanian newspapers should stop printing advertisements from non-Lithuanian firms. Instead, they should advertise new Lithuanian businesses in big letters. The press must support them!
Not one foot to the foreigners! The Jew will offer you a good price, but, citizen, you would be a traitor if you would sell him the country's richest treasure![2]

I closed the noxious little booklet. On the front cover, in the top right-hand corner, was the author's name, in bold capital letters. I didn't know how I had failed to see it: JONAS NOREIKA.

I dropped the pamphlet in a confusion of alarm and disgust. My head started throbbing. I did not want a grandfather who could have authored such a poisonous tract. I was tempted to burn the vile thing, to tear it into a thousand pieces. *Surely there must be some mistake. It couldn't be my grandfather who had written this!*

I stumbled out of my office and poured a glass of wine to steady myself. I had a wild impulse to drink much more of it to keep troubling thoughts at bay.

Jonas Noreika in uniform, perhaps in 1932, shortly before he wrote *Hold Your Head High, Lithuanian!!!*

It was several days before I returned to the pamphlet to reread it. This time, I found something that partially eased my anguish: a notation in pencil on the last page of the booklet, so faded that it was legible only through a magnifying glass. In my grandmother's handwriting were the words "22-year-old young man!" Clearly, she was indignant, rationalizing that her husband-to-be was then a naïve young soldier who had merely absorbed the pervasive sentiment that Jews were robbing Lithuanians of their economic self-sufficiency and dignity. In the two years since he had taken the army oath, Noreika had been surrounded by officers and impressionable young conscripts who, in turn, evidently had influenced his thinking. This rant did not necessarily reflect his true nature, Močiutė's comment declared. *In any case,* I told myself, *writing an anti-Jewish pamphlet was a far cry from killing Jews.* It was no proof of his having committed war crimes.

In the course of my research, I had learned that antisemitism was rampant in Europe at the time—a fact that did not exonerate my grandfather. The pamphlet he had authored was aimed at fomenting the hatred. I felt compelled to explore his motivation.

Clearly, by 1933, when he was a twenty-two-year-old soldier in Klaipėda, his antisemitism already was entrenched. Could I trace its development?

My task was made easier by a novel that my grandfather had written the next year, *Five Brothers*—a typed manuscript, not published in Lithuania until 2013, which my mother had maintained was a veiled autobiography. Over the past few years I had translated a number of passages from this novel and attempted to evaluate her judgment about it. Noreika had completed the manuscript while he was stationed in Klaipėda in 1934. I reviewed the original text of the sections that I had translated, comprising the accounts of a priest, a soldier, a lawyer, a farmer, and a high school boy who aspired to be a businessman. Studying the novel's themes and its structure, I endeavored to follow my grandfather's thought processes. I wanted to access his consciousness. Perhaps there was some explanation of his conduct, even a vindication.

I couldn't help but conclude that my mother had been right: the book's protagonist, Kaziukas, a soldier living in Klaipėda whose story was told in the third person, was essentially a self-portrait. Accordingly, I translated it in the first person.

Here weather and politics are often restless.

Listen to how the strong winds blow and how the white-capped sea screams, how quickly the two competing cultures wage war against each other.

To the north—seven kilometers of evergreen forest.

To the west—the never-frozen Baltic Sea.

To the east and south—flat, fertile land.

Where the forest meets the city stands the magnificent military district, where the Vytis Cross flag has flown since 1923, in honor of the seven cavalrymen who fought to reclaim this city for Lithuania. This is the Žemaičių Kunigaikščio Butigedžio Regiment.

Four years ago, I arrived to that same regiment. I had just finished military school as a young lieutenant of the first degree.

I remember kneeling on one knee before the nation's leader, who handed me a shiny steel sword, and how my chest filled with yearning for meaningful work. I looked earnestly at the calm, deep eyes of the man who gave his blessing: "Do not raise it without cause; do not lower it without honor!" Taking the sword and kissing its blade, I stood up, stretched, gave the salute, thrust my sword into its sheath, once more beheld my hero's eyes, then quickly turned to the right and with a bold step took my spot.[3]

This was a story of an ambitious man trying to make something of himself, a tale of sacrifice and an homage to the fatherland. I set down my reading glasses and sat back in my chair. The saga accorded precisely with everything I had heard about my grandfather from my family and the community.

I took a break and returned to the story a few hours later, a cup of coffee in hand. Kaziukas's student days in Šiauliai seemed to have a lot in common with my grandfather's time in high school there. Furthermore, "Kaziukas" was the diminutive form of "Kazimieras," my grandfather's middle name, honoring Lithuania's only saint, St. Casimir. I was reading the story, told in the third person, in the original manuscript.

I plan to be a businessman, mother! yells Kaziukas, who presses his lips together to observe what sort of an impression he's made upon his mother.

What kind of a businessman?

Similar to a Jew. Cha, cha, cha.

Go on now, she laughs.

Kaziukas wants to be a manufacturer in Šiauliai.

He thought to himself, If you point your finger in one direction, you're automatically an antisemite. They don't differentiate antisemitism from regular competition. If we ourselves avoid taking on the most profitable trades, we will always be oppressed.

I'll be the first to agree, God defend me, not to use violence or do anything evil to the Jews just because they're Jews. But if our own Lithuanians have to emigrate because they can't find work here while the new foreigners easily find a job, then something is not right. We ourselves are guilty.

We need to start a strong agitation, especially among the farmers and leaders, to avoid buying in non-Lithuanian stores.[4]

I almost spat out my coffee. Here were the very same views as those expressed in the pamphlet my grandfather had composed a year earlier: unrepentant antisemitism. How could my grandfather have left such a legacy?

I tried desperately to make excuses for him. He was a product of his time. After all, many—perhaps most—Lithuanians thought the same way. Surely my distinguished grandfather would not actually have used violence against the Jews; in the words of this very novel, he had promised not to: "I'll be the first to agree, God defend me, not to use violence or do anything evil to the Jews just because they're Jews."[5]

But I knew that my arguments were weak. The antipathy that Jonas Noreika had expressed toward Jews in the early 1930s could easily have flared into murderous violence a few years later, given the circumstances he would live through.

On my second trip to Murray, in the summer of 2010, I drove past rows of cornfields and thought of the photographs that I had recently assembled for the ten-year anniversary of my mother's death. One image showed her as an eight-year-old in Buenos Aires. She was standing with her mother, Uncle Stasys, and Aunt Antanina. Her face was round and puffy, like a cream pie, a large white bow fastened to her hair and a lacy collar carefully positioned over her dark dress. An earlier photograph showed her at the age of three, posed on a brocade ottoman, smiling primly, her hands tucked into a large fur muff. The picture must have been taken in 1942, when her father headed the Šiauliai District during the Nazi occupation. She looked like a princess.

I was still afraid that pursuing the rumor would rewrite my mother's family history and my own, disgracing both our family and our fatherland. Was I doing the right thing? As a journalist I had been trained to expose the truth, no matter how painful. Furthermore, I believed that Lithuanians should finally accept responsibility for their role in the Holocaust. Yet I knew very well how stubborn and proud they were. They could not endure the shame and embarrassment of acknowledging their part in the murder of Jews, and they dreaded the world's condemnation. Ironically, the Lithuanian people had always considered themselves victims of the Nazis, and therefore they fiercely resisted seeing the war from the Jews' perspective. Although Lithuania's history dated back to AD 1009, its land had been occupied or ruled by Russians, Germans, or Poles for most of its existence. Jews in Lithuania lived as a separate group that had only business dealings with the rest of the population; mutual distrust prevented social interaction.

Upon my return home from Murray, I dove more deeply into my mother's archive. There I found a book entitled *Masinės Žudynės Lietuvoje 1941–1944* (Mass Murders in Lithuania 1941–1944), published in Vilnius in 1973.[6] The book contained hundreds of documents signed by Lithuanian leaders during the Holocaust. To my revulsion, I found several that had been signed by my grandfather when he was chief of Šiauliai District.

On August 22, 1941, Jonas Noreika ordered that all the Jews in the areas under his control be moved to ghettos:

ŠIAULIAI CITY AND COUNTY
GOVERNOR
August 22, 1941
No. 962
    TO ALL CHIEFS OF PRINCIPALITIES OF THE ŠIAULIAI
COUNTY
    AND BURGOMASTERS OF SECONDARY TOWNS
    (Copy for Police Precinct Chiefs)
    By decree of Šiauliai District Commissioner, all citizens of
Jewish ethnicity, including half-Jews, must be removed from all
principalities and towns of the county and settled in one district:
the Ghetto. All Jewish property must be preserved and accounted
for by municipalities.

In accordance with this decree:

1. Jews of all principalities, secondary towns, and townships must be moved to the town of Žagarė in the period of the 25th to the 29th of this month. Requisites for resettlement will be provided by respective municipalities.

2. Lists of abandoned Jewish property must be delivered to me in 2 copies by August 29. Resettled Jews can take the most necessary household items and clothes and up to 200 RM in cash for each Jewish family.

3. In Žagarė, all Jews will be settled in a separate district which has to be fenced off by August 30. Fencing off the Ghetto district will be taken care of by the Žagarė municipality. Every day, district Jews in the Ghetto will be conveyed to work and back to the Ghetto by guards.

4. Non-Jewish citizens of the district appointed for the Jews are allowed to choose other locations in the county. If any of those non-Jews who are resettled have to abandon their real estate, they are allowed to choose real estate of corresponding value abandoned by the Jews in Žagarė or other townships.

5. Chiefs and burgomasters are obliged to inform me on the execution of this decree by the 29th of this month, including information on what has been accomplished, and how many Jews have been resettled. The Burgomaster of Žagarė must inform me how many Jews have been resettled to Žagarė.

◊

Jonas Noreika [signature]
City and County Governor

◊

Sekretorius Tamašauskas [signature]
Secretary

I could not believe what I was reading. This letter was in a book in my mother's archives; she must have read it. My grandmother, too, must have seen it. What had they thought of it? That it was Communist propaganda? That my grandfather had been forced to write this letter by Nazis holding a gun to his head? I was at a complete loss.

Later, a Lithuanian historian who had examined the Šiauliai archives sent me a brief letter with my grandfather's signature, one that hadn't been reprinted in *Masinės Žudynės*:

> August 9, 1941
>> To the Tryškiai Parish Elder,
>> Having come to an agreement with the Gruzdžiai Parish Elder, I am directing you to evict all citizens of Jewish nationality from the town of Tryškiai and transfer them to the town of Pakruojis/Gruzdžiai within three days from today.
>> Šiauliai, August 9, 1941
>> J. Noreika
>> District Chief
>> Tamušauskas
>> Secretary[7]

There could be only one reason for transferring a group of Jews during that period: to assemble them in a ghetto from which they would be marched into the woods and shot. My grandfather would have known their fate. Was he following orders from the Nazis? Presumably. Was he *happy* to comply with these orders? That was what I needed to find out.

Viktoras Ašmenskas's book rationalized my grandfather's conduct—Jonas Noreika was merely following orders, as if he were an automaton programmed to do the Nazis' bidding:

> Although Noreika was the Šauliai District Chief, he didn't have a lot of power, as we would imagine, and he wrote the orders under the instructions of the Lithuanian Chief Commissar Renteln, the Šiauliai Regional Commissar Gewecke, or the War Commandant.

Most of the orders concerned questions about the Jewish ghetto
and the cataloguing of their property.

There is no material in the archives that would compromise J.
Noreika as someone who personally participated in the Jewish
genocide. He never once gave the order to kill Jews and did not
participate in the Jewish actions. His young daughter, Dalia, according to Stasys Grunskis, gave Jews buns that her mother baked.[8]

I reread the phrase "No material in the archives that would compromise
J. Noreika." This official version of events was the one I had heard since childhood. And yet Noreika had written these letters, which bore his name and
signature clearly at the bottom. The letter in which he ordered Jews to be sent
to Žagarė had been available to the public since 1973; the book in which it was
published had been sitting in my mother's archives for years. So to which
archives was Ašmenskas alluding? Were the KGB transcripts his sole source?
The co-authors of *Mass Murders in Lithuania* had been able to access other
pertinent, detailed records. Apparently Ašmenskas, not wishing to find com-
promising information, simply hadn't looked for it, and when he was presented
with irrefutable evidence, he made excuses for my grandfather's conduct.

In *Mass Murders in Lithuania*, I found this testimony of a witness, describing my grandfather's role during the Nazi occupation:

Excerpted testimony by A. Gedvilas, born 1891 m. Šilalė region.
Joniškis city mayor from July to November 1941
1947, November 20.

A few days after the German Army came, I received an invitation from the Šiauliai District Chief Noreika. He told me that the
Germans saved Lithuania from the Bolsheviks, that Lithuania will
have its own government, and that the original ministers and
district chiefs can return to their former positions.

Besides, Noreika said, it's important to appoint the former
Lithuanians to their positions because if the Germans appoint

their people, it will be more difficult to get the country back. Noreika offered me to take my old position back—to become mayor of Joniškis. After thinking about it, I agreed, believing that Lithuania would be a separate country.

An "activist" staff led the city through specially appointed committees. I remember that the staff was comprised of these committee members: Personnel, Jewish Affairs, Economic Propaganda, Order and Justice. In the beginning, while there still wasn't any police [force], the activist staff arrested Soviet party activists, [and] later organized a ghetto, arrested Jews, took away their wealth, instituted a strict regime for Jews, imposed fines and so forth.

Around the month of August, through the district chiefs, the orders by the Gebietskommissar were distributed, and the mayors became responsible for forming the ghettos.

The orders categorically required to concentrate the Jews in one area—in a territory where they must be held and surrounded by a two-meter high fence, to forbid relations with Lithuanians, and not to allow Lithuanians to buy goods from Jews. As I followed that order, I created a list of Jews living in the city. I couldn't fully complete the order because our city didn't have the funds to build a ghetto, but I did everything possible.

I participated in several "activist" staff meetings where the ghetto matter was discussed. During the meetings, I would report on the Jews in my city. At the time, the list was given to the "activist" staff. When I participated, once we discussed fining Jewish national residents with 20,000 rb. I don't know how much money they collected because the fines didn't go to the district self-government, but to the "activist" staff funds.

As I said earlier, the Gebietskommisar's order to organize a ghetto wasn't fulfilled and the Jews still lived in their homes. In August, I received the District Chief's order to move all the Jews in Joniškis to Žagarė. To fulfill that, the police helped, and the district self-government provided the transportation.

During the second half of August, I mobilized the transportation. With the help of the police, all the Jewish national residents, except for a few families, were seated together with their remaining belongings into the wagons to go to Žagarė. Before sending them off, a truck of soldiers arrived to Joniškis lead by the Colonel's lieutenant. He told me to empty the articles on the wagon, as he needed them for another purpose. I fulfilled that order. We put the items in a warehouse and locked them up. The soldiers led the Jews into the synagogue, took away their gold and jewelry, which at first they sent to the police, but later the German soldiers forwarded it to Šiauliai. [Then] they sat [all the Jews] in the empty wagons, drove them to Vilkiauškis woods and shot them. That day, they shot about 300 people. The remaining Jewish families were driven to Žagarė, and later were shot.

When they appointed me as mayor of Joniškis, I thought the job would just be administrative, but events transpired in such a way that eventually instead of rebuilding the old Lithuania, I became an active German helper—not even feeling that I was standing on the guilty path, innocently fulfilling all of the occupier's orders.

It became clear to me that Lithuania wasn't becoming a bourgeois republic, but was instead taking the fascist path. That is why, more than once, I requested the district leader to be released from the mayoral responsibilities. He only released me at the end of August.

ADSR Fondas, r. 143, 1. 235-239.[9]

If my grandfather was disturbed by the letters he was signing, why didn't he step down, as the mayor of Joniškis had done? Other men, too, had left their posts. Why did Jonas Noreika choose to stay in his? I had discovered that he was one of approximately three hundred Lithuanians who worked in the district's government, all of whom answered to the Nazis.[10] The Germans couldn't possibly have run the country by themselves, without the help of these local mayors, vice-mayors, tax collectors, and monitors, because most of the German military and police forces had been sent to the war front.

After my third trip to Murray, in the summer of 2011, I renewed my investigation into the rumor about my grandfather and the Jews. This time, my mother's files yielded a clipping from the *Aušros Alėja* newspaper in Šiauliai, dated "April 2–9, 1993," with the heading "Don't Slander Captain Noreika, Sir!" Its author recounted how in 1942 there was an opening for a mayor in Skaisgirys, a town about thirty miles north of Šiauliai, and that my grandfather had asked him to accept the position:

> I remember in 1942, in the summer, how Noreika wanted to appoint me as Skaisgirys mayor. He told me:
>
> You are a good Lithuanian patriot and are not in favor of Nazis or Soviets. The Germans are killing the Jews. We Lithuanians are no different from Jews—we're kept against our will. The Nazis have decided to kill the Jews. But our destiny is no better than the Jews.
>
> Two world forces, Stalin and Hitler, divided Europe. As they were dividing, they got angry and went to war. We Lithuanians have to be united and wait until the bloodsuckers weaken. Then we will rebuild the Lithuanian nation. We will not capitulate to the brown or the Red occupation.
>
> I decided against taking the post. I didn't want to bow my head to the brown plague [Brownshirts]. Besides, if I worked for them, I'd end up being arrested and killed, which is exactly what happened to Noreika.
>
> Tadas Danta[11]

Why did my grandfather bow his head to "the brown plague"? Other men stepped aside. Why didn't he? Why was he recruiting for these jobs under Nazi jurisdiction?

I thought about my mother, who must have read the documents that she had compiled and organized into files, including the 1973 book detailing the mass murders. Until now, I'd assumed it was her illness that had kept her from writing the book for which she'd prepared so assiduously. Now I realized that she almost certainly had heard the rumor, had reviewed the documentation, and had been thwarted by her inability to find proof of her father's innocence. Had she abandoned her search in the hope that *I* would accomplish what she could not? What if, instead, the evidence that I found proved his guilt?

Vilnius
October 1, 2018

On his own initiative, J. Noreika, like other district chiefs, did not manage the ghettoization of Jews, nor the confiscation of their property. All the mentioned documents testify to the fact that H. Gewecke gave the orders to leaders, who were obligated to follow them. Therefore, J. Noreika, as a Šiauliai district chief, could not have initiated, organized, or executed any mass killing operations.

Vilnius Regional Administrative Court

File No. el-4215-281/2018

Response from the Genocide Resistance and Research Centre to the prosecution's claim against the Genocide Centre's refusal to change its historical conclusion on Jonas Noreika

CHAPTER THIRTEEN

Fault Lines

In the cornfields that I passed on my way to Murray each summer was an enormous cross, a steel structure that stood two hundred feet tall and dominated the landscape. It seemed so stark and incongruous. What was it doing there? Having driven by it several times on my previous trips, I now steered my car into the other lane for a closer look—almost crashing into a truck.

This towering symbol commanded my attention because I had been raised a good Lithuanian Catholic girl. It seemed significant that I found myself silently confronted in this manner expressly as I drove to sessions that would help me grapple with my grandfather's legacy. My reverence for his memory had always been an inextricable part of my faith and love for my homeland; after all, he was a national hero. He couldn't have killed Jews! As I contemplated the cross, I mused that where his legend and the rumor intersected was the crux of the matter. The cross itself, of course, represented compassion. Compassion and sacrifice.

Suddenly, a light flashed on my dashboard: a yellow halo around an exclamation mark. A moment later, my rear tire blew out. I got out of the car and stared at the damage.

A white Buick pulled over.

"Do you need help?"

I must have looked distressed.

"We girls gotta take care of ourselves!" the driver proclaimed. Her long blonde hair grazed her tattooed arms. She and her daughter stepped out of their car. The daughter jacked up my car and the mother pulled out a tire iron and set to work loosening the wheel lugs. Squatting barefoot on the asphalt, she assessed the situation. She pushed down hard on the tire iron and, straining with the effort, finally succeeded in loosening the wheel. "Damn screws tightened by a man," she grumbled. "They never think about us women."

Once the spare tire was properly snugged and lugged, she straightened up and said, "Just keep us in your prayers."

"I will. I promise," I replied.

It pleased me to believe that my mother had somehow sent this mother-and-daughter pair to that lonely stretch of road to replace my tire and encourage me along my path. I regarded the incident as a signal that any obstacles I encountered in pursuit of my story would be overcome, and that assistance might come from unexpected sources. Even now my fierce, tenacious mother would help.

My professors urged me to travel to the fatherland once again to investigate my grandfather's life during the Nazi occupation. I determined that, to accommodate my teaching obligations, I would go from mid-June to early August that year. This would afford me about seven weeks. It would be my fourth trip to Lithuania, but the first time that I would have to make all the challenging arrangements myself.

At first I thought I should stay in Vilnius, where my mother and grandmother were buried. My grandfather, however, had spent a lot of time in Klaipėda, in Žemaitija (the Lowlands). I made inquiries in the Marquette Park community and learned that a close Lithuanian friend had a sister who owned an apartment in Klaipėda. She offered it to me at a cost that was almost a gift. Its location would turn out to be providential.

Next I phoned my cousin Rasa Kovalenka, whose grandmother was my grandmother's sister. Rasa had recently moved to Klaipėda; her apartment was just a few blocks from where I would be staying. When I described my project to her, she sounded enthusiastic and offered to drive me to Stutthof and back.

A friend of mine, a Jewish journalist working for the *Chicago Sun-Times*, had recently returned from a trip to Lithuania, during which he had visited his relatives' burial sites. After requesting that he share the details with me, I contacted his guide to arrange a tour of the locations at which my grandfather might have been involved in atrocities against Jews.

Simon Dovidavičius was the director of Sugihara House, a museum dedicated to the Japanese vice-consul in Lithuania during World War II, Chiune Sugihara. This diplomat, in defiance of his government orders, had issued visas to six thousand Jews to enable them to escape the Holocaust. Initially, Simon was not sure whether he should help the granddaughter of an alleged perpetrator. He had heard of Jonas Noreika—as had all the Jews in Lithuania, he told me. But in a few weeks, he decided that he was up for the task and told me that he looked forward to working with me. He suggested that we travel around the country together for at least a week. As all these arrangements fell into place, I began to sense a guiding hand.

I phoned my indefatigable correspondent Damijonas Riauka in Kaunas— my grandfather's colleague in the five-day uprising against the first Soviet occupation, the one who had told me he would never cut his beard after my mother's death. Damijonas proposed that he and I spend a week together in Kaunas poring over the material in his archive—which he had been collecting for decades and which he planned to bequeath to me. He also recommended an excursion to Plungė, where he would give me a guided tour describing events before and during the uprising.

Then I called Nijolė Grunskis, in Šiauliai. She had been married to my grandfather's nephew Stasys Grunskis, the one who looked like Einstein. Stasys had passed away a few years earlier, but, as Nijolė had often spoken of her time in Siberia, I asked if I might interview her about that. She invited me to spend a few days with her.

I also contacted Sakalas Gorodeckis, whose father, Stasys Gorodeckis, had assisted my grandfather in leading the rebellion against the Soviets during their second occupation. Sakalas agreed to meet me in Vilnius.

Excited, I called my brother to ask whether he might meet me in Lithuania for a few weeks. He answered that, as a civilian working for the military, he had volunteered to be transferred to Afghanistan; his tour of duty would not end in time.

Finally I asked my daughter, then a college freshman, whether she wanted to accompany me. I hoped to transmit some of my heritage to her, but my main reason was a fervent desire to strengthen our bond. Our relationship had lately become strained. When she agreed to go, I was elated. I daydreamed about travelling through Lithuania together and becoming closer to each other.

As I prepared for the trip—purchasing a new laptop computer, a cell phone, a camera, and a voice recorder—I worried about all that remained to be done before my departure. I was still maintaining a full-time high school teaching schedule. I experienced a number of sleepless nights, perhaps as a result of subconscious anxiety about the trip.

Within a few months my daughter's life was spiraling out of control: she had acquired a heroin habit. Shortly before we were due to leave on our trip, she decided that she didn't want to go to Lithuania after all. When she stormed out of the house and was gone for nine weeks, at the age of I'm-an-adult-now-and-you-can't-do-anything-to-stop-me, my husband and I were desperate to understand and help her. We enrolled in couples' counselling.

One of the first questions our therapist asked was about how we met. This gave my husband an opportunity to vent all his pent-up frustration with Chicago's Lithuanian community.

I met Franco Foti in Buenos Aires, Argentina, on January 1, 1985, when I was living with my great-aunt Antanina and freelancing for the *Buenos Aires Herald* and *Argentine News*. On one of our first dates, Franco held my hand and led me down a trail through the tall grasses of Ezeiza Forest. A World War II buff, he wore a camouflage T-shirt under a blue denim jacket, a short hunting knife suspended from his belt, and a rosary in his right pocket, along with a book of matches. I carried a blanket, a thermos of hot water, and ingredients and tools for *maté*, a local kind of tea: a *bombilla* (a metal straw) and a *matero* (a hollow gourd) to hold the green tea and sugar.

After we had hiked down a trail for twenty minutes, gathering dry sticks along the way, Franco found a secluded clearing with a fire pit. Once we had settled in and begun sipping our *maté*, he pulled out a brown leather-bound book from his jacket.

"What's that?" I asked.

"A poetry book."

"Wonderful! Nobody has ever read poetry to me before."

"I'm glad to be the first!"

He opened the volume to a passage that he had already selected and began to read aloud slowly, since I was still learning Spanish:

> How beautiful you are; how pleasing my love, my delight!
> Your stature is like a palm tree, your breasts are like clusters.
> I said: I will climb the palm tree. I will take hold of its branches.
> Now let your breasts be like clusters of the vine
> And the fragrance of your breath like apples,
> And your mouth like an excellent wine. (Song of Songs 7:7–9)

He paused to observe my reaction.

The verse sounded racy yet tender. "What is that?"

"It's called Song of Songs." He handed me the book for my inspection, and I immediately recognized it as a Bible.

"You're reading from the Bible? Breasts are in the Bible? I can't believe that!"

He nodded, laughing. "I had a feeling you wouldn't recognize it. Would you like me to read some more?"

As he read, I listened to his deep voice and noted his broad hands. He held the Bible lovingly, I thought, and turned the pages gently, absorbed in the words and the moment.

Franco's parents were Sicilians who had left Italy during World War II. He was unlike anyone I had ever met.

He paused to sip the *maté*, clearly pleased with my response to his recitation of suggestive verses from the Bible. He struck me as masculine and kind-hearted, a strong-willed man who read from the Bible. This was an intriguing combination.

A few months later we announced our engagement. My mother and grandmother lectured me, long-distance, about how disappointed they were that I wasn't marrying a Lithuanian. But they were thousands of miles away, in another hemisphere. Nonetheless, I knew I'd pay a price for renouncing my implicit obligation to transmit my precious heritage. "This is a slap in the face to the community," my mother pronounced.

Franco and I married in Chicago on August 23, 1986, the forty-seventh anniversary of the signing of the Molotov-Ribbentrop Pact. The non-aggression agreement between Germany and the Soviet Union provided for the secret division of six European countries between the Soviets and the Nazis, with Lithuania falling to Germany. Subsequently, Lithuania found itself under Soviet control. Just as Lithuanians had felt betrayed in 1939, my family regarded my marriage as an insult to its proud history.

My wedding day was also the day that neo-Nazis assembled in Marquette Park to protest the movement of more African Americans into the neighborhood. I remember looking out of the window of my limousine on my way to church and seeing white men dressed in brown uniforms and gleaming black boots marching down Marquette Road.

Notwithstanding all of this, I had a splendid day. I treasure the photo taken when my five giggling bridesmaids spontaneously crawled under my long, billowing veil. Once vows were exchanged and champagne uncorked, everyone finally seemed to relax. We danced, drank, and sang in Lithuanian, Spanish, English, and Italian until well past midnight.

Yet Franco never forgot how rejected he had felt by my mother and grandmother simply because he wasn't Lithuanian. And, at a party held by my Lithuanian friends shortly after our wedding, an incident occurred that left a lasting impression on us both. An inebriated guitarist in a band that had performed at countless Lithuanian weddings made his way unsteadily toward us. "Silvia! I heard you got married," he slurred. I introduced him to my husband. The Lithuanian looked Franco over from head to toe and sneered, "*This,*

this is who you married? I thought you'd marry a tall blond with blue eyes; not—not—someone like *him!*"

I turned to Franco, who looked as if he would explode. As the drunken musician stumbled away, Franco grabbed my wrist and said, "We're leaving!" Two of our friends from Argentina who had overheard the exchange walked out with us.

In the car, Franco swore in Spanish and pounded the steering wheel, then leaned over me and pulled a gun he'd bought without my knowledge from the glove compartment. "I'm going back in there to shoot that damn Nazi!" he stated.

I tried to wrest the gun from his grasp, but he was too strong for me. As he was about to return to the party to confront the musician, our mutual friends tackled him and tore the gun from his hands.

"Calm down," one of them said in Spanish. "Just think about what you're about to do. No matter what that drunk said, it's not worth ruining the rest of your life." Franco returned to his senses. "God help me," he sighed. Then, to me: "I'm sorry. I didn't mean to frighten you."

"I've never seen you like this!" I answered. "Honestly, I barely know that guy. I never want to see a gun in our car or our house ever again. Promise me."

We drove home, and Franco explained that it was a pump-action BB gun—not a real gun, as I had thought. He claimed he'd intended only to scare the drunk, to "make him piss in his pants"; not to murder him.

In the years that followed, Franco continued to maintain that the musician's words reflected the thoughts of the entire community. No matter how much I attributed them to the musician's crudeness or drunkenness, it would never mitigate the damage they had done. Franco was convinced that the community's attitude was that if he wasn't Lithuanian, he was unworthy.

Sitting near me on the therapist's pillow-laden couch, Franco admitted, "I could never get over the rage and resentment I've always felt toward the Lithuanian community. And to think that your mother and grandmother and the rest of the community compared me unfavorably to your grandfather—only to find out that he was a damn Nazi! It's unbelievable! Who the hell do they think they are?"

"I'm sorry, I'm sorry," I repeated in tears. The therapist handed me a box of tissues. "I'm sorry. I wish I could change it, but I can't. What do you want me to do?"

"Why do you have to go to Lithuania *now*?" Franco demanded. "Why *now*?"

It was a difficult question to answer. I gazed at the little desk on my right, with its stack of books and Freud bobblehead toy. I wanted to tap Freud's head, to watch it wobble. "You know why," I replied slowly. "You know how long it's taken me to get here, how important this is to me."

"More important than our children? Than me?"

"I'll be back in seven weeks."

The therapist's eyes widened. "Seven weeks? You'll be gone for seven weeks? But we just started!"

"It's a project I've been working on for many years," I explained. "I'll be conducting research."

"I wish I was there when your mother asked you to do this," remarked Franco. "If I'd known it would take this much time and energy, maybe I could have stopped it."

"Some of the most important witnesses are in their nineties," I pointed out. "I've already made so many preparations and arranged so many schedules with relatives and my grandfather's colleagues. I've come this far; I have to go there. I'm sorry. I know it's a bad time—but it's *always* a bad time. You and the children won't change in seven weeks. We'll resume therapy when I get back."

Franco was unhappy about being left alone with our son and daughter, but eventually he gave me his blessing. Literally. Four years earlier, he had been ordained as a Catholic deacon. Now he made the sign of the cross over me, murmured a few words of prayer, and wished me Godspeed.

I scarcely knew what awaited me.

PART III

LAYERS OF TRUTH

CHAPTER FOURTEEN

An Unreliable Witness

*Today we stand in war against one common double-dealing
enemy. That enemy is the Red Army, Russian Bolshevism, wild
Asian gangs, who in the summer of 1940 invaded our land. Using
a handful of "Lithuanian" degenerates and traitors, they killed
our nation's independence, ushered in the so-called Soviet order
and—every day and every hour—ground our nation deeper into
slavery and poverty, while sinking us into terror, oppression,
torture, and extortion.*

—"For All Posterity, Let Us Remove Lithuania from the Jewish Yoke,"
Lithuanian Activist Front, Document LXIV, 1941

I n Vilnius I was greeted with far less fanfare than my brother and I had
received thirteen years earlier, when we'd gone to bury our mother's and
grandmother's ashes. I had arrived exhausted. Travelling on frequent-flyer
miles to save money had compelled me to take a long, complicated route: a
flight from Chicago to Newark, a bus from Newark to New York, a flight
from New York to Berlin, a ten-hour layover in Berlin, and then a flight from
Berlin to Helsinki, with an overnight layover there. The booking agent had
promised a hotel for the night but, to my consternation, no such accom-
modation awaited me. I phoned my husband in tears. He had worked at an
international travel-insurance agency for twelve years, and so was eminently
qualified to assist in booking a hotel in Helsinki. But the cost of my trip was

escalating even before I had reached my destination. After a fretful night I flew from Helsinki to Vilnius.

Damijonas Riauka, my grandfather's colleague in the rebellion against the Soviets, stood waiting for me at the airport with two of his friends. He greeted me with a kiss, a bouquet of flowers, and a small Lithuanian flag with its three stripes of gold, green, and red.

He was rail-thin but spoke energetically, nonstop. "I can't believe you're finally here! I'm so happy you're here! I've been so sick the past few months, just lying in bed, thinking about this moment when you would arrive. It was the only thing that kept me alive. I was so worried I would die before you arrived, but God had other plans."

It was difficult to get a word in edgewise. "You cut your beard," I said, smiling, remembering that he had vowed never to shave again after my mother's death.

"I had to. I was so sick. There is so much to share about your grandfather. The campaign by the Jews against your grandfather is getting worse. It's more important than ever that you publish that book!"

One of his companions, a former journalist who asked not to be named, had been serving as a go-between for Damijonas and me over the past few months. As Damijonas did not have access to the internet, he had enlisted his younger friend to send emails on his behalf. I shook hands with our intermediary, pleased to meet him in person. He requested a payment of $100 to cover gas and expenses for the one-hour drive to Kaunas. Damijonas took me aside to apologize for his friend's demanding such a high fee, but said that he had been unable to find anyone else. I assured him that the cost was not a concern—while privately resolving not to depend upon private chauffeurs for the remainder of my trip.

Damijonas had brought a second Lithuanian flag, which he affixed outside the car window for our journey from Vilnius to Kaunas. As it flapped in the wind, I felt rather like a visiting American dignitary.

I checked into my hotel room and was pleasantly surprised at its spaciousness. My first phone call was to Remigijus, the son of my father's second wife. His mother had entrusted me with $2,000, mostly in $20 bills, a gift to her son. I had kept the envelope of cash next to my bosom during the flights and layovers and was relieved to hand it to him at last. That afternoon, he drove me to the Akropolis, a huge shopping mall in Kaunas, where I acquired a new SIM card for my phone and converted dollars from my checking account to Lithuanian litai. That evening I fell asleep early in a comfortable bed. The next day I would begin learning about the June 1941 uprising.

Eighty-nine-year-old Damijonas was the last living participant in the five-day uprising against the Communists in 1941 and the only person who could tell me firsthand about my grandfather's role. Immediately after that uprising, Jonas Noreika had become chief of Šiauliai, a position he continued to hold during the Nazi occupation until 1943. Very little had been written about this controversial period of his career. I wanted to understand the precise nature of my grandfather's actions during that brutal time. Damijonas was crucial to my inquiry. I spent my first week in Kaunas, discussing with him the uprising that had preceded both Lithuania's freedom from the Soviets and involvement in the Holocaust.

Aukštieji Šančiai, where Damijonas had a one-room apartment in a house owned by his married daughter, was a neighborhood of modern mansions mixed with humble older dwellings. Still grieving the death of his wife seven years before, he had covered his walls with about fifty framed photographs of her; his bedroom nook was part sleeping quarters and part shrine. I pitied him. He seemed to live only to memorialize his wife and my grandfather. Damijonas was nicknamed "the Computer" because of his reputed ability to recall the past in minute detail.

For much of our week together we sat in the middle of his apartment in two chairs at a small table. He had single-mindedly been accumulating documents, as well as audio and video broadcasts of memorials about my grandfather, for more than twenty years. One wall was covered by a curtain that he grandly pulled aside, like a boastful wizard, to show shelves filled with binders of newspaper articles and letters, in addition to books and leaflets he'd written about the uprising. It was an astonishing amount of material about those five momentous days. He promised to give it all to me. Secretly, I felt overwhelmed.

To my surprise, his account of those five historic days in June 1941 seemed disjointed and riddled with inconsistencies. He jumped from one topic to another, comparing the 1941 uprising to the rebellion of 1946. I stopped him to request clarification, but his explanation of events only went around in circles. Feeling dazed, I listened dutifully, enduring this for hours on end.

Each day's marathon session was punctuated by Damijonas's coffee-preparation ritual—usually around the third or fourth hour. Throughout the day he sat on an old black rolling chair, wheeling himself around the room to access this archive, that document, this photograph, or that letter. When it was time for coffee, he rolled up to a shelf near his desk, which he called the "partisan shelf," where he hid treasured items from his family. Taking a tall white mug, he mixed one teaspoon of finely ground Indian coffee with one teaspoon of coarsely ground Brazilian coffee, then added three teaspoons of sugar, one tablespoon of apple jam, and a dash of cinnamon and blended them together. As the water boiled, he beat the contents vigorously for precisely three minutes, until the mixture had become creamy. The extraordinary beverage was poured into porcelain teacups, where a lovely froth formed at the top. As we sipped this delightful concoction, Damijonas resumed his story of the uprising.

According to Damijonas, the June 1941 uprising was part of a master plan coordinated by the Lithuanian Activist Front (LAF). Various stories reported the number of participants as ranging from 10 to 100,000 men. Damijonas produced a document containing sophisticated cartoon drawings depicting most of the pertinent facts. One image portrayed Hitler and Stalin stomping on the globe, with tears falling from Europe. Another showed a long train of boxcars headed to Siberia, with a sorrowful mother and child looking on.[1]

The LAF was represented as having been created in Berlin on November 17, 1940, by Colonel Kazys Škirpa and other Lithuanian leaders in exile after the Communist invasion.[2]

"Why in Berlin?" I queried.

Damijonas explained patiently that these men couldn't possibly have met in Lithuania without risking being killed; since they all had fled to Germany, they met up in Berlin. Their plans were coordinated with the Wehrmacht,

Germany's armed forces from 1935 to 1945. All members swore an oath of loyalty to Hitler. *Oh, so they were Nazis*, I thought.

The LAF's two main planning centers for the uprising appeared in these illustrations: the one in Vilnius was designed to oversee its activities in three regions, while the Kaunas branch orchestrated events in four regions, including Žemaitija. The frame concerning Žemaitija boldly stated that Captain Jonas Noreika was the leader of that region, which encompassed Šiauliai, Telšiai, Mažeikiai, Kretinga, Tauragė, and Raseiniai. Plungė was not mentioned—although it, too, was in his sphere. My grandfather's involvement seemed incontestable. If he had truly led the uprising in Žemaitija, as Damijonas asserted, he must have wielded an enormous amount of power.

The truth is that Lithuania was forced to make an excruciating choice between the Communists and the Nazis. As a child, while completing homework for Lithuanian school under my grandmother's guidance, I had asked her who the Lithuanians hated less: the Russians or the Germans. After some hesitation—as if carefully weighing her answer—she replied that the Germans were less objectionable because they were more like us: so neat, so organized, so smart, so efficient. "We liked their order," she asserted.

The Lithuanian Activist Front's plan was to instigate the uprising when Germany attacked Russia.

This coordination was crucial. Colonel Škirpa chose several translators for the German Army, whose identities never were disclosed.[3] *Was my grandfather one of them?* I wondered. Damijonas admitted that Jonas Noreika had served as a translator for the Nazis within months of the uprising, when he assumed the role of Šiauliai district chief.

After sorting through the evidence, I concluded that it was more than likely that my grandfather had actively assisted the Germany Army as it invaded Lithuania and took it over from the Russians.

When Damijonas refused to confirm my suspicion, I presented him with everything that I had learned about Jonas Noreika's acts as chief of the Šiauliai District.

"When he became chief, he took Nazi officers to several cities and translated their speeches to the locals," I persisted. "Ašmenskas says this in his book.

My grandfather must have been translating for the Nazis at the time of the uprising, too."

"Ašmenskas was a double agent. How can you trust *anything* he put in that book?" Damijonas snapped. "After I read it, I threw it in the trash."

"Why would you do that?" I exclaimed.

"He tried to kill me, you know!" Damijonas strode to a cabinet and rummaged through one of its drawers, then held out a round, palm-sized item from which wires protruded. "This is the bomb he tried to use. He stuck it on my stove when I was out—but I discovered it before it went off."

I was dumbfounded. I began to question Damijonas's sanity.

He handed me the alleged bomb. "Don't worry. It's defused."

I photographed the unrecognizable object and carefully handed it back to him.

"Why would he try to kill you?"

"He was the one who ruined my pension. I could have had a good pension."

Now I was doubly confused. "How is your pension connected to any of this?"

"The bomb was planted when my wife was still alive, and she was scared out of her wits. I miss her so much! Can you believe he would do that to me?" he demanded, his eyes glistening in frustration.

Was he attempting to distract me from my pursuit of the truth with these irrelevant accusations? He seemed desperate to discredit Ašmenskas.

I followed him over to his wife's shrine to admire her photos. As a young woman she had dressed very stylishly. In later pictures she looked tired, defeated.

I had met her on previous trips and remembered how gracious she had been. Again I felt sorry for Damijonas. But his efforts to sidetrack me only increased my determination to confirm my suspicions at a later date.

Almost more tiresome than my host's eccentricity was his discomfort with any pocket of silence. As an introvert, I needed intervals of quiet to process all the information I was acquiring, but he never accorded me more than a minute or two of silence. Consequently, I always left his home with a pounding headache.

In my hotel room at night, often with a glass of wine to calm my nerves, I combed through his scattered accounts, spending hours rearranging my notes into a coherent chronology—fighting against fatigue, resolved to complete the task that had somehow fallen to me: to set straight my grandfather's record.

Later, in Chicago, I continued to scrutinize these notes over a period of years. I eventually realized that this charismatic, exasperating witness was deliberately telling only half the story. He was giving me the Lithuanian nationalist version of events. My grandfather's colleague was complicit in the nation's cover-up of its role in the Holocaust, a whitewash that possibly extended to the highest levels of government.

Vilnius
March 27, 2019

Lithuania experienced a different type of Nazi-occupation than other European nations. When deliberating the question of collaboration during the Nazi-occupied years, it is necessary to take into consideration the type of regime the Nazis introduced. Lithuania was the only country in Europe that tried to use the German invasion to free itself from Soviet occupation, announcing its independence and restoring its structures of self-government.

"On the Accusation of Jonas Noreika (General Storm),"
Genocide and Resistance Research Centre of Lithuania

CHAPTER FIFTEEN

Groundwork for a Rebellion

I sought to:
a) Wash the shame off the face of Lithuanians for
succumbing on June 15, 1940, without firing a shot in resistance.
b) With weapon in hand, make it abundantly clear to Lithuania's
friends as well as enemies, the Lithuanian nation's unwavering
will to seek freedom and the right to be an independent state.
c) Thereby reveal for all time Moscow's lies about Lithuania's
allegedly voluntary entry into the Soviet Union in 1940.
—Kazys Škirpa[1]

After the Soviet Union seized control of Lithuania in 1940, it proceeded to rid the country of potential opponents. My grandfather, by then a captain teaching cadets at the Kaunas Military School, was released from the Lithuanian army on October 28, 1940—a stroke of luck for him, as otherwise the Communists would almost certainly have killed him or sent him to Siberia.[2]

My mother was one year old at the time. The young family had to decide quickly where they should live. They moved to the home of his wife's parents, in the town of Barstyčiai, in Žemaitija, along with Noreika's sister Antanina. But the young couple yearned for their own home. My grandmother soon received an offer from the Soviet government to teach at an elementary school in Mardosai, a small village outside Plungė. The life that would be afforded them by this position was a far cry from the comfortable

My grandfather holding my mother as a new-born just home from the hospital

and esteemed existence they had enjoyed as army officer and officer's wife in Kaunas. But there were few opportunities available to them, and they had no wish to live with her parents forever.

My grandmother taught students in several elementary grades, while her sister-in-law Antanina took care of my mother, Dalytė. Damijonas, who was attending Plungė's high school at the time, said that his two younger sisters were both taught by my grandmother, who was reported to be strict and exacting.

My grandfather saw the schoolhouse as a perfect place in which to establish a base for the future uprising, which potentially would encompass the entire region of Žemaitija. Mardosai had twelve farms, providing twelve men who joined the troop headed by Captain Jonas Noreika.[3]

Damijonas was then seventeen years old; Noreika, thirty-one. Damijonas's cell comprised four men, including his father, Liudvikas Riauka; his brother, also named Liudvikas; and Pranas Blaževičius from the village of Juodeikiai. My grandfather's leadership role was kept secret to prevent his capture by the Communists.

The Mardosai school was owned by a Jewish man named Bertė Pelcas, who maintained the building and its small yard and repaired the furnace. He lived on one side of the structure; the other side contained the single schoolroom, a kitchen, a bedroom, and a basement. The fact that the owner was Jewish made the Russians unlikely to suspect any underground activity there; had Bertė Pelcas known about the covert goings-on, he would have informed the NKVD, Damijonas claimed. He maintained that all Jews were Communists; consequently, they all were mistrusted.

"All of them?" I asked.

"Unfortunately, yes," he answered. Then, after a moment, "Are you still planning on taking that Holocaust tour?"

"Yes."

"Why do you need to take it?"

"I think it's important to find out about Jewish history during World War II. There might be a connection to my grandfather's story."

"I'm not sure you need to do this. How long is the tour, anyway?"

"A week."

"A week? Why a week? You don't need a whole week. Maybe a day, at most."

I eyed him curiously, wondering why he was so concerned about the length of the tour. This conversation took place during my visit to Lithuania. He seemed to want to exert control over me for the rest of my stay in Kaunas. I would have to extricate myself as soon as possible—but not until I'd heard his account of the uprising.

As the schoolhouse could not hold the number of men expected at the clandestine meetings, the Mardosai troop met at the Kijauskas family's farm in the village of Šiemuliai. Noreika stipulated repeatedly that no documents be left anywhere, that everything must be kept in strictest confidence, and that all orders were to be given orally. No photographs portraying him as the group leader were permitted.[4] The only photograph I had of him during this period showed him sitting in the schoolhouse next to a chess table, holding my infant mother.

One of the principal men in the troop was Kazys Kijauskas, who had taken Captain Jonas Noreika's law course when he was a cadet at the Military Aviation School of Kaunas from 1939 to 1940. After he was dismissed from the Lithuanian army by the Communists in October 1940, Kijauskas returned to his homestead, heard about the uprising, and joined the Mardosai troop. His father's house eventually became the primary meeting place for this unit of the Lithuanian Activist Front.

In 1931, Jews in Plungė owned 87 percent of the trade businesses and 74 percent of the factories.[5] A newspaper report Damijonas had given me stated that Kijauskas had been arrested when, at a dance outside Plungė in 1941, he had shouted, "We have worked so hard, brothers, that now the Jews lead us!"[6] His meaning was clear: the Jews—all of them presumably Communists—had overtaken Lithuanians both economically and politically. The Communists arrested him for his inflammatory outburst; he was jailed for two days.

These were the same sentiments my grandfather had expressed in the leaflet I had been so distressed to find. Here was another one of the rebels proven to be an antisemite by the written record. And perhaps Kijauskas was following my grandfather's lead in this, as in the rebellion. As his granddaughter and a Lithuanian patriot, I was loath to face this possibility; it felt almost treasonous.

Damijonas and I had been sitting reviewing piles of documents and photos as he droned on for hours. I could no longer bear the sound of his voice. I asked if I could take a short walk around the neighborhood to stretch my legs. He led me outside, past the ditches in his neighbor's yard.

"What are the ditches for?" he asked.

"We're fixing the plumbing," his neighbor replied. "Sorry for the inconvenience."

"They'd be good for burying Jews, wouldn't they?" Damijonas responded, laughing loudly at his own joke.

I glared at him. Did he not understand why I was here? I had told him I was hunting down the rumor, seeking to dispel it—to prove that my grandfather was a hero and not a Jew-killer. Damijonas seemed oblivious.

I needed silence and time to myself. Turning on my heel, I left his yard and walked down the street. Was he covering up for Jonas Noreika? Was he counting on my loyalty as the granddaughter of a hero, trusting that I wouldn't dare—or want—to discover the truth? When I returned an hour later, still perturbed and angry, I told Damijonas that I had decided to go back to my hotel room early to work on my notes for the rest of the day.

The 1941 uprising against the Soviets had an unimaginative name: Tautinio Darbo Apsauga (TDA), or "Defense of National Labor." According to historian Andrius Kulikauskas, this was the Lithuanian version of the National Socialists.[7]

Colonel Kazys Škirpa, Lithuanian leader in exile, created this military section of the Lithuanian Activist Front and selected about forty soldiers to receive special training from the Germans in Klaipėda (Eastern Prussia). In May 1941, Škirpa met them during their training near the Karaliaučius farm.[8]

Much of the propaganda designed to foment the uprising came from Germany. Jonas Noreika travelled there at least once a month by secret routes. He was often escorted by the head of the German-Lithuanian border police, Kazys Šilgalis, and by men from the Mardosai troop. Occasionally a few of Lithuania's intellectuals crossed the border with him to evade the Communists. On his return trips, my grandfather brought political literature and news from the Germans: war was imminent.

It certainly seemed that Jonas Noreika was a Nazi collaborator. But Damijonas refused to acknowledge any wrongdoing by my grandfather.

How did he manage to avoid this obvious conclusion? Damijonas conceded that Noreika had travelled monthly to meet the Germans in order to help them plan their invasion of Lithuania. But he insisted that the Germans had promised not to occupy the country, only to liberate it.[9] My grandfather had simply failed to foresee their treachery, Damijonas avowed. My host put the whole blame on Germany's deceit and utterly denied Lithuania's collaboration.

Noreika met with LAF operatives at the Dovykas home, near the border. Sometimes he rode in a German truck; at other times he walked or used a thick-tired bicycle. He invariably came back with instructions, maps, pistols and light arms, proclamations, and radio equipment. He established radio stations in Barstyčiai, his wife's hometown, and in the schoolhouse in Mardosai. These stations enabled him to receive instructions from Germany in Morse code, and to broadcast messages from the LAF to the locals.

"What did those messages say?" I asked.

"I don't remember. Just that war would start soon."

Listening to Damijonas, I had conflicting feelings. While I was grateful for his firsthand report of the long-ago uprising, his denial of the obvious conclusions to be drawn from the evidence sent waves of nausea through my body. Increasingly I sensed that I was being told only half the story, that he was consciously misdirecting me, obscuring all connections between the Lithuanians and the Nazis. But I had no definitive proof.

Didn't he understand that having a grandfather who was a Nazi collaborator had changed my whole sense of who I was? Maybe he *did* understand, and for precisely that reason told me nothing about my grandfather's complicity in murder. Or perhaps he was concerned that such revelations would reflect badly upon him.

Later that afternoon, I met Holocaust researcher and guide Simon Dovidavičius at the Chiune Sugihara museum. He gave me a quick tour of the premises, plus several books about the Holocaust in Lithuania. When I mentioned Viktoras Ašmenskas's book, he asked if I could assist him in locating a copy of it. Later, over a dinner of mushroom *koldūnai* (dumplings) at a restaurant in the Akropolis, we began planning the itinerary of my week-long Holocaust-themed tour.

I lamented that the apartment in Klaipėda in which I would be staying the following week did not have internet access—something that would significantly hinder my research. Simon responded by taking me to an electronics shop in the mall and showing me a device called a Vodafone. He explained that it could be plugged into my computer, and—for a monthly fee—provide access to the internet anywhere in Lithuania.

After our pleasant evening, I braced myself for the next day with Damijonas.

Vilnius

1941

During the time period of the Provisional Government, the German SD and Gestapo special units introduced the majority of the Jewish discrimination orders, albeit with the help of locally created governments. They created ghettoes on their own volition—with a few TDA forces—and commenced to slaughter Jews on a massive scale. Throughout the entire six-week period of the Lithuanian Provisional Government, the Jewish mass murders could not be stopped (one even wonders if it were possible). Thousands of Lithuanian citizens—Jews—were sacrificed to the Holocaust by August 5, 1941.

Lithuanian Provisional Government meeting minutes June 24–August 4, 1941

CHAPTER SIXTEEN

A Slaughter of Innocents

We all believe that this [Soviet] enemy's greatest and most helpful
assistant was the Jew. The Jew does not belong to any national
organization. He doesn't have a homeland or country. He is
always and everywhere just a Jew.... During the last twenty
years of our independence, the Jews—as "equal citizens"—peeled
off nine fur coats from the Lithuanian nation. The Jews imme-
diately dominated our domestic and foreign businesses, trades,
banks, farms, and professions. All of our cities and towns became
Jewish. The Jews openly bragged, "Lithuanians get the streets, but
the Jews get the curbs [with the houses and other buildings]."
—"For All Posterity, Let Us Remove Lithuania from the Jewish Yoke,"
Lithuanian Activist Front, Document LXIV, 1941

O n June 13, 1941, ten days before the uprising, Damijonas's father asked
him to come home early from Plungė High School. The teenager was
handed his birth certificate as identification and instructed to ride his bike to
Klaipėda, observing everything along the way. His father was trying to decide
whether the family should cross the border to escape the Communists. Damijonas noticed Russians on the road under the hot sun, and twice was actually
interrogated by Soviet soldiers demanding whether he knew of any underground activity. He lied and said, "No."

Two days later, pedaling his bike back from Klaipėda, he slowed down to observe Soviet trucks containing wailing children whose families were being deported to Siberia. Gripped by dread, he returned home to report to his father what he had seen. Nonetheless, after some deliberation, the family gambled on staying to fight for their country.[1]

Six days later, when Jonas Noreika was at the Kijauskas farm, a boy from the nearby Meškauskas farm arrived there breathlessly. Meškauskas's farm was situated near the underground German radio outpost, where it had just been learned that Operation Barbarossa, Hitler's invasion of the Soviet Union, was to be launched on June 22. Thus, Commander Noreika was informed, the rebellion must begin on that date.

To protect his family, Noreika asked Kazys Kijauskas to convey his wife, daughter, and sister from the Mardosai schoolhouse to the home of his in-laws in Barstyčiai, twenty-four miles north, through secret paths in the forest. Kazys departed at once with a pair of horses and a carriage. According to Damijonas, my grandfather's family in Barstyčiai was unaware that Jews were being slaughtered in Plungė. He reiterated a few times that even Jonas Noreika himself, travelling from Plungė to Barstyčiai to Telšiai during this terrifying time, would not have known about the murder of Jews in Plungė. I jotted in my notebook, "Why does he keep repeating this?"

On the day before the uprising, at nine in the morning, Damijonas's mother was tending her garden when police chief Edvardas Martišius, Noreika's main LAF messenger, appeared. Damijonas overheard Martišius's announcement to his father: "Tomorrow, war begins. Your group is expected to come with weapons to the agreed location at 11:00."[2] Damijonas jumped onto his bike and rode to his aunt's home in Plungė to tell her the news. As Russian soldiers marched down the road, preparing for the invasion, he rode the five miles back and found his family staring toward the west at the terrible black smoke rising from Klaipėda. The war had started.

That evening, upon my grandfather's orders, the partisans of Žemaitija received their weapons. The arms had been hidden in the schoolhouse and then transferred to Plungė. Seventeen-year-old Damijonas was given a

7.65-caliber pistol; his friend Pranas, a German carbine. His older brother and his father already had guns of their own.[3]

As Damijonas passed the rectory of St. John the Baptist Church, where my grandparents had been married five years earlier, he saw Father Lygnugaris, who was pale, sweating, and mumbling incoherently. The priest had just returned from Kaušėnų, a village two miles from Plungė, where he had attempted to baptize Jews in the desperate hope of preventing their murder by local partisans. His efforts were in vain; by July 13, 1,800 Jews had been shot dead.

Days later Father Lygnugaris, who had witnessed the atrocity, had a nervous breakdown and isolated himself in a monastery, refusing to speak to anyone.

"Since Noreika was the leader of the partisans in Žemaitija, wouldn't he be responsible for their killing the Jews?" I asked Damijonas.

"Noreika didn't know about any of this. Povilas Alimas and Arnoldas Pabrėža were in charge of Plungė. Many men acted independently in killing Jews. Your grandfather had nothing to do with it. Besides, he was going back and forth, visiting his family in Barstyčiai."

I felt uneasy. My fear regarding my grandfather's involvement in the Jew-killing grew steadily, despite Damijonas's denials. I studied the face of my grandfather's friend and colleague, wishing I had a lie detector, or some more sophisticated device that could scan his brain to identify and extract the truth. How could my grandfather, whom Damijonas had described as the commander of the partisan uprising in Žemaitija, not have been aware of his followers' actions? As none of his directions were recorded on paper, there was no evidence that he had ordered—or that he had tried to stop— the slaughter of Jews. At this point, Germans had not yet arrived in great numbers, so the mass murder could not have been committed by them; clearly, it was perpetrated by Lithuanians. And who was the Lithuanians' leader in that area at that time? Jonas Noreika. As the evidence accumulated, I hardly needed a smoking gun. And, God help me, did I even want to find one?

Vilnius
March 27, 2019

Lithuania's purpose was to serve Lithuania—not the Third Reich—
during the June 1941 uprising and afterward, when it restored its
self-government. However, Germany was perceived as an ally in
the struggle against the Soviet Union.

"On the Accusation of Jonas Noreika (General Storm),"
Genocide and Resistance Research Centre of Lithuania

CHAPTER SEVENTEEN

A Maze of Alibis

Lithuania's Communist Party, the true Russian Bolshevik agents,
and the gang that shoved Lithuania's independence into the pits,
is comprised of 80–90 percent Jews.
—"For All Posterity, Let Us Remove Lithuania from the Jewish Yoke,"
Lithuanian Activist Front, Document LXIV, 1941

On the first day of the uprising, Sunday, June 22, 1941, the Russians burned the Martynas windmill. Damijonas attended Mass at St. John the Baptist Church to strengthen himself spiritually for the battle to come. His mother wept as his father proclaimed, "Now we are left to die or achieve Lithuania's freedom. If we die, Lithuania will still live! Don't cry, Mother; we will return safely."[1]

Damijonas and the rest of the Mardosai group met at the town's school-house as agreed. Upon entering my grandfather's bedroom there, Damijonas was impressed to find a copy of *Mein Kampf* sitting on my grandfather's desk, looking like a splendid prayer book. I gazed incredulously at Damijonas's reverential expression. He knew what a mention of *Mein Kampf* meant today, didn't he? He was openly stating that his hero, Jonas Noreika, had treasured Hitler's vile argument for eliminating the Jews.

My host read to me from a newspaper article describing his first impression of the uprising's leader:

He was an unusually interesting person. He wore part of the Lithuanian army uniform, with a jacket, but it was clear he was a soldier.
He was energetic and very demanding. His speech was short and
to the point.

"Have all of you men taken the oath?" Noreika asked his
troops.

"We have."

"Do you all understand the assignment?"

"We do!"[2]

Noreika issued them white armbands stitched with the initials TDA
(Tautinio Darbo Apsauga, or "Defense of National Labor"—which, as we
have seen, can be read as the Lithuanian version of "Nazi"). Alert to this
detail of the account, I surmised that the sewing probably had been done by
women. Had my grandmother and aunt sewn those armbands? Damijonas
didn't know. My grandfather instructed his soldiers to wear them only when
near German soldiers, and to carry them in their pockets when ambushing
Russians. This instruction could have engendered confusion, as Russians
and Nazis, facing off against each other, sometimes occupied the same field,
and the partisans would not always know whether or not to wear their
armbands.

The partisans moved into a tall field of rye and crouched, pointing their
pistols, about two feet from each other. The Meškauskas family home overlooked the road; when a family member opened a window, this would signal
that Russians were advancing. A Russian tank rolled by, but my grandfather
signaled to his men to let it pass, so as to allow the Germans to attack it by air.

Jonas Noreika had arranged that a Wehrmacht four-engine plane carrying weapons and supplies would land at a makeshift airfield nearby. But
the plane sent a yellow rocket, indicating that it would not land as expected.
Instead the pilot flew over the field, machine-gunning Russian Communists
and causing them to flee toward Plungė. Then the pilot began shooting at the
Mardosai troop, which felt confused and betrayed. Its members ran for their
lives, crossing the woods and the Babrungas River, where they huddled to

determine their next move. The problem, Damijonas opined, was that the pilot had not seen any white TDA armbands, the agreed-upon sign.

That evening Noreika and a band of his followers went to guard the electric tower, each of them carrying two wooden boards. My grandmother's brother, Vladas Krapavičius from Barstyčiai—who had been the best man at their wedding—was there to help; he was an electrician. When the Russians came to bomb the tower, the partisans clapped their boards rapidly together to simulate the sound of machine-gun fire. The ruse succeeded in repelling the Russians.

At 9:28 a.m. on the second day of the uprising, June 23, 1941, Leonas Prapuolenis, a Lithuanian Activist Front leader, announced Lithuania's newly won freedom from the Communists over the Kaunas radio station. The nation that had been brutally tortured during the Bolshevik terror, he proclaimed, now dared to rebuild its future. The Lithuanian anthem triumphantly sounded as listeners exultantly stood at attention. The declaration was repeated in German and Russian.[3]

When I compared the Lithuanian account of the speech broadcast that morning with the Jewish account, I noted a significant omission. According to Jewish reports, Prapuolenis continued with the following statement:

> Brothers and sisters, Lithuanians! The destined final hour of revenge against the Jews has arrived. Lithuania must be liberated not only from the slavery of the Asiatic Bolsheviks, but also from the longstanding oppression of the Jews. The Lithuanian Activist Front, in the name of the entire Lithuanian nation, solemnly declares:
>
> 1. The rights given to Jews during the ancient times of Vytautas the Great have been totally and completely revoked.
>
> 2. Every Lithuanian Jew, without exception, is immediately warned to leave the Lithuanian land.
>
> 3. The new Lithuanian state will be restored through the energy, work, heart, and wisdom of the Lithuanian People. Jews are completely and totally excluded from this task.

> So let us all prepare for battle and victory for Lithuania's free-
> dom, for Lithuania's cleansing, for its independence, for its sound
> and happy future.[4]

When, weeks after hearing Damijonas's curtailed version of this announcement, I learned of this second half of it, I was stunned. And appalled. I wanted to stop my research. *Is this what Holocaust denial looks like? Where is this story going to take me?* But by now the story had a life of its own, a magnetic power. Compelled in equal parts by fascination and by a reluctant moral obligation, I slowly pieced together the confused narrative from the new facts that were emerging. Many details suddenly seemed charged with new meaning, acquiring a darker significance when considered in a larger context. I rewrote, restructured, and refined my notes, increasingly convinced that the result would not reflect well upon my grandfather and other Lithuanian nationalists.

About three hours after Prapuolenis's announcement, the Mardosai squad set out to guard the Santykis Bridge, which still stands today. They did not believe the Russians to be nearby. Noreika decided to cross the bridge first. As soon as he stepped onto it, machine-gun fire erupted. He fell onto his hands and rolled three times from side to side to evade bullets. Damijonas was pleased to reenact this moment, screaming *ra-ta-ta-ta* to imitate the sound of the guns. Noreika told his men to run.

As the young Damijonas raced through rye fields, he felt a tug at his coat. A bullet had gone right through it, grazing his skin. A second bullet struck his knee. Yet despite claiming that there had been two hundred Russian soldiers around the bridge, he maintained that no partisans had been killed.

He rolled up the leg of his outer pants and then of his pajamas, proudly displaying the scar to me. "I never showed this to anyone because it would get me in trouble," he declared. In all the years that he had lived under Communist rule, he had not divulged his participation in this anti-Communist rebellion.

On the third day of the uprising, everything was quiet in Plungė. The Russian soldiers, disguised as civilians, had departed. That same day, Noreika was driven to Klaipėda by a Wehrmacht soldier in a car belonging to the German government. There, as previously arranged, the Lithuanian Activist Front appointed him as leader of Šiauliai. He was then taken back to his Mardosai headquarters.

On June 25, the fourth day, Bertė Pelcas and his wife fled the Mardosai schoolhouse by horse-drawn wagon. Noreika, noting Pelcas's intended route, yelled, "Hey, where are you going? The Germans are shooting Jews. Don't go down that road. Run away from that road! Go to any Lithuanian farmer and hide there. Try the Stanevičius farm."[5]

Pelcas, trembling, thanked Noreika for the warning.

This anecdote was intended to demonstrate my grandfather's kindness to Jews, to prove that he wouldn't have harmed them. Yet it utterly contradicted Damijonas's earlier story; Noreika could not have been both in Barstyčiai, unaware of the massacre, and simultaneously in Mardosai and knowledgeable about it.

That very day, Jews were being packed into the synagogue in Plungė, directly across the street from the police station. They would soon be executed. Damijonas continued to insist that my grandfather had been ignorant of this fact.

"How can that be true, if Noreika was the leader of the region?" I asked once again, my frustration evident.

"The Mardosai squad had nothing to do with it," Damijonas insisted. "It was all Alimas, Pabrėža, and the Germans."

I realized that he was covering up not only for Noreika but for himself. I felt ready to throttle him.

Noreika instructed the villagers to raise a white flag to indicate that the Russian Communists had left. The Lithuanians wanted to regain control of their country without shedding any more blood. A number of Lithuanian Communists were caught and brought to the Mardosai schoolhouse basement, where Noreika judged them. He ordered them to stop being Communists and released them. They gratefully kissed his right hand.

Damijonas's glowing portrait of my grandfather only prompted questions to race through my mind. *Jonas Noreika had instigated an uprising against the*

Communists, but treated some of them kindly? He had no control over what was happening to the Jews, who were regarded as Communists, but he had the authority to release Lithuanians accused of the same crime? None of it made sense—unless I accepted the interpretation I feared most.

Vilnius
March 27, 2019

J. Noreika's colleague Damijonas Riauka testified, "Jonas Noreika did not separate the occupiers' adherents into us and them: When we asked him how we should act with the Germans, Noreika stated, 'The Russians are not our friends, nor the Germans our brothers.'"

J. Noreika, along with ten other Žemaitija intellectuals, demanded that the German leadership prohibit its genocide against Lithuanians and Jews, and that it grant Lithuania independence.

In February 1943, he wrote an article, "Today's Germany," in which he exposed the Nazi regime's destruction of Lithuania and Germany itself.

In his final speech to the Soviet court, J. Noreika agreed with all charges made against him concerning his fighting against the Soviet regime, except for its accusation that "he voluntarily served the Germans."

(LYA, f-Kl, ap. 58, b. 9792/d, t.4, quoting Viktoras Ašmenskas, *Generolas Vėtra* [General Storm] (Vilnius: Lietuvos Gyventojų Genocido ir Rezistencijos Tyrimo Centras [Lithuanian Genocide and Resistance Research Centre], 1997), 359, 384.

"On the Accusation of Jonas Noreika (General Storm),"
Genocide and Resistance Research Centre of Lithuania

CHAPTER EIGHTEEN

Lost Credit

The new Lithuanian nation will be rebuilt through the efforts,
works, hearts, and minds of Lithuanians. Jews will be completely
excluded from Lithuania forever.... In the newly rebuilt Lithu-
ania, not one Jew will have rights to citizenship, nor the means
to make a living. This is how we will remedy the past mistakes of
the Jewish nonsense. This is how a strong foundation will be laid
for the future happiness and creation of our Aryan nation.
—"For All Posterity, Let Us Remove Lithuania from the Jewish Yoke,"
Lithuanian Activist Front, Document LXIV, 1941

To visualize the area in which the uprising had been staged, I hired a chauffeur named Mykolas to drive me and Damijonas to Plungė. When we
stopped at an automated teller machine so that I could withdraw cash to pay
him, I couldn't find my bank card! With shaking hands, I pulled everything
out of my purse and scoured every pocket of my wallet—to no avail. The two
men eyed me suspiciously, and I felt mortified. *How could I forget my bank card?*
What could I possibly have done with it? When did I last use it? Eventually, I
recalled with dismay that I had used it at an ATM in the Akropolis shopping
mall a few days earlier and hadn't remembered to retrieve it from the machine.

"I'll pay you somehow, but it will have to be after our trip, if that's alright,"
I faltered.

"What about gas for the trip?" asked Mykolas.

"I still have a credit card," I replied. I tried not to think about its high interest rate, which would cause me to spiral ever more deeply into debt. This story was ruining me financially. The calculator in my head tabulated the expenses to date. The trip alone would cost more than $10,000. I had also taken out $60,000 in student loans in order to obtain two more master's degrees: one in education so that I could teach high school and have my summers free to work on the book; and the other in creative nonfiction, to facilitate its writing. I had gambled so much on the completion of this story that the current crisis made me feel as if I were about to implode.

I strove to maintain my usual stoic and gracious facade. Stifling my sense of rising panic, I assured Mykolas that he would be paid. To my great relief, he grudgingly agreed to continue driving us. Here I was, seeking to establish my grandfather's and Lithuania's credibility, and I could barely establish my own with my chauffeur!

We headed northeast, to Plungė.

The ever-changing scenery provided a welcome diversion: lush vegetation, pine forests, winding rivers, and a profusion of white storks. The white stork, Damijonas informed me, was the national bird of Lithuania. Everyone regarded a stork as a good omen, especially if its nest was built near one's home. The nests, about four feet wide and equally deep, were generally perched on top of telephone posts or man-made pillars with platforms.

I had never seen so many storks in my life. With their long legs and thin beaks, they looked like white flamingos.

Damijonas resembled a stork himself, I thought, with his gangly legs. He couldn't weigh more than 110 pounds. He wore a thick, faded, blue, long-sleeved cotton shirt; green pants held up by red, white, and blue suspenders; and flannel pajama bottoms as insulation under his pants. While I was sweating in a sleeveless blouse in the eighty-degree weather, he sported a furry vest and a jacket and begged me not to open the car window because the wind would cause him to catch cold. The combination of the stifling heat and his old-man's breath in the enclosed car made me feel nauseated. I opened the window a crack, telling him that I was too hot and felt faint. He shook his head, but granted me the inch of fresh air that streamed in.

He interrupted his own constant chatter to point to a stork. "Look! There's one—no, two! Oh, it's a family of four! We're up to thirteen now! The parents are known to kick out a weak chick, you know." He so enjoyed counting the storks we saw along the way that I soon joined him in pointing them out.

We stopped at the Mardosai schoolhouse. It had been renovated and was now owned by two separate families. Thanks to Damijonas's efforts, it bore a wooden plaque, dated 1995, that commemorated my grandfather—in honor of what would have been his eighty-fifth birthday. We drank coffee with one of the building's owners, Povilas Navickas, who told us about the radio that Noreika had hung from a tree near the schoolhouse. He showed us the woodshed that my grandfather had used to store weapons obtained from the Nazis for the partisans' use during the uprising.

A family of storks nesting on a telephone pole next to the schoolhouse craned their necks to observe us. We raised our cups, then stood to admire the faded plaque:

> In this home 1940–1941 lived
> Žemaitija Uprising
> June 21–25, 1941
> Leader Captain
> Jonas Noreika
> Generolas
> Vėtra
> 1910–1947

Back in the car, a 2005 Skoda, I resumed my queries and scribbling. Damijonas didn't give me a minute of peace: "I'm going to keep talking; I don't care who's listening! I'm going to die this year, anyway. Oh, look! Another stork! If you have money in your pocket and you see a stork in a nest, you'll have enough money this year. If you don't have money and you see a stork flying, you won't have any money this year." He threw me an aggrieved look, no doubt to remind me about the lost bank card and how much money I was going to owe him. Having lost access to my checking account, in which I had managed to accumulate several thousand dollars, I glumly envisioned my steadily mounting credit card charges. *At least people are no longer sent to debtors' prison.*

By the time we'd counted seventeen storks, we had arrived in Plungė. Mykolas parked next to St. John the Baptist Church. In addition to its bell tower, in 1941 this church had a gong to announce the beginning of worship, a wedding, or a funeral. *Was the gong sounded at the beginning of the uprising, a call to arms? Could it be heard eight kilometers away, in Mardosai?*

We strolled down Vytautas Street, the town's main road, toward a statue of St. Florian, the patron saint of firemen. Shaking his head in disapproval, Damijonas remarked that the saint had not done a good job of guarding the city; the Jews, he said, had burned it several times. He offered no elaboration. Then he pointed out the police station, an imposing white structure with blue trim which seemed to dominate the town. Across from it, in the central square, were once booths called *kromai*, where Jews and Lithuanians sold goods. I glanced back down Vytautas Street at the path we'd just taken, viewing the church from a distance. This was where my grandparents had embarked upon their married life.

Damijonas proceeded down Freedom Avenue, stooping to pick a tiny white edelweiss flower. Balancing himself with the aid of his cane, he secured his prize and rose stiffly. German soldiers, he informed me, traditionally presented their beloved with an edelweiss bloom from the mountains before going off to war. He bowed gallantly and offered me the flower. Amused, I accepted his delicate gift with an exaggerated curtsy and a giggle, then tucked the blossom behind my right ear.

Near the end of the avenue and close to the Babrungas River stood a bookstore that had been a printing shop at the time of the uprising. Damijonas recounted that, three months before the rebellion, he and two other men had taken a mimeograph machine from this shop to print proclamations. An employee had set the machine on a basement windowsill to allow it to be carried to the home of Damijonas's aunt at Vaižganto 63, four blocks away. Damijonas had obtained a thousand sheets of paper, which he said he had purchased by soliciting donations from Plungė residents. Later I would wonder if he had really received the paper from the Germans.

Damijonas Riauka—at eighty-nine years old in 2013—who was my grandfather's close friend and colleague in the uprising, standing in front of the window of the former bookstore in Plungė where he had picked up the mimeograph machine so many decades before

The three-man team used a stencil to copy the proclamation's text and then took turns hand-cranking out a thousand sheets through the night.

Afterward, they wiped the stencil with kerosene, "so that not even a dog could smell that it was used during the night." At dawn, one man returned the mimeograph machine to the windowsill while another stuffed copies into strategically placed bundles of straw throughout town. The next morning the townspeople searched the bundles for directives. Sometimes they would find a snake that had crawled into the straw, said Damijonas, chuckling.

"What did the directives say?" I inquired.

"I don't remember. The proclamations came from the LAF in Berlin."

He was unusually quiet.

"Don't you have any copies in your archives?" I persisted. "You made a thousand copies! That big wall in your apartment, behind the curtain, that's filled with paper? Didn't you save at least one of the directives?"

"Unfortunately, I didn't."

"What a shame!"

I found it odd that Damijonas couldn't remember the content of the directives that he had gone to such trouble to produce; he seemed to recall everything else in minute detail. I consoled myself with the thought that somebody must have a copy somewhere.

Later during my trip, I found what I was looking for in a book entitled *ŠOA Holokaustas Lietuvoje: Skaitiniai I dalis* (SHOAH Holocaust in Lithuania: Readings Part One). Then I understood the reason for Damijonas's pretended memory loss, and I was furious. The proclamation whose contents he had "forgotten" declared:

Lithuanian Information Bureau in Berlin

Fight!

Enslaved Lithuanian countrymen

1941 March 19

Dear enslaved brothers!

Lithuania's hour of freedom is approaching. In a few months, the outcome of our diligent work against your sufferings under the Asiatic oppression will be delivered. We are ordered to quickly inform you of these matters:

....

2. As was mentioned, the hour of Lithuania's freedom is almost here. Once the march has started from the west, you will be informed within the same minute by radio or other means. At that moment, Lithuania's enslaved cities, churches and villages will be in the uprising, or better said, the government will return to its own hands. At once, you need to capture the local Communists and other Lithuanian traitors, so that not one will avoid what's coming.

3. We are sure that you are ready and organized, but those who are not ready, organize yourselves into small secret groups. You

have learned that among Lithuanians there are traitors, so at this time be very careful.

5. Once the activities begin, take over the bridges, important railroads, airports, factories, etc. Do not destroy them or let the Russians destroy them. These are important economically and for the soldiers.

6. Today you can inform the Jews that their destiny is clear. Whoever can should leave Lithuania so there will be no unnecessary victims. At that moment, you should take their property so that nothing will go to waste.

Lithuanian Information Bureau

P.S. This notice should reach the farthest corners of Lithuania by spoken or written word.

Having read this, give it to another.

Go away, Jews!

Having slaved for centuries, Lithuanian, go to war for freedom. The time for revenge has come. There is something that is blocking us.

Let us take revenge a hundredfold upon the Jews and Communists for the innocent blood shed by our nation's people.

We've had enough of the Jews baking their matzah bread in Lithuanian blood.

Lithuanians, whoever is alive, go to war against Jewry.

Lithuanians, let's lead our nation out of Jewish slavery.[1]

Years later, historians investigating my grandfather's role in the Holocaust in Lithuania would tell me that they believed many of these LAF directives had been written by my grandfather himself.

As our day trip to Plungė neared its end, Damijonas was uncharacteristically quiet. We were lost in our thoughts during the ride home, speaking only when we spotted another stork. Mykolas played a CD of German waltzes and Lithuanian folk music to fill the silence. We counted fifty-three storks in all.

Once back at my hotel room, I called my husband and told him, in tears, that I had stupidly lost the bank card, and that this was going to add to the expense of the trip, already so much greater than planned. He calmly assured me that he would send a new card. Neither of us had any idea that it would not arrive until the last week of my trip. In any case, all of my careful financial planning had suddenly gone up in smoke; I was at the mercy of a credit card with a nosebleed interest rate. Sick with anxiety at this and other uncontrollable turns of events, I cried myself to sleep.

During the remaining weeks of my trip, I attempted to find answers to the continually multiplying questions. *Who wrote those directives? Had the orders to shoot Jews come from my grandfather? Even if they hadn't, how could he not have known about the killings? And if he knew, why didn't he stop his men from committing these heinous crimes?* I did not let Damijonas know that I was losing my trust in him. I needed his testimony for the record; its degree of credibility could be assessed later.

There were other troubling questions, too: *Did my grandmother know what was happening? Could that have been why she told me, "It's best to just let history lie"?*

Vilnius
March 27, 2019

In the first days of the occupation, the Nazis shattered the Lithuanians' hope for independence.... The Jewish massacre, planned by the Nazis—even before they attacked the Soviet Union—was especially surprising for Lithuanians. This plan was executed by Special Operations Group A, led by SS Brigadeführer Walter Stahlecker in the occupied territory of Lithuania. The German Nazis organized the slaughter of Jews within the borders of

Lithuania. It occurred very swiftly in the cities of Gargždai, Kaunas, Vilnius, and Plungė, where identical instructions appeared by the Germans to restrict the lives of Jews and establish ghettos. From secret German documents, it is obvious that W. Stahlecker's tactic was to kill as many Jews as possible in the first days of the occupation, while Lithuania's residents still believed Germany was an ally against the Soviet Union.

"On the Accusation of Jonas Noreika (General Storm),"
Genocide and Resistance Research Centre of Lithuania

CHAPTER NINETEEN

Murder and Celebration

Stasys Patackas: Earlier, you stated that Noreika received
news of the war's beginning from Germany. Yet later he took a
stand against them, against the Germans in war. How can you
explain this?
Damijonas Riauka: Noreika said, "Neither the Germans nor the
Russians are our friends! We have to fight for independence."
—"General Storm: Who Is He?" December 9, 1993, Lithuanian
radio transcript[1]

According to Damijonas, Jonas Noreika led eighty-seven men in the Mardosai-Plungė region in the 1941 uprising against the Soviets.[2] On June 26, the day after the uprising ended in victory in Plungė, my grandfather departed for Telšiai, nineteen miles to the northwest, escorted by a German in a truck.

After the success of the uprising, partisans across the entire Žemaitija region reportedly rounded up and massacred large groups of Jewish civilians. I found it difficult to believe that the men under Jonas Noreika's command would have perpetrated such acts on their own, without his knowledge or instructions.

On June 29, Damijonas crossed the Stalgenas Bridge over the Minija River between Rietavas and Plungė and was stopped by two German soldiers. He showed them his white TDA armband and told them that he had helped to protect the bridge from the Soviets. Upon hearing this, they released him, saying, "Good! Good! Super partisans!" Damijonas smiled as he recounted the story. I pictured the Nazis slapping him on the back and giving him the "thumbs up" sign.

That same day a fire broke out in Plungė, which Damijonas attributed to a Jew. In retaliation, Plungė's commandant, whom Damijonas named as "Arnoldas Pabrėža or Povilas Alimas, but absolutely not Noreika," ordered all of Plungė's remaining Jews to be gathered into the synagogue and detained there without food and water. They were executed on July 12 and 13, at Kaušėnai.

Damijonas took me to the home of Albinas Kijauskas, the younger brother of one of my grandfather's men. We were served a delicious meal of *cepelinai* prepared by his wife—large potato dumplings stuffed with meat, named after zeppelins because of their shape.

On June 30, 1941, five days after the uprising, the Germans appointed Kazys Kijauskas, the elder brother of our host, Plungė's head of police. Kazys understood that his new post would require him to supervise the liquidation of Jews. He consulted his mother about this, and she advised him not to accept the position. So he declined it and chose to work on his farm.

I pushed the food around on my plate. *Why had Kazys felt the need to ask his mother whether he should agree to murder Jews?* Apparently such brutality was so accepted by the local culture, so entrenched, that Kazys had seriously considered carrying out this "duty." And evidently other men had no such qualms; enough of them said "yes" to carry out these heinous murders.

By July 13, three weeks after the uprising, all of Plungė's two thousand Jews had been shot and buried in ten pits on the outskirts of Plungė. The town had just lost half its population. Officially, all blame was cast upon the Germans.

Two weeks after this mass murder, an enormous party was held at the farm of Pranas Blaževičius. Damijonas showed me a brochure about the uprising that featured a photograph of the festivities.[3] About one hundred people sat in seven rows, squinting in the bright sun. I noted my grandfather sitting in the third row on the right, wearing a business suit. My grandmother was seated near him, across from Aunt Antanina, who was holding my mother (then two years old). They were celebrating the successful uprising, rejoicing at their freedom from the Communists.

A celebration in 1941 in Plungė. Jonas Noreika is the second from the right in the third row from the front. The description below the photograph reads: "Žemaitija uprising, June 21–25, 1941, led by Lithuanian army captain Jonas Noreika (later the leader of the anti-Soviet Resistance of 1946–1947, becoming its general after having given himself the code-name 'General Storm'). Defense of National Labor uprising company, 13 men who participated in two battles: June 22, 1941, Mardosai-Nausodžiai village junction, and June 23, 1941, by the Santakos Bridge, along with the region's Lithuanian Activist Front participants and their family members. A gathering in Nausodžiai village two weeks after the uprising (in the same place where the first battle took place), in Plungė's district, at the farmstead of upriser Liudvikas Meškauskas."

I surveyed the throng, with their jubilant faces, and was appalled. I asked Damijonas, "How could they throw a party so soon after two thousand Jews—half of the town's residents—were killed? Who killed them?"

Damijonas merely shook his head and said that the Nazis did all the killing, and the merrymaking was to commemorate the locals' having chased out the Communists.[4]

On our last day together, Damijonas presented me with two cardboard boxes packed with a large portion of his personal archive. We took a taxi to the post office, where I arranged to have the boxes sent to my home; the postage cost $300. Back in his apartment, he gave me a few more personal items, saying that he didn't know when he would see me next.

I had given him a few hundred dollars for his trouble, and he was tremendously happy. We had tears in our eyes as we said goodbye.

I'd had to exercise extraordinary patience to endure the week with him. I had done so for the sake of Lithuania; I needed to discover the truth. I already knew that writing the truth would mean betraying Damijonas. And not only him. It appeared that, in Lithuania during World War II, everyone had rationalized their motives and actions. They had had to pretend to sympathize with the Germans or the Russians simply to survive. Some pretended so well that they eventually took the side of the enemies they had set out to placate. Then the political winds shifted, and personal histories had to be reinvented or hidden. Thus I was taught to revere a grandfather who, it now seemed, had played an active role in the Holocaust.

I slept fitfully.

Vilnius
October 1, 2018

The petitioner's [Grant Gochin's] reference to the city's celebration was not at all connected to the Holocaust. The newspaper *Žemaičių Land* (1941, July 30) stated that the celebration, which occurred in Plungė on July 27, 1941, was intended to support the Lithuanian Provisional government.

Vilnius Regional Administrative Court
File No. eI-4215-281/2018
Response from the Genocide Resistance and Research Centre to the prosecution's claim against the Genocide Centre's refusal to change its historical conclusion on Jonas Noreika

CHAPTER TWENTY

The Blood Libel

The war against the Bolshevized Jewish world demands
taking a clear stand against the Soviet Union. You cannot
drive out the devil with Beelzebub.
—*Žemaičių Land*, July 7, 1941

At the end of my week in Kaunas, my father's second wife's son, Remigijus, offered to drive me to Klaipėda. A friend of his accompanied us on the two-hour trip.

The apartment lent by my Chicago friend was situated in the middle of Old Town, on Turgaus (Market) Street. Remigijus, his friend, and I sweated as we struggled up the four steep flights of stairs with my heavy luggage. I had brought a backpack full of electronics; a fanny pack containing my important documents; and three suitcases bulging with thick history tomes, a Lithuanian-English dictionary, and an excessive amount of clothing. I found the keys to the complicated German multiple-dead-bolt lock, but was confronted by another lock with a four-digit access code. At last I remembered the owner's detailed instructions and succeeded in entering.

The apartment was spacious but smelled stuffy, as though it had been closed up and vacant for several months. We immediately opened all its thirteen windows. A soothing sea breeze rushed in. The kitchen window faced the green Klaipėda Sea. I watched the waves crashing to the shore and admired the two hotels whose shapes together formed the letter *K*, for Klaipėda. Behind them, tall construction cranes bobbed ceaselessly as old cement structures were replaced with bronzed-glass towers. The view from the other side of the apartment, looking east, was of a cobblestoned boulevard with fashionable tourist shops.

The bathroom had a large, extra-high tub and a German-made washer and dryer with a bewildering array of buttons. Remigijus's friend kindly showed me how to operate them.

I walked through the living room and the two bedrooms looking for a place where I could write. I was disappointed not to find a proper desk; I would have to do my writing at the kitchen table. Positioning my laptop on one side of the extended oak table, I plugged in my Vodafone device. Within minutes I had access to the internet and had informed my husband of my new location.

This apartment would be my work headquarters, my writer's retreat between research trips to Kaunas, Plungė, Stutthof, Šiauliai, Šiluva, Šilutė, Telšiai, Tytuvėnai, Vilnius, Žagarė, and Žemaičių Kalvarija in order to examine the suppressed details of my grandfather's complex life. I was eager to conduct interviews, to translate passages of books and newspaper articles, and to construct a narrative about the most significant aspects of his life from my notes.

Remigijus and his friend, both about twenty years younger than I, invited me to go dancing with them at a nightclub. They seemed relieved when I declined. Once they had left, I unpacked and treated myself to a bubble bath. As I soaked in the tub and inhaled the soothing lavender scent, I reflected upon the past thirteen years. I knew that I couldn't possibly have addressed the rumor about my grandfather if my mother and grandmother were still alive. I wouldn't have dared. I still ached from their loss, but it accorded me the freedom to ask bold questions and pursue a course that still frightened me.

I also thought about my daughter. My husband reported that she had returned home but was staying out late at night with friends of questionable character. Had I made a mistake in taking this trip now? What would happen to her? Would my marriage withstand the choices I was making? How great an emotional cost would this story exact? My tears fell into the bathwater.

Remigijus and his friend came back late and returned to Kaunas the next morning. I had plans to meet my cousin Rasa Kovalenko for dinner at her home, a few blocks away. I decided to spend the day perusing my notes from the previous week, exploring the neighborhood, and going grocery shopping.

The owner had left coffee on the shelf and beer in the fridge. I drank a cup of coffee, powered up my laptop, and viewed film footage of Hitler addressing an enthusiastic crowd from the balcony of the theater square, just a block away from where I now sat. He had sailed in on the battleship *Deutschland* with an escort of German soldiers and, on March 23, 1939, announced his bloodless reconquest of Klaipėda. As he paraded to the balcony, he was greeted by residents who lined the streets and raised their right arms in salute. A banner proclaimed, "This land remains forever German." A man could be seen painting over the city's Lithuanian name on its signs while the Nazi flag flapped brazenly above the theater. Curtains emblazoned with swastikas were unfurled with great fanfare from the second floor.[1]

Most of the city's six thousand Jews fled in terror to Žemaitija—only to be massacred there three years later.[2]

I walked out to the square, envisioning all of this.

Today, beautiful women walked past in high heels, navigating the cobblestoned streets without a second thought. Tourists were browsing the displays of souvenirs in the scattered booths: amber jewelry and figurines of castles, trees, and hedgehogs. This last item was a popular Lithuanian memento. I bought lacy crocheted fingerless gloves for my daughter and a baseball cap in the Lithuanian colors of yellow, green, and red for my son.

In my olive-green cotton pants, sleeveless top, and flat, brown leather shoes whose thick rubber soles resembled tire treads, I felt overweight and rather self-conscious. I anticipated having to do a lot of walking. I had been wearing a pedometer to count my steps, and routinely reached ten thousand steps a day. On several days, the count had surpassed fifteen thousand.

From the theater square I walked two blocks to a corner grocery store called IKI (an abbreviation of "Iki pasimatymo," or "See you soon"). It had three long aisles of packaged foods, a delicatessen counter, and a refrigerated section featuring ready-made Lithuanian specialties such as dumplings, savory potato-bacon-and-egg cakes called *kugelis*, and beet soup. Lithuania had been independent for twenty-three years now, and the stores were better stocked than during my first visit in 1989. This store looked positively capitalist.

I was startled to see the word "Akcija!" ("Action!") posted next to several food items. Wasn't that the same word that the Nazis had used when relocating Jews to ghettos, marching them into the woods and killing them? To prepare for my trip, I had read several books about the Lithuanian Holocaust, which included accounts of Nazis and their Lithuanian collaborators bellowing "Akcija! Akcija! Akcija!" as they forced Jews into a ghetto at gunpoint. When the soldiers shrieked this fearsome word, Jews were required to run into the street, assemble into a line, and wait to see who among them would be taken away and shot.

"Akcija!" screamed out on grocery shelves alongside labels identifying a particular brand of yogurt, cheese, or wine—causing me to recoil. The other shoppers seemed either ignorant of or indifferent to the word's historical connotation; in fact, they tended to select the products flagged in this manner. I soon realized that the term now meant "Sale!" Amoral capitalists had chosen a loaded word with an ugly association merely to induce the contemporary masses to buy a product. If I wanted to save money on food purchases, I would have to acclimate myself to their thoughtless practice.

I reluctantly chose a bottle of red wine marked "Akcija!," black bread marked "Akcija!," butter marked "Akcija!," and a can of herring marked "Akcija!" Already, I was becoming inured to the impact of that hideous word.

That evening I walked down a busy, six-lane street lined with businesses, shops, and restaurants to my cousin's apartment. Rasa had offered to drive me to her home, but I'd replied that I enjoyed walking. The stroll would allow me to surpass my daily goal of ten thousand steps.

When I arrived, Rasa's ten-year-old daughter, Eva, was waiting for me at the bottom of the stairs. A lively and intelligent girl, she escorted me to their third-floor apartment. As we climbed, she told me that she liked hip-hop dancing and wearing makeup.

Rasa, wearing an apron over an elegant dress, greeted us at her apartment door. She had long, blonde hair and a svelte figure. She gave me a quick tour of her modern, uncluttered premises. To my surprise, they also contained a small beauty salon where she earned a second income as a makeup artist. Her full-time primary job was as a border-patrol agent on a ship in the Klaipėda Sea, apprehending people who attempted to enter the country illegally.

Rasa's seventeen-year-old son, Viktoras, played with their well-behaved white poodle for most of my visit. Her husband had been living in Ireland for the past three years, she said; it was the only place where he had been able to find a job.

Shortly afterward, Aunt Rūta (technically my first cousin once removed) arrived from Rietavas. Her mother, Marija Krapauskaitė Budrienė, and Rasa's mother, Aldona Budrytė Bruzienė, were two of my grandmother's sisters. Aldona lived only a few blocks from Rasa, but she was too ill to come that evening. Rūta had taken a bus for the thirty-mile trip and had brought an overnight bag. Apparently she travelled here for most holidays. She opened a side closet to hang up a sweater and store her bag.

Rasa had prepared a delicious meal, including pickled vegetables, cheese and crackers, and champagne, in honor of my arrival. As we drank, we spoke excitedly about our trip to Stutthof the next day. My grandfather had spent two years there in prison in the Nazi concentration camp. Rasa had reserved a rental car for the three-day journey; her daughter and Aunt Rūta would join us. Viktoras would stay home and take care of the dog.

My cousins asked me about my daughter, as I had announced months earlier that she would be accompanying me. Draining my glass more quickly than usual, I explained that she'd changed her mind at the last minute, as teenagers do. I was too ashamed to admit that she had developed a heroin habit. Aunt Rūta said that my daughter's decision not to come may have been wise; she probably would have found the trip very demanding.

Changing the subject to that of my upcoming Holocaust-themed tour, I described my first meeting with Simon Dovidavičius, the Holocaust researcher and guide at the Chiune Sugihara museum, explaining that he had been unable to find Ašmenskas's book about my grandfather. I asked my cousins whether either of them had an extra copy. Rasa took a volume from a bookshelf and handed it to me, saying that this was their only copy and that it would have to be returned. I thanked her, hoping that Simon would have time to read it during the next few weeks; perhaps I could eventually find another for him to keep.

We sat down to a dinner of chicken and rice with white wine. Aunt Rūta suggested that I meet her sister Jadvyga, who could describe my grandparents' wedding day. Jadvyga lived in Šilutė, thirty miles south of Klaipėda. We decided to visit her by bus after our trip to Stutthof.

Rūta excused herself from the table and walked to the closet to retrieve some photos from her bag. She returned smiling, holding a sepia photograph of her childhood home in Plungė, where my grandparents' wedding reception had been held. She remembered guests talking, years afterward, about how my grandparents had waltzed so gracefully to "The Blue Danube" on the polished wooden floor that my grandmother had so admired.

Aunt Rūta slipped me another sepia photo, which showed my grandmother stylishly dressed in a velvet hat and a coat with a large fur collar into which a plaid scarf had been artfully tucked. My grandfather stood next to her, clad in his military uniform, with a cap bearing the double cross surrounded by a crown of rue. On the back of the photograph was written: "Memory of our first meeting on October 22, 1932, Antosėlė." This was a diminutive of my grandmother's name, Antanina; most of her friends and family called her "Antosėlė." My grandparents had dated for four years, Aunt Rūta said, before marrying on December 26, 1936.

I told them that my grandmother had given me a piano on the condition that I learn to play "The Blue Danube" waltz for her, to evoke the happiest day of her life. Then I mentioned her strange request, shortly before she died, that I not write the book about my grandfather that my mother had beseeched me to undertake. "Do you think that might have had anything to do with his killing Jews?" I asked.

Everyone shrugged, shook their heads, and suddenly decided that the table needed to be cleared right away.

Rasa and her daughter brought out three types of dessert and a honey liqueur called *krupnikas*. Halfway through my first glass of *krupnikas*, I inquired, "What was Lithuania like before the Nazi occupation? What did Lithuanians think of Jews?"

Everyone turned to Aunt Rūta. Born in 1942, she was the eldest person present. She had been an elementary school English teacher for thirty years and had a dramatic flair for telling stories that reminded me of my grandmother.

She gulped down her *krupnikas*, shoved her glass across the table for a refill, and demanded, "Have you ever heard of the blood libel?"

"No. What is it?"

Aunt Rūta launched into a macabre tale about the matzah that Jews eat during Passover, when they commemorate the Exodus from Egypt. Before God sent the final plague upon the Pharaoh's land, Moses instructed the Jews to mark their doorposts with the blood of a lamb to signal to the Angel of Death that their families should be spared the killing of their firstborn sons. The next day, the Jews fled Egypt in such haste that their bread did not have time to rise. They ate unleavened bread—"matzah" in Hebrew. Thousands of years later, Aunt Rūta's tale continued, it was rumored that Jews kidnapped innocent Lithuanian children, the little lambs, to drain them of their precious blood to make the Passover matzah. Whenever a Lithuanian child was missing, adults blamed the Jews.

"It's crazy," said Aunt Rūta, "but a lot of people believed that story. I *still* meet people who believe it."

Back at my borrowed quarters in Klaipėda, I packed a few belongings for the next day's trip and tried to fall asleep. The monstrous blood libel swirled in my head. *How could such an absurd claim have been handed down from generation to generation like some perverted Bible story? It sounded more like a tale written by the Brothers Grimm.*

When sleep came, I dreamed of a blond boy named Kaziukas, with hair so long it covered his eyes.

One cool spring day, Kaziukas failed to show up to do his farm chores. The soil had to be plowed and the rye seeds planted. His mother, frantic, screamed, "Kaziukas is missing! He's been gone all night!" She wrung her hands fearfully. Everyone assumed he'd been kidnapped by a Jew.

I was a dove, hovering above. The enraged villagers gathered in the square, shook their heads, raised their fists, swung their axes and knives, and furiously marched off to the Jewish part of town, intent upon finding Kaziukas. They stormed the synagogue. A frightened rabbi greeted them, asking what they wanted. The men rudely pushed past him and gawked at the rows of matzah piled high on tables against the wall. An angry cauldron simmered and then boiled over, spilling what looked like bubbling blood.

"We're looking for Kaziukas. We know you sacrificed him for his blood, to make your matzah! Look at all this matzah! It's proof!"

"No, no, I didn't!" shrieked the rabbi, cowering, covering his face to protect himself from their blows. But he had no chance against the angry mob.

The furious villagers took turns slashing and stabbing him, until a pool of blood inundated the synagogue, rising as high as its windows and spilling over its ledges like a crimson waterfall.

I woke up in a sweat, my heart beating rapidly. This dream didn't prove anything! It didn't mean that my grandfather had killed Jews. But how large a role had he played in stoking the ancient hatred that had boiled over during the war years?

Two months later, at home in Chicago during a Labor Day barbecue in my backyard, I struck up a conversation with my father's second wife. She was born in Kaunas in 1939, in the same town and same year as my mother. The subject of the matzah story came up, and she told me in no uncertain terms that Jews undoubtedly kidnapped children to use their blood for matzah.

"But surely you can't believe that!" I exclaimed.

She shook her head resolutely, dismissing my protest. "Oh no, my father told me so!"

I wiped up the wine I had inadvertently spilt in my indignation and replied that maybe her father had been mistaken, deceived by Nazi propaganda. She glared at me as if I'd committed a sacrilege by suggesting her father could have been wrong.

The conversation was clearly over. I crumpled my soaked napkin onto my empty plate and left the table.

Vilnius
February 28, 2019

The petitioner [Grant Gochin], together with his supporting documents, did not provide any meaningful or credible proof that J. Noreika (General Storm) was a participant in the Holocaust (genocide), as the act is assessed under the provisions of the Criminal Code of the Republic of Lithuania, by the provisions of the United Nations' Conventions on the Crime and Punishment of Genocide, nor by the statutes of the Nuremberg Tribunal or the United Nations' Criminal Tribunal.

> **From the attorney's office of Liudvika Meškauskaitė in the name of Lithuania's Genocide and Resistance Research Centre**
> **To the Vilnius Administrative Regional Court, the petitioner Grant Gochin, and his representative and attorney Rokas Rudzinskas**
> **Responses to additional documents submitted by the petitioner**
> **(Administrative case Nr. eI-534-281/2019)**

CHAPTER TWENTY-ONE

A Privileged Status in Hell

When I received Jonas's first letter [on his way to Stutthof], I
appealed to the Šiaulių Police Chief. He declined to interfere on
my husband's behalf. In fact, he told me that, since Jonas wasn't
careful, he should have expected something like this to happen. I
was despondent. I didn't know what to do. I continued teaching
German to the grade-school children. At the same time,
I had to take German language courses. And as the best student,
I received Mein Kampf.
It was awful to wait and not know where Jonas was. Was he
alive or not? Most of our friends and acquaintances began
to avoid talking to us. My mother-in-law, sister-in-law,
daughter, and I were still allowed to stay in the government
house, although after a month, we had to give up half of it
to German officers.
—diary entry of Antanina Noreika, my grandmother

O n June 30, 2013, the day after my dinner at Rasa's home, she arrived early
to pick me up for our trip to Stutthof. She was driving a rented Renault
Peugeot stick shift. I sat in the passenger seat, and her ten-year-old daughter
and Aunt Rūta were seated in back. Travelling from Klaipėda to Gdansk,
Poland, we cruised in the rain along two-lane highways under construction
and a number of side roads. I was thinking about how I would construct the

narrative of my grandfather's time in the Nazi concentration camp in 1943. In addition to the information I expected to gather from this road trip, I had memoirs written by three other Stutthof prisoners—playwright Balys Sruoga's *Forest of the Gods*, A. Gervydas's *Beyond the Barbed Wire*, and Father Stasys Yla's *A Priest in Stutthof*—in addition to my grandfather's own seventy-seven letters to my grandmother.

Jonas Noreika had been arrested with forty-five other prominent Lithuanians in retaliation for their country's being the only one whose citizens refused to join the Schutzstaffel, better known as the SS. He was the only person from Šiauliai to be arrested; sixteen men seized were from Kaunas; twenty-four from Vilnius; and five from Marijampolė. All were members of the intelligentsia: five university professors, four high school directors, four government assessors, three lawyers (including my grandfather), two priests, and several teachers, soldiers, and business leaders.[1] My grandfather was perhaps fortunate to have been apprehended at home. Most were arrested at their places of employment and thus did not even have an opportunity to say goodbye to their friends and relatives. I wanted to see where he had been taken and to visualize his life at the camp.

Klaipėda is 137 miles due east of Gdansk, Poland, but we drove a distance four times greater than that. We had hoped to travel through Kaliningrad, the Russian exclave between Poland and Lithuania, but we discovered that this would require Russian visas with a myriad of mandatory stamps, which would have taken three months to procure. We were obliged to circumnavigate Kaliningrad. At crossroads along the way, we passed six- to twelve-foot crosses decorated with ribbons and flowers. I wondered whether they were commemorating Saints Peter and Paul, whose feast day is June 29. There were so many of these crosses that we soon began counting them as a diversion; they totaled thirty-four by the time we'd reached our destination.

As we drove past Kaunas, I recalled that my grandfather had been driven from Šiauliai to the Gestapo headquarters here, situated in a building that now housed the Darbo ir Kultūros Rūmai (House of Labor and Culture). A few hours after his arrival, a guard had brought him a package from my grandmother, which contained a house key, a comb, and a photograph of the two of them with my mother.[2]

That evening guards ushered the prisoners to the SS dining room, which had clean tablecloths and comfortable chairs. They were served by polite young civilian girls. Balys Sruoga recalled in his memoir that the prisoners found this humane treatment from the Germans very odd; they suspected that it was a ruse, a prelude to execution. The next morning, the Germans served them a breakfast of bacon with bread and butter, followed by cigarettes from the SS's own stock. At eight o'clock, a young guard announced, "Men, your journey continues to Germany. Anyone who tries to escape will be shot." Several guards appeared holding automatic rifles. Two soldiers with machine guns led the prisoners to a civilian bus.[3]

I noted that the Lithuanian author of this memoir referred to the Nazis simply as "Germans" rather than as "Nazis."

In 1943, Kaliningrad, Russia, was Königsberg, Germany; the Nazis were able to convey their prisoners to Gdansk by a far more direct route than the one we had to take. They stopped at several prisons along the way. Sruoga's memoir states that the trip took eight days.[4] From Kaunas, the prisoners travelled west to the town of Tilžė, East Prussia, now Sovietsk, Kaliningrad. When the bus arrived at a church in Tilžė, the Germans led their captives into an airy hall on the fourth floor of a brick building, where each received a blanket and was instructed to write a letter to his family.[5] My grandfather's letter, dated "March 19–21, 1943," was written in blue ink on a thin sheet of paper measuring 5½ x 8 inches. Receiving it prompted my grandmother to pen the sole entry she ever made in her journal.

Jonas Noreika had steady, even handwriting that slanted to the right, his lines spaced exactly one millimeter apart, as if guided by a sheet of lined paper beneath. The flow of his well-proportioned letters often broke after the letter *i*. I read easily:

> Hello. I'm fine. I feel great. I barely had to touch the food you packed. They feed us well. There are a lot of people from Vilnius and Marijampolė with me. I'm the only one from Šiauliai. We'll

be here one more day. After that, we're going somewhere else.
What we're guilty of, I have no idea. I am very sure that we'll see
each other very soon. Maybe in our beloved homeland, or maybe
they'll let you visit me.

Now it is just after prayers, and we have a priest among us. It
felt like we were in the men's Mass in Šiauliai; we are lodged in a
small wool-gatherer's chapel. It is so refreshing to have my mind
fly to you. My spirit has strong wings that fly freely like the wind
in the hills, a whirlwind. I will be with you. My thoughts and feelings will visit you. You will feel my kisses and caresses.

Please tell my friends to stay calm, to never lose faith. Europe
will be happy. Don't worry about me. Annie, my love, your uneasi-
ness troubles me. Give my best to Dalytė and Antosėlė.

In Kaunas, I received the photograph, key, and comb. Please
believe that I feel fine. I wish you hope and health. I have faith that
people everywhere and at all times will help you as much as they
can. Maybe even the region's Commissar. Because he must truly
know that my arrest was just a misunderstanding. Maybe he could
check with the chief security officer in Tilžės.

I wish everyone in Šiauliai and Žemaitija success.

I kiss you and kiss you,

Your Jonas N.[6]

The letter arrived in an envelope bearing a red 12-Reichspfennig stamp
depicting Hitler's face over the phrase *Deutsches Reich*.

Father Yla asserted in his memoir that, during the Lithuanian prisoners'
brief stay in Tilžė, Vladas Jurgutis—one of the professors who had been
arrested, the man would become something of a father figure to Jonas
Noreika and whose daughter would get very close to my grandfather—was
told that the prisoners would all be shot.[7] Most of them were unaware of this.
And for some unknown reason, Heinrich Himmler, the ruthless concentration camp administrator, delayed signing the execution order and instructed
that the Lithuanians be sent to Stutthof. On March 26, the Germans loaded

the captives into a third-class passenger train, handing them sandwiches in waxed paper. Upon arriving at the Gdansk railroad station they were met by Gestapo soldiers.[8]

An eerie calm surrounded the dense forest landscape. The soldiers herded their charges into small trucks, cursing and bludgeoning them, according to Sruoga's memoir. The prisoners scrambled in one on top of another. The trucks headed east, to the town of Stutthof.[9]

The Nazis had finished erecting the concentration camp there by September 1939. The site was bordered on three sides by water: the Baltic Sea; the Gulf of Gdansk; and the vast, two-forked Vysla (Vistula) River with its channel and canal system. A narrow peninsula separating the Baltic Sea and the Gulf of Gdansk flanked the camp's fourth side. Any prisoner attempting to escape would encounter water in every direction. And it would be impossible to dig a tunnel. The camp covered 120 hectares (296.5 acres), measuring 1,350 meters (1,476 yards) long by 900 meters (984 yards) wide. At present, the site comprises twenty hectares (49.4 acres), including a museum and four of the original barracks.[10]

It was late when Rasa, Eva, Aunt Rūta, and I arrived in Gdansk and checked into the Pension Studijat. Our room had purple walls and white curtains, a double bed and two single beds, a refrigerator, a hot pot, and a table with four glass mugs.

The next morning we feasted on a breakfast of cold cuts, bread, butter, cucumbers, and tomatoes. Then we took an old-fashioned cable ferry across the Vysla River and drove another seven miles to meet our guide, whose services I had booked months earlier. Tomasz Swigon was a primary-school instructor who taught Catholic theology. He led us to the entrance of the Stutthof concentration camp, a tall, barbed-wire gate known as the Death Gate. Above it was the phrase from Dante's *Inferno*, "Lose all hope, ye who enter here." I shuddered as I thought of all those forced to enter during my grandfather's time. Tomasz said that prisoners were told bluntly, "This is the entrance to the camp, but there's no exit for you except through that chimney. If anyone tries to get close to the fence, you will be shot." He directed our attention to the black watchtower at which a guard had stood day and night, armed with a rifle and ready to shoot at the slightest provocation.

Behind the watchtower was a long, narrow yard lined with shacks. Our guide told us to imagine twenty black dogs barking in their kennel; they might be set upon the terrified prisoners on any pretext. The camp had been built expressly to annihilate Communists, Jews, and any other resistors to the Nazis. Its crematorium burned continually. Tomasz spoke of the gray smoke that floated over the camp, the smell of burning flesh that assailed the inmates' nostrils, and the ashes that descended upon them day after day.

We walked through the first barracks house, where prisoners were registered. "Each person was called by his assigned number, not his name," said Tomasz. "He had to memorize his number. The intent was to rob him of his dignity and identity. Everything was taken from the prisoners, even their shoes."

A mountain of shoes was visible behind a glass wall. "These symbolize the many who walked through these gates and who died here," our guide solemnly informed us.

Balys Sruoga's vivid memoir describes how German officials lined newly arriving prisoners up along the barbed-wire fence. Four prisoners carrying typewriters were followed by two uniformed SS men from the political division, who led the inmates into the nearby barracks.[11]

I visualized my grandfather approaching a table at which an official recorded his information.

"Stand straight! What's your first name?"

"Jonas."

"Last name?"

"Noreika."

"Address?"

"265 Vilnius Street, Šiauliai."

"Why were you arrested?"

"I don't know."

The official handed him a number: 21330. "This is your pass; don't lose it."

The pass read *Schultzhaft-Politisch*, meaning "political custody arrest."

The prisoners were led to the bathhouse, where they were weighed, their hair was shorn, they were chased through a cold shower, and their bodies were sprayed with disinfectant. Their clothing and other belongings were taken away, and each was issued a cloth triangle with a number to sew onto his uniform.

A red triangle signified political prisoners; green, criminals; yellow was for Jews; black for sociopaths; violet for Jehovah's Witnesses; pink for homosexuals. The prisoners were ordered to sew a letter on the triangle indicating their national origin: *P* for Polish, *R* for Russian, or *L* for Lithuanian.[12]

Each barracks block housed from five hundred to seven hundred prisoners in two sleeping rooms, a dining area, and a lavatory. The head of the political division was SS master sergeant Ludthe, whom Sruoga portrays as a wrinkled man with a hat tilted over his eyes. Ludthe screamed at newcomers, "He who blocks the road for Germans must be destroyed!" He was fond of ordering prisoners to perform humiliating tricks such as "leaping like a frog." Prisoners who failed to leap across the camp yard in a squat position had their heads battered with a rifle butt and their ribs kicked with a heavy boot. Ludthe might stab them with a knife and strike their heads with a stone, or he might whip them mercilessly before hitting them with a brick.[13]

I stood in the wide, green field and tried to imagine my grandfather crouched and hopping like a frog. I was reminded of the fairy tale he had written for my mother in this camp. It described a witch who cackled in glee as she commanded her prisoners to leap like frogs.

At five each morning the prisoners were roused from sleep and ushered into the lavatory, which contained several cement fountains. The camp's fifty thousand inmates were allotted forty minutes in the morning and evening for washing. As they fought for their turns, the guards stood by, ready to shoot anyone who attempted to escape. The workday began at 6:00 a.m. Father Yla recalled that prisoners were put to hard labor: building roads, pouring gravel, and working on the water line or on engines at the factory near the canal. A few of them seem to have been engaged in carpentry work.[14]

The Nazis ordered the lawyers, professors, and priests to run with logs for a distance of five hundred meters and back. With each successive leg of the relay, the guards made the prisoners run faster. When Professor Vladas Jurgutis, the oldest of them, moved slowly, he was beaten.[15] An economist and a graduate of St. Petersburg Theological Academy, he was a former Catholic priest and a professor at the Universities of Kaunas and Vilnius. He had been the first governor of the Bank of Lithuania, in 1920, as well as the minister of finance and foreign affairs in 1922. As Lithuania's economic counselor during the German occupation, he had been critical of Nazi politics, writing an angry letter and resigning his post.[16] He and my grandfather became close friends at the camp, where they spent many hours together.

The prisoners were required to march in unison in their clumsy clogs. They had to master the art of standing at attention. "Mützen ab!" came the order. My grandfather, along with his fellow prisoners, pulled his hat off his head, slammed it against his thigh, and froze. "Mützen auf!" He shoved his hat back on. This senseless routine was repeated for hours every evening.[17]

Afterward the inmates shuffled to their sleeping quarters. Their mattresses were sacks filled with wood shavings. There was one thin blanket for every three men.[18]

Father Yla's memoir asserts that by their fifth week of captivity, nine of the forty-six Lithuanians who had been arrested on March 16 and 17, 1943, had died. Between April and June of that year, 43 percent of the camp's four thousand prisoners perished of cholera.[19]

On the evening of April 28, the surviving members of the group arrested with Noreika were "promoted" to a higher prisoner status. Their beatings stopped, and they were given easy jobs. My grandfather and Professor Jurgutis were assigned to the construction bureau. They were permitted to bathe and wear clean clothing. They decorated the triangles affixed to their garb to indicate their increased standing. Their food rations, however, remained meager, and they still slept on filthy mattresses and took part in endless marches, which they termed "goose races."[20]

Six weeks after his arrest, Jonas Noreika wrote a second letter to his wife, which she received with an official letter from Danzig (the German name for Gdansk):

I miss the homeland, and I trust I'll see you all soon.

You, my love, I feel so close to my heart that sometimes I can't believe you're not with me.

Mother, daughter, sister, brother—I deeply feel you all near me.

I believe you are strong and bold enough to look destiny in the eyes. Never lose faith or courage. For technical reasons, I can't write to you in Lithuanian. You'll have to write back in German. I'm happy you packed a sweater and extra underwear. I'm allowed to receive a package once a week. It's forbidden to send money, a letter, or matches in the same packet.

Yours, Jonas N., April 30, 1943

We don't know [our] release date. It is forbidden to visit the camp. It is useless to ask questions. They will not be answered.

Each prisoner can receive two letters of four pages each month. [Each] page should have no more than 15 lines. It should be easily legible. Whoever will not follow these rules will not have their letters delivered. It is forbidden to send money. It is forbidden to write anything on the postal orders. Prisoners are allowed to purchase goods from the camp store. They can read national socialist newspapers, but the prisoner must order the newspaper from the camp's leaders. It is forbidden to send pictures or photographs.

Kommandant

You can write to Schutzhäftling

J. Noreika

Nr. 21330 Block VI

Concentration Camp

Stutthof b. Danzig[21]

One month later, on May 31, there was another improvement in my grandfather's situation. The Lithuanian prisoners were instructed to stand in line along a fence outside their barracks in Block 8A. Captain Mayer, a Bavarian with "SS" tattooed in tiny letters just below his eye, made an announcement. According to Sruoga's memoir, Mayer moved like a stork, standing first on one leg and then on the other, pacing as he announced his orders: "I don't know why you've landed in camp, but it seems you're different from the others. A document has been received stating that, from this day forward, I have to keep you as honorary prisoners—*Ehrenhäftlinge.* You'll all be housed separately."[22]

Work was no longer mandatory, but the Lithuanian prisoners could volunteer to work to alleviate boredom. They were provided with a new striped outfit and proper underwear and did not have to display a red triangle with a number. Instead they were permitted to wear their own jackets, as long as they sewed on a yellow armband. The striped prison pants remained compulsory, and camp discipline was still enforced.[23]

The group was moved into a newly renovated barracks with two-tiered bunks. Each man had his own bed with clean sheets, a covered pillow, and three woolen blankets. This was Block 8E, formerly the sewing center. It had been freshly repainted. A radio loudspeaker transmitted music. The doctor was told to accord them special attention to ensure their health.[24]

As Rasa, Aunt Ruta, my niece, and I stood in the spot where the barracks would have been, our guide declared that the Lithuanians' "prisoner of honor" designation had saved their lives. Such status was unusual at Stutthof, he said; the only other prisoners there to be accorded such preferential treatment were Latvian statesmen and Norwegian policemen.

My grandfather was now allowed to write and receive letters every week. I suddenly thought of the letter to his wife dated May 1, 1944, and wondered what it might signify:

I couldn't sleep or think clearly last night, after reading your letter from April 23, 1944. My heart was so heavy and uneasy, like yours was on April 10, 1942, when I was completely broken and came home and told you everything. Two years have gone by since. I think that destiny has punished me enough.

Yesterday, as I read, "When you return and I won't be here anymore—" To tell the truth, that raised a big worry. "The poor child will only stand in your way." "Don't be angry, I only returned what you gave me." These sentences are completely incomprehensible to me. I spoke with you all night. I wrote you many letters last night. We'll read a sea of letters in eternity. In every letter, you will find: To my dearest Tonute, in this full-suffering night, I feel guilty. With an outstretched hand, I ask you: Come, come to me. I'm waiting for you impatiently. I love you unconditionally. Tonute! Do you hear me? With every step, I call for you. In the streets filled with leaves outside: Tonute! Tonute! Your Jonas is calling you. Whether you're rich or poor, young or old, beautiful or ugly before my eyes, innocent or stained with sins, I call you! Come to me! I will strengthen you. You will rest. My love is endless like God's blessings. You are my only one! Tonute, do you hear my call? Do you doubt it? Oh, no, no! You feel in these lines my blazing heart, blood and soul. There's nothing so bad in this life that you could have done that my love wouldn't try to melt and love anew.

I called for you all night. Today I prayed to Mary, and always you were on the altar.

Then I read your letters from beginning to end: April 17, April 23, May 1, and others. April 17, you wrote, "Believe me. You are and will remain until my life's end the only beloved man and father, and after death." How am I to understand this? It is as if I'm bewitched. And until you tell me everything that weighs down your heart, I shall remain bewitched. You feel my love. I could renounce many things, but not you. Amazingly, I receive much energy from you. God has chosen us for each other. If one of us commits some sort of a foolishness, we both suffer. No storm is too awful for us. I am sure we both accept this path. That's what

you said on February 16, 1933. I believed you then. Much is suffered
in every step, if that intention weren't there.

Who better can understand a sinner than another sinner? Tell
me everything that happened to my Tonutė. Has she taken a mis-
step on the path? I wait for you with outstretched arms, and I call
you today and always: The world is ours, Tonutė. We're insepa-
rable, in space or eternity. We'll win. We have to win.[25]

What did he tell her on April 10, 1942, when he unburdened his heart?
At that point he had been chief of the Šiauliai District for nearly a year.

By June 1944, at Stutthof, his thoughts had turned to the Communists,
whom he and his countrymen presumed would invade soon. On June 18,
1944, he wrote, "One or another fateful moment is not far in the future. On
June 15, at 23 hours 40 minutes, I heard that England was in flames from new
weapons. That should substantially speed up these historical events. We will
either die or develop into a happier Europe. Where and how our place will
be will depend, in part, on our bearings, our preparedness, and our plan.
Being a small country, we must learn to use other weapons: education, high
culture, unity, spiritual and physical strength."[26]

Only days later, Russia marched into Lithuania, occupying it for the second time that decade. According to their program of historical revision, the
Communists had come to liberate Lithuania from the Nazis. Everybody
became a Soviet citizen, forced to embrace Russian as their language and to
revere Joseph Stalin rather than God.

As I gazed at the pile of shoes behind glass in the Stutthof museum, I
asked myself what the forty-six Lithuanian prisoners had done to merit
privileged treatment in a concentration camp at which Jews were being
cremated. As Jonas Noreika's granddaughter, I wanted to dismiss any
notion that Noreika might have been rewarded for killing Jews. It wasn't
possible! But as a journalist, I was obliged to regard it as an eminently logi-
cal explanation.

Vilnius
March 27, 2019

J. Noreika, as chief the Šiauliai District, resisted the Lithuanian mobilization into the German Army and the establishment of an SS legion in Lithuania; therefore, he fought against Lithuanian collaboration with the Nazis—which is why he spent two years in the Stutthof concentration camp. J. Noreika "led the Lithuanian resistance movement, especially agitating against the Reich Komissar's announcement of Lithuanian mobilization," stated the German security police and SD chief Karl Jaeger (Stutthof concentration camp card, Archiwum Muzeum Stutthof, Sygn., I-III-11224).

"On the Accusation of Jonas Noreika (General Storm),"
Genocide and Resistance Research Centre of Lithuania

A Torrent of Questions

God, I'm terribly sad that such a destiny has befallen our country. An indescribable storm in our country's history. My heart breaks as I think of Mother, my sister, and brother. I'm unbelievably happy that you are my eternal friend, my dearest and my sun. Tonutė, you with our daughter and Antosėlė fled and wrote me. I have your letters from Tauragė, Tilžės, Elbing-Danzig, and yesterday from Oppeln. I can imagine your path. I know. We'll clench our teeth. A tough and unmerciful war. Only God can save us.

—Jonas Noreika, August 13, 1944[1]

My mother told me that, in July 1944, she and other children in Šiauliai were trained to locate a trench and claim it, laying down grass in it. She thought these scouting expeditions a grand adventure. One night when bombs started raining down she, her mother, and her aunt left home to find the trench that she had claimed a few hours earlier. To their dismay, another family had already occupied it. No amount of invective from my grandmother would persuade the squatters to leave. Angry, her family managed to find another trench, albeit without fresh grass; they spent the rest of that terrifying night sleeping in the dirt.

On July 28, 1944, my mother, grandmother, and Aunt Antanina fled
Lithuania, along with a few friends, each carrying a small suitcase. The
police chief of Šiauliai appeared at their home and offered to give them a
ride. Perhaps my grandfather had written him a letter from Stutthof,
appealing for his help. My grandmother studied the small car, an Opel,
and protested, saying that there wasn't enough room. Somehow, though,
eight people and eight pieces of luggage squeezed into the vehicle, with
children sitting on adults' laps. My grandfather's mother, Anelija, decided
to remain in the fatherland. She suggested to the travelers that they go to
Argentina, where my grandfather's brother Stasys had settled, if they were
unable to get to America.

In Stutthof, Jonas Noreika kept apprised of events in his homeland
through newspapers and a radio in his barracks. On October 1, 1944, he wrote:

> According to *Völkische Beobachter* [the National Socialist German
> Workers' Party newspaper] Sept. 28, 1944, a Lithuanian committee
> approached President Roosevelt, asking him to protect Lithuania,
> telling him that the Bolsheviks drove out Lithuanians [to Siberia,
> as my grandmother added to her translation] from four big Lithu-
> anian cities. It didn't state from which cities, but the talk is it's from
> Vilnius, Kaunas, Panvežys, and Šiauliai.
>
> So if you wouldn't have fled (!) what type of situation would
> we be in (!) The war is in a decisive phase and nearing the end, but
> it's not completely clear how it will end. Otherwise, everything in
> my daily life is the same as earlier. I read, I read. Not always what
> I want to, but what I can get. I have in my account 900 RM. Per-
> haps I can send you a portion. I don't need it.[2]

These letters reveal my grandfather's love for my grandmother and his
struggle to serve as the head of the family from afar. On October 15, 1944, after
he learned from his family that bombs had fallen where they were staying in
southwest Germany, he wrote:

Death passed you by on Sept. 30, 1944. Your brown dress has a
hole from the English-American terrorism. Death missed you by
a hair. I still can't think of it calmly. Millions are dying in the
name of justice. Be careful, Tonutèle. Don't drive. We often hear
"a caravan of planes above SouthWest Germany." My heart trem-
bles. I'd advise you to leave the spot where you are now, to go
somewhere else, but I don't know where. We know so little. Most
of our country's people want to leave Vienna. The newspapers are
writing that the strongest attacks against Germany have begun.
We're like a pot on a fire. From the "Lithuanian Union" in Berlin
we hear little. And the news that does reach us is contradictory.
For example, "You'll be released soon." Another time, we hear,
"Little hope." Or "You can count on the war's end."³

After the New Year, rumors spread throughout the camp that the Soviets
were advancing and that the Nazis would flee. All newspapers, letters, and
parcels were banned, and all radios in camp confiscated. As the inmates
waited anxiously, trying to plan for their unknown future, they were directed
to build sleds to transport their belongings.⁴

On January 14, 1945, just before he was evacuated, my grandfather penned
his last letter from Stutthof:

I am fully healthy, I have clean underwear, a warm room, a soft
bed, free time, fresh news, good books, just friends, and 85 of
your letters. Aren't I wealthy? I want to use all opportunities
available to me for our benefit. If you ask me how long can I
withstand this, I can answer that if I remain under these circumstances, not only will I last until the end, but in some respects I
will be stronger than the day I arrived in this prison. I want for
nothing but freedom. I want to tell you again, to repeat in no
uncertain terms that you [should] not move from the place you
are now in Lausheim. If for some time you do not hear anything

from me, I will find you. I will come. Sooner or later. I trust the
loving God will allow it.[5]

On January 24, 1945, an announcement was made in camp: "Tomorrow at four o'clock in the morning, we're leaving."[6] During our tour of the
camp, Tomasz told us that all Jews and all persons too ill to walk were left
behind in the camp. Eight marching columns were formed, each with a
name, an SS sergeant, a group of guards, and a canine detachment. The
Lithuanian prisoners of honor were placed in a column of 1,600 male
prisoners, and they were the first to be marched out toward the railroad
tracks, less than a kilometer away, where they crowded onto freight cars
and platform cars.[7]

The ailing Professor Jurgutis was too frail to climb onto the crammed
train on the night of the evacuation. Jonas Noreika stayed with him, nursed
him through the night, and managed to get with him onto the train heading
west the next day. On the third day of their journey, they met up with fellow
inmates in an old school in Zukowo, nineteen kilometers southwest of
Gdansk. At that point Jurgutis had a temperature of 104 degrees and could
barely walk. Everyone suspected that he had typhus. Once again my grandfather chose to remain with him.[8] Once the professor was strong enough,
guards took both men to the Lauenberger evacuation camp, from which
Noreika addressed another letter to his wife. It was dated February 23, 1945,
and postmarked "Goddentown—Lanz, b/ Lauenburg R.A.D Lager": "My
beloved! I couldn't write you for a long time. I was and am, thank God,
healthy. But still not on my own. In that respect, my circumstances have not
changed. For now I don't know when I will be able to write you again. Try
to write me immediately. How are you, how is our daughter and Antosėle,
Eugenia, and dear Jonas? Professor Jurgutis is with me. We are on the road,
but to where? For how long? We don't know. Stay where you are and wait
until I arrive or until you get news. With the warmest regards and the best
hopes we look to the future."[9]

My grandfather clearly wanted to rejoin his family, as several of his companions had already been able to. Yet he had resolved to return to Lithuania.

To fellow Stutthof inmate Pilypas Narutis, Jonas Noreika declared, "Not everyone will flee. Most will stay, suffer and fight. Why should we run away? No, we need to stay with them. To suffer with them, fight, and if necessary, die."[10]

I grew up hearing those words proclaimed fiercely by my mother and grandmother, always with a catch in their voices.

While nursing Jurgutis, my grandfather had contracted typhus or pneumonia, which he endured for forty days, until the end of April 1945. It was now the professor's turn to nurse my grandfather. By the time he recuperated, the Soviets had arrived; they promptly conscripted him. Jurgutis, at age sixty too old for military service, was left to return home alone.[11]

On August 24, 1945, my grandmother received this telegram: "Noreika on transport Stutthof to west seized by Russians remained in Russian zone compatriots from Stutthof now in Sweden—Martin Brakasa."[12] My grandfather had become a Red Army private in the 732nd Infantry Regiment, 238th Riflemen's Division, under a false name: Dimitrov. From May 5 onward he marched with Russian troops through Poland, Germany, and perhaps also Norway or Sweden.[13]

After our tour of Stutthof, Rasa, Eva, Aunt Rūta, and I spent the afternoon strolling through Gdansk, a quaint city on the Baltic Sea. We saw a faux pirate galleon, high-spired cathedrals, and souvenir stalls bursting with amber. With cobblestoned streets and churches on every corner, the city reminded me of Vilnius, although it was rendered more striking by its seafront.

"You're lucky you were born in America," my cousin remarked. "By the time my grandparents decided to leave, it was too late."

I shrugged in agreement, knowing that Rasa's life in Lithuania under the Communist regime had been far more deprived and challenging than mine in the United States. I didn't dare express this; it might have felt like gloating, and I had survivor's guilt. As a child of immigrants, I had often been told how lucky I was to grow up in the United States. Had my parents ended up in Siberia, I might never have been born. My mother and grandmother left their homeland a month before the Russians sent soldiers to secure the border.

During our drive back to Klaipėda, Eva subjected us to a torrent of questions prompted by our tour: "Why did they kill the Jews? What happened to the victims of medical experiments; are they still alive? Who was the leader of the Germans who did these terrible things?"

We told her that his name was Adolf Hitler. "Is Adolf Hitler dead? What happened to all the bad people who helped him? What about those who tortured people in the camp?"

Eventually we settled into silence. I had questions of my own. Chief among them was this conundrum: Why was my grandfather spared the heavy labor on low rations? The gas chamber and the crematorium? Why was he treated as a "prisoner of honor"? Jonas Noreika had arrived at Stutthof on March 26, 1943, and acquired privileged status on May 31. He and fellow Lithuanian prisoners endured a hellish existence for sixty-seven days; they were worked to exhaustion, beaten, starved, and terrorized. Only thirty-five of the original forty-six men survived this period. Balys Sruoga lost sixty-three pounds,[14] and Father Stasys Yla nearly starved to death.[15]

But after those sixty-seven days, their lives greatly improved. They were permitted to read, write, and go for walks. They worked only if they chose to, to stave off boredom—and were given easy work, in an office or a library. They could create their own schedules; they had the luxury of choice. They were entitled to receive packages from home. They were even allowed to visit women in a neighboring barracks, according to Sruoga's memoir, although apparently the married men abstained.[16]

On July 25, 1944, 3,800 Jews arrived at Stutthof from Šiauliai. Within two months, 40 percent of them had died of starvation and disease.[17] At the camp, many of those Jews lived a mere 150 meters from the Lithuanian prisoners of honor.[18] Tomasz had shown us canisters of Zyklon B gas, a cyanide-based pesticide used to kill Jews; others perished on the gallows.

For most of my life I had felt proud of the fact that my grandfather was a "prisoner of honor." The title seemed to radiate prestige. I would have liked to hold this title, I had thought: imagine being held in high esteem even under captivity! But now I wanted to know why Himmler had been so impressed with my grandfather.

A Response to the Statement of the Genocide and Resistance Research Centre of Lithuania of 27 March 2019, "On the Accusations Against Jonas Noreika (General Vėtra)" April 10, 2019

There is no question that the Nazis stood at the apex of the power structure during the German occupation of Lithuania and held ultimate authority over the fate of the Jews, but this in no way diminishes the responsibility of the native collaborators. After World War II international courts have consistently rejected the argument of "following orders" as a defense, most recently in cases of crimes against humanity in Rwanda and the former Yugoslavia. In Lithuania, local officials often acted against the Jews with minimal German supervision and at times even on their own. There is no record of any ranking Lithuanian official executed or imprisoned for refusing anti-Jewish German directives during the height of the genocide in the summer and fall of 1941. The fact that the Nazi administration suppressed Lithuanian anti-Nazi activists during the latter part of the occupation is not relevant to Noreika's history of anti-Jewish actions as District Chief of Šiauliai.

> **The International Commission for the Evaluation of the Crimes of the Nazi and Soviet Occupation Regimes in Lithuania**
> **The Sub-Commission for Evaluation of the Crimes of the Nazi Occupation Regime and the Holocaust**

The Candle That Went Out

All for Lithuania!
The German nation with its grand army has saved Europe's cul-
ture and civilization.
Brother Lithuanians! Take up your arms and help the German
Army in its work of liberating our country.
May friendly relations continue to prosper with the Great Ger-
many and her Leader Adolf Hitler!
—Lithuanian Front Activist Headquarters
Authorized Leader Leonas Prapuolenis

A unt Rūta came to my apartment the next evening to enable us to get an early start for her sister's home in the morning. After a quick breakfast we made ham-and-cheese sandwiches to take for lunch so that Jadvyga, who was frail, wouldn't have to prepare a meal for us.

We took a taxi to the Klaipėda bus depot, about three miles away. The taxi driver noticed my American accent as I greeted him in Lithuanian, and complimented me on my knowledge of the local language. I told him that I had been raised in Chicago and that my facility in the language of my family's homeland was a point of pride for my parents. Then I asked him what changes he had seen in the country since independence. He replied that he now drove for sixteen hours a day and yet was barely able to cover his living expenses; he hadn't had to work so hard during the Communist era.

When he dropped us off at the bus depot, we bought tickets to Šilutė, thirty miles south. We boarded a clean, modern, blue-and-white bus and found comfortable seats together. Aunt Rūta spoke of having visited Chicago shortly after Lithuania's independence, recalling that a journalist had come to my grandmother's house to interview her about her life without her heroic husband. My grandmother had answered, "If you are young and have a family, don't get involved in politics." After a moment's pause, Aunt Rūta asked me, "What do you think of her advice?"

"It wasn't an easy life for her," I answered. "By the time she came to America, she was in her forties. She could speak Lithuanian, German, Polish, a little Russian, French, and Spanish. But she couldn't learn English; she always said that the spelling baffled her."

My aunt, a former English teacher, remarked that her students also complained that the spelling didn't make any sense.

The bus rumbled southward. We saw stacks of hay dotting the landscape and fields with cows grazing. Aunt Rūta remembered that shortly after independence she had watched a TV show featuring Stasys Gorodeckis, who had been in the KGB prison with my grandfather. Gorodeckis asserted that several of Jonas Noreika's friends in prison had tried to convince him to say whatever would get him a lighter sentence. Their exchange was conducted in Morse code, tapped on the prison walls. Noreika tapped back that he had sworn an oath of loyalty to Lithuania and would tell the truth to the KGB; he was prepared to die for his country.

"I heard a similar story," I told Rūta. "Ašmenskas's book said the same. What did your family think of my grandfather?"

"My father thought Jonas Noreika was too much of an idealist, that he went too far. That's why he got in trouble. That's what killed him."

Her father had worked for the police in Plungė when Noreika led the uprising against the first Soviet occupation in 1941, and he had remained with the police during the Nazi occupation. Police were known to participate in the killing of Jews during the Holocaust. I wondered what role Rūta's father had played, but I didn't dare to ask. Aunt Rūta's niece Ina would later tell me

Aunt Rūta Budrytė and Aunt Jadvyga Budrytė Bivainienė at the home of Aunt Jadvyga in Šilutė. This photograph was taken in July 2013.

that her father Vladas remembered that his and Rūta's father had gotten drunk during the *akcijas* in Plungė and so had not been involved in the killing.

Our bus reached Šilutė and we walked the few blocks to Rūta's sister's apartment. We climbed three flights of stairs to meet Jadvyga Budrytė Bivainienė, born in 1929. Her twin brother Vladas Budrys lived in Vilnius. Eighty-four-year-old Jadvyga had medium-length gray hair and blue eyes. She was wearing an oversized white cotton shirt with purple stripes. Her hands were stiff with arthritis, and she could stand only in a bent position. She hadn't climbed down the stairs in three years; she counted upon her family and neighbors to bring food and run necessary errands.

She invited us to sit in her small kitchen. We took out the sandwiches we'd brought, and my aunts set the water to boil for instant coffee. Jadvyga opened the gas line for the stove while Rūta struck a match and held it to the burner until a flame appeared. It reminded me of Aunt Antanina's stove in Buenos Aires so many years ago.

I had brought Jadvyga cookies and chocolate, too, as well as some money, but she implored me to take back the sweets, saying she had diabetes.

She seemed eager to tell me everything that she remembered about my grandparents' wedding. "I was six or seven years old when they got married. My family sat in the first row, so we could see everything. Your grandmother had bridesmaids who held her long wedding train. I remember many soldiers. Did you hear about the candle?"

"What candle?"

"Do you know what it means when a candle blows out at a Lithuanian wedding?" Jadvyga asked.

"No. Tell me."

She took a deep breath and exhaled dramatically. "It's bad luck," she said. "It's a terrible omen. She never told you about that candle?"

I searched my memory. "She made rather an odd fuss over the fact that no candles blew out at *my* wedding, saying that this was a sign of good luck," I said. "I never understood why. I never asked her about it."

Aunt Rūta raised her eyebrows and smiled.

"What happened?" I demanded.

My grandparents had been married in Plungė on Saturday afternoon, December 26, 1936. I had read, in a brochure entitled "Welcome to Plungė," that the town, which stands on both banks of the Babrungas River, was designed in the sixteenth century and boasted a radial layout. It had a triangular Market Square near the main crossroad and a long, single-story building housing shops called Didieji Kromai (The Great Stores) at its center. Until World War II, Plungė was renowned for its fairs.

Among my grandmother's family members living there was her older sister, Maria, who was married to a policeman named Aleksas Budrys. The couple had four children: Aldona, Jadvyga, Vladas, and Rūta. Their large house at Telšių 65 sat on an acre of land that included a vegetable garden, an orchard, a cow, and a pig. This was the family home where Aunt Rūta had grown up and where my grandparents' wedding reception had been held. Rūta showed me a photo of the house, which had a brown wooden-slat exterior, pointed roof, and windows trimmed in yellow. The shiny wooden floor of the interior was ideal for large receptions and for waltzing. When the Soviets occupied the country eight years after Močiutė's wedding, they divided the home into four separate residences to accommodate four families.

On the day of the wedding, snow was piled high. Many guests came by horse-drawn sleigh. My grandmother kept looking out the window, beyond the fence quivering in the bitter wind, anxious for the groom to arrive. The Mass was to take place at three in the afternoon at John the Baptist Church at the center of town, on Vytautas Street. Jadvyga's father relentlessly teased the bride, "And what if he doesn't come? Maybe he won't come! Then what will you do?" Jadvyga chuckled, "It was so easy to tease her that day."

At last my grandfather, who was about to become a lieutenant, arrived from Kaunas with a retinue of soldiers. One of them went to Jadvyga's house to tell the bride that Jonas was waiting for her at the church. Močiutė and her bridesmaids arrived in grand fashion, having rented the only car in the city from a neighbor.

"What kind of car was it?" I asked.

"It might have been the same model Hitler rode in," replied Jadvyga. "It looked like that." I later learned that Hitler rode a Mercedez-Benz 770.

Plungė, in the upper northwest corner of the country, was in an area known as Žemaitija (the Lowlands). Its residents were stubborn and hardworking and spoke an odd dialect. When my grandmother occasionally spoke Žemaitiškai to me and my brother in Chicago to demonstrate how strange it sounded, we found it so different from standard Lithuanian that we couldn't understand it. But Jonas Noreika and Antanina Krapauskaitė were both university-educated and had acquired an upper-class academic pronunciation, said Jadvyga.

Later I learned that, before World War II, 43 percent of the population of Plungė had been Jewish. The town had six Jewish study and prayer houses, including the Great Synagogue; a Hebrew elementary school and high school; a Jewish library; and a Jewish bank. The chocolate factory, the flour mill, and an electric-power station had all been owned by Jews, but most Jews earned their living in agriculture or as artisans. Many of their businesses were in the Kromai, in the center of town.[1] Because they lent money with interest, a practice not in accordance with Catholic custom, Jews were resented and envied by many.[2] Antisemitism was prevalent. During Lithuania's years of independence many Jews were forced to give up their businesses, either because their Gentile neighbors pressured them to do so or because of the global economic depression. Later, most of Plungė's 1,800 Jews were murdered while the region was under my grandfather's control.[3]

I was interested in learning how my grandparents' deep roots in Plungė had enabled my grandfather to establish himself as a leader in the district. I also enjoyed hearing about their wedding and wondered what other details Močiutė might have withheld.

Jadvyga told me that she had been overjoyed to attend the wedding ceremony. She had insistently begged her mother to let her go until her mother finally relented. The other children remained home as they probably would have been restless during the solemn Mass. Rūta had not yet been born at the time.

Jadvyga sat next to the mother of the bride, whom she called Babytė (Grandmother). The church was filled to capacity, with soldiers standing at attention on either side of the pews. Having visited the church with Damijonas the previous week, I knew that it could hold at least three hundred people. When the organ music began, Jadvyga said, everyone stood up, and my twenty-seven-year-old grandmother walked down the aisle on her father's arm. Clean-shaven Jonas, twenty-eight years old, waited at the foot of the altar. My grandmother looked regal in her wedding gown and trailing veil. She must have been shivering as she stepped across the pink marble floor of the unheated church.

The black marble altar featured a statue of Mary at its center. Two angels stood guard on towers on either side of the tabernacle, each flanked by six long white candles burning brightly. Two smaller angel figures flanked the altar, each bearing a lit candle. Jadvyga affirmed that Babytė kept a close eye on all fourteen candles, casting an eye to the couple, scanning the candles, listening to the music, then checking back on the flames.

The heavyset Father Pukys stepped down from the altar to prompt the couple's recitation of their vows. After my grandparents had kissed, sealing their union, the soldiers in attendance clicked their heels and raised a salute to Jonas Noreika and his new bride. "I remember how loud that click was," Jadvyga remarked, trying to smack her hands together to replicate the sound.

But a moment later, a stream of wind unexpectedly blew through the church. It might have been a gust caused by a late guest opening a door, or a draft from a cracked window. The air current seemed to snake its way to the altar, where it extinguished one of the candles as if by design, leaving only a wisp of smoke. The mother of the bride gasped, then began to weep.

"I looked around at all the dismayed faces and asked my grandmother why everyone was crying," Jadvyga continued.

It was a catastrophic sign. "It's a terrible, terrible omen," wailed Babytė.

According to Jadvyga, everyone believed that the altar candle had been blown out by the breath of the Holy Ghost, who was signaling that this marriage was doomed. The couple might be separated, or one of them might die early, or they might not have children, or one might be unfaithful.

"Well, as you know," I said, "my grandfather ended up in a Nazi concentration camp seven years later and died in a KGB prison after being tortured."

Jadvyga and Aunt Rūta nodded.

"How did my grandparents meet?" I asked. Jadvyga told me that they had met four years earlier at a military chapel in Klaipėda. For centuries Klaipėda had belonged to the Germans, who named it Memel; it would be seized again in 1939 in a fashion similar to the invasion of Austria, known as the Anschluss. When my grandparents met there, just as now, the city had a German character, and they both admired the German language and the German capacity for organization and neatness. My grandfather had graduated from the Kaunas Military School and was spending his first year in the Lithuanian army with the Seventh Grand Duke Butigeidis Regiment. My grandmother was studying at the Klaipėda Pedagogical Institute to become a teacher of the German language. The red-brick buildings that had housed both these institutions were now part of Klaipėda University on the north edge of town near the forest.

My grandparents on their first date, October 22, 1932

The ambitious Jonas Noreika had been courting the daughter of a wealthy and prominent family at the time, but he noticed my grandmother as she entered the army chapel on October 22, 1932, and was drawn to her. Močiutė later told her relatives that she felt his penetrating gaze, blushed, looked away, and then glanced back at him. He was wearing an impressive uniform, his cap adorned with the double cross.

"She was worried about that noblewoman he was dating," Jadvyga observed. "She said, 'I'm just an ordinary girl, and she's a rich woman. I don't think he'll choose me.' He dated both of them for a while, before he chose your grandmother."

Even in romantic matters, my grandfather was the consummate patriot. He proposed to my grandmother on February 16, a day of national celebration. After their engagement, my grandmother taught German at the Vytautas Magnus High School. She lived at Turgaus 29, just two blocks from where I was staying now. The couple visited their relatives on both sides of the family. Danutė Noreikaitė Nausėdienė, the daughter of Jonas's older brother Pranas, was about three years old when her Uncle Jonas first brought his fiancée for two nights. As was the custom for betrothed couples, they were chaperoned, but also were given some privacy. They had separate beds in the corner of a

My grandparents in Klaipeda, when they were dating, perhaps in 1933

larger room and were given a sheet to hang up as a room divider. Danutė
peeked in to see what her Uncle Jonas and new "aunt" were doing and accidentally brought down the sheet. Jonas grabbed the leather shin-covering from
one of his military boots and hurled it at her.[4]

Aunt Jadvyga described how the bridal couple waltzed to "The Blue Danube," never taking their eyes off each other—perhaps trying to forget about
that ominous candle.

"Once they were married," she said, "they lived in Kaunas. He bought her
a fur coat, which cost 1,000 litai. A cow cost 200 litai at the time, so you can
imagine how we all talked about that fur coat. They would visit us often in
Plungė. But then the Russians came, and your grandmother ran away. We
didn't hear from her until 1957."

At the end of our visit, Jadvyga, with enormous effort, launched herself
out of her chair so that we could hug and say our goodbyes. She asked me to
send her pictures of my family.

On the bus drive back to Klaipėda, Aunt Rūta disclosed that her family had tried to escape Plungė when the Russians invaded in 1944, perhaps because her father was afraid of the consequences of having worked for the police during the Nazi occupation. But the Budriai family vacillated for too long; the Russians had secured the borders, and they sent the family back. The family members separated, assuming new identities and going to live with different relatives and friends.

Once we were back at my apartment, Aunt Rūta decided to take a nap. I went for a walk to sort my thoughts about my grandparents' wedding. The significance of that snuffed-out candle had grown to wild proportions among my relatives in Lithuania, while Močiutė had never even mentioned it. But perhaps she had secretly feared that her marriage was cursed from the start.

Vilnius
February 28, 2019

The interrogator's [Grant Gochin's] request to indicate who in Germany organized the shooting of Jews in Plungė did not prove in and of itself that the investigators did not know who did it.... The interrogator's question of who among General Stahlecker's team organized the shooting of Jews obviously confirms that there were no doubts among the German prosecutors that the Germans themselves organized the shootings—not the Lithuanians.

From the attorney's office of Liudvika Meškauskaitė in the name of Lithuania's Genocide and Resistance Research Centre to the Vilnius Administrative Regional Court, the Petitioner Grant Gochin, and his representative and attorney Rokas Rudzinskas

Responses to additional documents submitted by the petitioner

(Administrative case Nr. eI-534-281/2019)

Pilgrimage

I had so much to pray for. My nights were restless, tormented by anxiety over my daughter's worsening heroin habit. My husband had told me during our last long-distance conversation that she was sleeping until late in the afternoon, then staying up late watching television, playing video games, or talking on the phone. She would go out at night and come home only in the early morning hours, and occasionally she was gone for days at a time. She never left a message so as to spare him worry.

Her behavior had become more erratic and sullen, and utterly unreasonable. My husband reported that she had begun to smoke cigarettes in the house during my absence despite our rule against it. She claimed that she couldn't help herself. I argued that he should establish stronger boundaries for her—but he said that he felt overwhelmed and wanted me back home.

"Do you think it will make a difference?" I asked.

He replied that he didn't know.

And so, halfway through my trip, I was torn between either suspending my project and flying home or pursuing my investigation in the fervent hope that my daughter's situation wouldn't have deteriorated by the time I returned. The truth is that I didn't want to face my inadequacies as a mother, nor the shame of having a daughter addicted to drugs. I convinced myself that she would straighten herself out. I doubted that my presence would have any real impact upon my defiant daughter, and I reasoned that for the next four weeks my energy would be best spent in uncovering the truth about my grandfather—a reckoning that was long overdue.

If the rumor about Jew-killing turned out to be true, it would be a hideous stain on my family's history—but not necessarily a reflection upon Lithuania itself. I would have to relinquish a cherished fairy tale, to sacrifice my crown as the granddaughter of a national hero. Surely the lionization of Jonas Noreika was based upon ignorance of his worst deeds; the entire country could not have been complicit. Yet I realized that my inquiries would unearth facts that inevitably would drag down others. *I wish I didn't have a deathbed promise to fulfill*, I thought. I ended up crying myself to sleep.

I was ill-prepared for my pilgrimage the next day to Žemaičių Kalvarija and Šiluva, both of which were on the way to Nijole Grunskienė's home in Šiauliai. I had asked some of my relatives if they wanted to join me, but they demurred, saying they were busy and that they weren't churchgoers. As I felt uneasy at the prospect of travelling on public transportation all by myself, I hired Mykolas as my chauffeur again—resolving that after this excursion I'd find a way to curtail my expenses.

When Mykolas arrived in the morning, I was morose and withdrawn. Our journey to Žemaičių Kalvarija was quiet. We drove northeast for about an hour, passing through Plungė. On the way, we stopped at Žemaičių Park to see the largest boulder in Lithuania. Presumably deposited by a glacier, it was roughly fifteen feet high and forty feet long. We watched children clambering up it and standing on top, pounding their chests and yodeling like kings of the rock.

We arrived in Žemaičių Kalvarija around noon. The town hosts pilgrimages on twelve consecutive days every July. The devout flock to twenty chapels on twenty hills, each representing a station of the cross, detailing Christ's passion. Some come to express their piety or to atone for sins, others to plead for relief from maladies or to pray for the dead. An enormous crowd had assembled, eager to follow the bishop through the stations of the Last Supper, the crowning with thorns, the Crucifixion, and the burial. The bishop was flanked by four altar attendants, who held a red canopy over him as he proceeded. He carried a vessel displaying the Blessed Sacrament, the consecrated bread. Incense wafted from an attendant's bronze censer as the bishop stopped at each chapel, circled it, and recited the adoration.

I was sweating as I climbed each hill amid the throngs praying and singing and kneeling. It was the tradition to prostrate oneself at three of the twenty chapels on one's first visit, so I sank to my knees and then lay on my stomach on the grass, inhaling its fragrance. *Dear God, you know how frightened I am about my daughter. She has changed so much, and I don't know what to do. Why am I here? Is this trip worth it? What will happen to her? What will happen to my family?* When I rose, I was crying. I wiped away my tears and rejoined the procession. I noticed that several people were weeping. Evidently, I wasn't the only one struggling with private suffering.

We moved to the next station on a hill, the crowd surrounding the chapel from all sides, then on to the next, and the next—where I prostrated myself for a second time. The day's heat was oppressive. I slapped a mosquito on my neck and listened to the bishop's prayer. My anguish over my daughter turned into acute distress about my grandfather's legacy. *How am I supposed to write my book? What kind of hero killed Jews? And if he is a Jew-killer, what does that make me? Flesh and blood of a monster! I carry his sins! How can I be forgiven?* Again, I stood up in tears.

By the time I lay down in front of a third chapel, my thoughts had circled back to my grandmother's perplexing words. These instilled my greatest doubt about Jonas Noreika's heroism. "It's best to just let history lie," she'd said. "There's no need to dig around." I now intuited this meant that she hadn't wanted me to discover her husband's involvement in the Holocaust. *How am I going to live with this? It's not my fault! I had nothing to do with it! Besides, it can't be true! He's innocent! The Communists just made up this story so that Lithuanians wouldn't have a hero.* I wept again as I got to my feet. The bishop walked through the crowd, pronouncing his blessings and sprinkling us with holy water.

When the twenty stations had been completed with a final prayer, I met up with Mykolas and we walked through the marketplace of religious items. I noticed his discomfort.

"Do you ever go to church?" I asked.

"No; I grew up in Soviet times. There was no faith. And by the time we got our independence, I didn't see any point in it. Too much time had passed."

As we wandered between the tables of religious articles, I mentioned that I was looking for a *Rūpintojėlis* (a little worrier).

"What's a *Rūpintojėlis*?" he asked.

"You don't know? In Chicago, all Lithuanian families have one. It's a carving of a troubled Christ." I demonstrated the statue's pose, placing my hand against my cheek and closing my eyes as though lost in deep thought.

Mykolas smiled. When I found and bought a few of these figures, he purchased a small one.

The next day we drove to Šiluva, where the Virgin Mary is believed to have appeared in 1608 to a group of children who were tending sheep in the field. They reported seeing a young woman in a white robe and blue veil standing on a rock, holding an infant and weeping inconsolably. Word spread rapidly in the Calvinist village. The Catholic church built in 1457 by Vytautas the Great, which contained an icon of Our Lady, had been destroyed by the Calvinists in 1532 as the Reformation spread. However, a parish priest had managed to bury vestments, gold chalices, church deeds, and a painting of the Madonna and Child in an ironclad box near a large rock. A blind man recalled burying the holy treasures with the priest seventy-five years earlier; when he returned to the rock to help the villagers find the box, his sight miraculously returned. The Catholics rebuilt the church around the rock where the Virgin had appeared. Our Lady of Šiluva Shrine was now one of Lithuania's holiest places. Pope John Paul II had held a Mass there.[1] I visited this sacred space to petition for a miracle of my own. To my surprise, Mykolas joined me.

Mary, how am I going to write this story? I don't know how to present all this complicated information. I would have to pretend that Jonas Noreika was a stranger. Lawyer, soldier, husband, father, charismatic regional commander, Nazi collaborator who enjoyed privileged status in a concentration camp, and author of an unfinished fairy tale—his vaunted heroism itself now seemed a fairy tale. I had a document proclaiming his motive and intentions: a brochure in which he had directed his compatriots to seize Jewish businesses.[2] I had several directives bearing my grandfather's signature demonstrating that he had the power and the means to carry out Jew-killings; as chief of Šiauliai, he forced Jews to be sent to a ghetto, inevitably to their deaths.[3]

As a journalist, I knew I had sufficient proof of the rumor's truth. And yet I also knew that there was more, that something crucial was missing. I was in a high-stakes game of blindman's bluff, my eyes covered, patriots pushing me in every misdirection. I had to run from this crowd and get these blinders off somehow.

Like a Method actor tentatively reciting her lines, weighing their impact, I struggled against my rising doubts:

No, *not my grandfather.*

No, not **my** *grandfather.*

No, not my **grandfather.**

It didn't matter which way I said it. *Yes, my grandfather.* Eight months after my mother's death I had been told by Boleslovas Tallat-Kelpša, at the school in Šukioniai named after my grandfather, that Jews had not wanted the school to be named after a Jew-killer. I rubbed the rock in the Our Lady of Šiluva Shrine and, tears coursing down my cheeks, begged to be shown how to proceed.

CHAPTER TWENTY-FIVE

A Desperate Rationale

When Lithuania joined the USSR in 1940, I took that as an occupation. For example, when from July 1940 the Soviet organs began cleansing Lithuania of anti-Soviet elements, deporting them to work camps, I took that as the destruction of the Lithuanian nation and then fully and finally joined the side of the enemy of the Soviet government.
—Jonas Noreika, KGB interrogation transcript, 1946[1]

It was an hour's drive north from Šiluva to Šiauliai. Here the summer greenery was bursting forth like a luscious utopia, an irresistible invitation to leap and prance among ferns and peek slyly behind birch trees.

Virtually every Lithuanian family had at least one member who had been sent to Siberia. In my family, that person was Nijolė Grunskis. Her late husband Stasys Grunskis was the son of my grandfather's sister, Onutė. Nijolė had never met my grandfather, but Stasys had talked continually about General Storm, whose romance was central to family lore.

Lithuanians tend to blame the Russians for their problems. Or the Germans. Or the Poles. The enmity between Lithuanians, Russians, Germans, and Poles preceded World War II, and it had complicated every aspect of Jonas Noreika's life.

Nijolė Grunskis and I had been writing to each other since my mother's death. I'd been preparing for a long time to interview her about her memories of Siberia. More recently, I had become used to hearing that Lithuania had suffered under the Communists as badly as the Jews had suffered during the Holocaust.

On June 15, 1940, Lithuania was occupied by 150,000 Soviet soldiers.[2] They had wrenched Vilnius from Poland and returned it to Lithuania—but with the proviso that Communist troops be allowed into the country. Lithuania, having little choice, agreed.

Ten days later, the Communists declared the Catholic Church separate from the state. They confiscated parish lands, abolished state salaries for the clergy, and destroyed religious books. Although Catholics were 80 percent of the country's population, the state began discriminating against them.[3] Many synagogues and Jewish schools also were closed, and many Jewish religious books were defiled. And yet when the Communist government began exiling Lithuanians to Siberia, many Lithuanians accused the Jews of being Communists who had betrayed patriots to the Russian soldiers.

June 1941 in Lithuania became known as "Black June." That was when the Communists sent 17,500 so-called enemies of the state to Siberia to work in mines and forests in extreme cold on near-starvation rations.[4] The same month, Lithuanians staged the five-day uprising against the Communists and Germany launched Operation Barbarossa, invading Lithuania. June 1941 was also the month in which all of the country's 200,000 Jews were targeted for extinction by the Nazis and their Lithuanian collaborators. They very nearly succeeded in achieving their horrific objective of eradicating Jews from Lithuania; 95 percent of Lithuanian Jews perished.

Black June. Its enormity was too devastating to contemplate. Growing up in a nationalistic bubble in Chicago's Marquette Park—intentionally isolated from the more diverse outside culture—I had heard countless tales from my family about Siberia, and nothing whatsoever about the Jewish extermination. In my family and in my Saturday classes at Lithuanian school, Jews were portrayed as Communist spies, the enemies who had denounced Lithuanians to the Russian soldiers who sent them to Siberia to die. I reasoned: *This was probably my grandfather's thinking, too, at the time.*

Vilnius
March 27, 2019

J. Noreika belonged to the anti-Nazi Šiauliai underground, which helped Jews.

The Šiauliai Jew-helpers trusted J. Noreika, appreciating him considerably. D. Jasaitis described J. Noreika as a resistor, one who "vigorously defended the country's concerns against occupiers." [Another] Šiauliai anti-Nazi underground participant was Šiauliai vice mayor Vladas Pauža, who handed out more than 300 identity papers to those persecuted by the Nazis, for which he was questioned by German security agents on more than one occasion. He characterized J. Noreika "as a grand patriot—not too cautious when speaking, with an impulsive and fiery temperament—a national hero who died for our and Lithuania's freedom." (Domas Jasaitis, "The Jewish Tragedy in Hitler-occupied Lithuania," *Draugas*, Chicago, 1962.)…

J. Noreika's colleague Damijonas Riauka testified that in the first days of war J. Noreika convinced a Jewish family in a carriage to turn away from the road and to quickly hide from the Germans (*Genocide and Resistance* Nr. 1 (30), Vilnius, 2016, p. 50).

"On the Accusation of Jonas Noreika (General Storm),"
Genocide and Resistance Research Centre of Lithuania

CHAPTER TWENTY-SIX

Exile

Oh Fatherland, our most beloved,
We are torn away from you.
We vow with our heartfelt love
To never forget you.
—"Song of the Exiled in Siberia," author unknown[1]

S tasys, Nijolė's late husband, had erected a six-foot-tall cross dedicated to my grandfather on Šiauliai's Hill of Crosses. My mother, brother, and I had visited it, one of several thousand crosses there, in 1997. Afterward, we were invited to the Grunskių home, where we sat at a long dinner table with relatives from Vilnius, Klaipėda, and Šiauliai. Stasys poured vodka into everyone's glasses, raised his own glass in a toast, and launched into a long, impassioned speech about Jonas Noreika's noble fight against the Communists to bring freedom to Lithuania. Then he veered onto the subject of his own wife's miserable years of exile in Siberia. All of Lithuania had suffered under the Communist occupation for fifty years, he declared, including—as he looked pointedly at the three of us—those who'd managed to escape and live abroad, while longing for the homeland. Everyone was in tears when he finished.

"Į sveikatą!" ("To your health!") we cried, as we clinked our glasses together and proceeded to drain them. Stasys began singing Lithuania's national anthem. We all stood up and joined him. He poured another round of vodka, and we toasted again. As we were about to sit down, my mother, the opera diva, burst

Aunt Nijolė Grunskienė in Šiauliai. Photo taken in July 2013 in front of the building where Jonas Noreika worked during the Nazi occupation

into an ardent, mournful rendition of "Lietuva Brangi, Mano Tėvyne" (Dear Lithuania, My Fatherland), and we all joined in. Some guests were moved to tears. By the time we finally sat down to eat, the food had become cold, but we didn't care. Vodka, black bread, and patriotism were all we needed.

Now, sixteen years later, Nijolė greeted me warmly and beckoned me into her home. She lived in a spacious three-room apartment in Šiauliai, across the street from the hospital where she had worked for thirty-three years as a physical therapist. She and her husband originally rented the apartment from the hospital union, and then eventually bought it outright. After Stasys died in 2007, Nijolė shared the apartment with their fifty-three-year-old son, Artūras, who was unemployed. Her other son, Gerardas, lived in England with his wife and child.

Despite my protestations, Nijolė insisted upon giving me the best bed in the house for my three-day stay. It was in the living room, and had orthopedic features to address her osteochondritis, spinal stenosis, and hip arthritis. I felt guilty about taking it, but she was so insistent that I realized it would be a breach of her hospitality to refuse. She slept in a side room, which she called "the Jonas Noreika room," where her husband had created a shrine to his uncle. Clearly, the couple had felt that their relationship to him was an inestimable asset, conferring honor and distinction. It bound their identities still more firmly to their homeland, as it always had for me. A three-foot-high wooden representation of Vytis that had adorned Jonas Noreika's office when he was the head of the Šiauliai region during the Nazi occupation now hung on the wall of this shrine. My grandfather's beloved chess pieces, which he'd often used when playing with guests, also were in this room. It was astonishing, the number of family members who cherished my grandfather's belongings as if they were religious relics—as if he were a deity.

Nijolė told me about Siberia as we drank coffee and ate biscuits at her small dining table.

"Well before dawn, on June 15, 1941," she began, "six Communist soldiers with raised machine guns arrived at our home in Šiauliai. Four soldiers stood, one at each corner of the house, surrounding us as if we were terrorists, while two commanded the family to get dressed. I was seven years old; my sister, Silvia, was ten.

"I often wondered how we were chosen to be sent to Siberia. This is what I've decided: My father loved politics and he talked too boldly and loudly against the Russians—which, as you know, is a Lithuanian pastime. He often had this conversation with a Jew, who warned him, 'Wait, wait, you'll see! You're going to take your words back!' Perhaps this Jew betrayed us, pointing out my father as an anti-Communist to authorities.

"Our family of five was roughly herded into a truck and driven to the Šiauliai railroad station. Our father was separated from us and led into another train, headed for Krasnouralsk. We had no way of knowing that we wouldn't see him for fifteen years.

"After two months, our train stopped in Biysk. We couldn't believe we'd finally arrived and that we could get off. For a moment, we rejoiced that the journey was over. When we disembarked, taking our few belongings, we spotted trucks and carriages in the distance. A rumor spread that getting onto the trucks would be better, so we made that our target. I felt lucky and hopeful because our family landed on an open truck. But unfortunately, it became horrifyingly apparent the carriages would have been the wiser choice. The carriages brought people near Biysk, where there was a school and a hospital. The trucks, on the other hand, drove 300 kilometers away, far from any city, and deep into the tundra. We had no luck, after all.

"We arrived at a wide passage between the Altai Mountains, a range where Russia, China, Mongolia, and Kazakhstan meet.[2] We moved into a primitive barracks, occupied by calves, with ten other families. We were part of a collective, like farm animals.

"Our first order of business was to shoo the calves and grab shovels to scoop out manure. We laid hay on the floor to sleep. We were so tired we didn't care about any manure left under the hay, as disgusting as that was. Eventually we found logs, which we cut up to make beds. In a corner stood a little stove. Cockroaches scampered behind it. They made my skin crawl. In the center of our barracks, we had four bricks in a pit where we cooked. Oh, how we all fought for a piece of potato! The hunger was gnawing and constant. It made us all crazy.

"We found vermin in our beds, which we killed by squeezing them with our fingers or boiling them in water. We often painted the walls with quicklime; if we didn't, the parasites appeared again, crawled into our beds, and refused to let us sleep.

"I was in charge of the cow. My brother helped me to build a woodshed. We used manure from the cow as cement between pieces of wood. The cow needed hay, so my brother and I cut grasses. Our mother taught us to count how many square meters we needed to cut to make enough hay. As I swung the scythe to cut the grass, I heard the howling of wolves not far off.

"I remember a kind rabbi there, who prayed constantly, but he had bronchitis, and coughed from the bottom of his lungs. In the winter, he asked us to bring water. We ran to the frozen river, chopped the ice with an axe, tied a cup to a string, and dipped it into the hole. When we brought him the water, he thanked us with a piece of chocolate. Oh, that chocolate meant so much to us! We would have brought water to him all day long for chocolate. But one day, he disappeared. We don't know what happened to him.

"My sister got sick almost right away. She kept saying, 'I'm going to die here,' and wouldn't leave the barracks. She suffered for six years, wasting away to nothing. She died in April 1947 when she was sixteen. She was so beautiful. I made a little crown for her out of wildflowers, weaving them slowly so they would look perfect. I helped my brother make a coffin. Our mother said prayers over her and we sang hymns. We borrowed a wagon, then drove into the woods, where we buried her. At least winter was over, so we could dig in the dirt.

"One day, while climbing a mountain to look for food, I tripped and fell, tumbling through bushes and trees until I hit my head on a rock. I was unconscious, and the other children carried me home. I don't remember how long it took to recover. For some years after that, I talked nonsense."

When Nijolé's bleak tales became too distressing, we sought diversion. As we sat down to a meal of herring, cheese, black bread, butter, and tomatoes, I surveyed her bookshelf. It was adorned with a cross and held books, family photos, and china, including porcelain tea sets that had been purchased by my grandfather on his many trips to Germany. I wondered about these trips. Why did he travel to Germany so often? Whom did he meet? How did he acquire all those dainty tea sets? My grandmother also had elegant Weimar-era porcelain tea sets; I never understood how she had managed to take them with her when fleeing Lithuania.

We nibbled and talked for the rest of the afternoon, as the sunlight shifted from one end of the room to the other.

"Mother and Father reunited fifteen years later," Nijolé told me, "but by then they were strangers—too traumatized; too different from their younger selves and from each other. They couldn't live with each other anymore. Siberia changed everyone."

Trying to fall asleep in Nijolé's bed that night, I thought of the thousands sent to Siberia for no reason at all, and of the countless lives shattered because of the Communists' cruel whims.[3] My head was full of images of snow and dead horses.

I knew that my father had escaped deportation to Siberia as a child. He never spoke of those years. His tears were frozen, buried, inaccessible. Shortly after my mother's death, I convinced him to go to grief-counselling sessions with me, thinking that these might draw us closer. During one such meeting he tried to share a memory of his escape from the Communists, when he was nine years old. But even fifty-five years later, in the safety of a therapist's office, his repressed terror would not permit him to do more than stammer, "I remember my father hiding."

"Hiding?" I prompted.

Dad struggled to elaborate, but no further words emerged.

The psychologist queried, "You were born in 1935, right?"

Dad nodded.

"And you left the country in 1944?"

Dad managed another nod. Our therapist, also born in Lithuania, offered, "I think I have an idea of what happened to your father. Stalin began denationalizing the country in 1941 by sending the top political, cultural, and religious leaders to Siberia. After that, he went after farmers who owned a lot of land."

"Yes," Dad said softly. "My father owned a lot of land."

"Stalin instituted land reform," the therapist continued. "He parceled land previously owned by the farmers whom he'd deported. If I share my family's story, it may help you share yours."

Dad nodded once again, seeming relieved.

"My father was a lieutenant in the reserves. That meant he was an enemy of the Communists; his whole family was guilty by association. We were all in danger of getting deported to Siberia. I remember, as a child, how trucks drove by, every day, to collect our neighbors and send them to Siberia. We were warned that they were coming down our block, so we ran into the fields to hide. We watched soldiers enter our house, then leave. The truck drove up the street. About a half-hour later, we watched the truck drive back in the opposite direction, filled with neighbors. We felt horrible."

"We were all so scared," Dad whispered.

The therapist responded, "I grew up scared, too. We were scared of Russians, scared of Germans, scared of leaving Lithuania, scared of not being able to finish school in America, scared of not being able to get a job or to keep it. I only knew how to be scared."

We waited for Dad to divulge more. The silence soon became uncomfortable. Evidently, he could not retrieve the memory without its undoing him.

I had noted that Lithuanians commonly referred to the deportations to Siberia as a national genocide. That shocking, chilling word fed a desire for revenge against the Communists. It gave rise to a sense of moral outrage that served as inspiration for the uprising Jonas Noreika led in Plungė—and as rationale for the murder of the falsely accused Jews. A facile—and false—equation was born, "justifying" atrocities as self-defense: Jew=Communist=Enemy.[4]

As a journalist, I rejected the use of the word "genocide" to describe the Lithuanian experience—unless in reference to Lithuanian Jews. The Lithuanians sent to Siberia had endured enforced dislocation, mass detention and internment, and bitter deprivation, but not genocide—not targeted mass extermination. Nearly half of the Lithuanians deported to Siberia survived their ordeals and returned home; perhaps as many as half a million escaped to the West.[5] They were scarred by painful memories, but alive.

Vilnius
March 27, 2019

The nation's reaction during the uprising was to kill Jews; however, they killed them not as Jews, but as Bolsheviks. More Lithuanians than Jews suffered under the [Soviet Union's] wrath. Morally rotten Lithuanians helped Nazis kill Jews and steal their property, but those who acted in this manner, comparatively speaking, were rare—fewer than in other countries. (Mykolas Krupavičius, "Lithuanian and Jewish Relations during Hitler's Occupation," *Letters to Lithuanians*, Vol. 37, 1986, Nr. 6–7.)

"On the Accusation of Jonas Noreika (General Storm),"
Genocide and Resistance Research Centre of Lithuania

Playing for Power

[Leonid] Olschwang [whose article "Die Mörder werden noch gebraucht" (The murderers are still wanted) appeared in Der Spiegel on April 23, 1984] blamed the local Lithuanian commandant, Jonas Noreika, for the killings. Noreika later ran the Šiauliai district, and was eventually imprisoned by the Nazis at the Stutthof concentration camp. After the Allies liberated him, Noreika returned to Lithuania and became a noted resistance fighter, dying at the hands of the Soviets. His case is a typical example of the historical divide between Jews and Lithuanians— he was a hero to Lithuanians, but to Olschwang—a criminal.

—Alfonsas Eidintas[1]

Nijolė took me around Šiauliai, showing me the high school my grandfather had attended and the house in which he had lived and worked as the district chief during the Nazi occupation. We also visited our remaining relatives in the area, who seemed pleased to share their childhood impressions of Jonas Noreika. Since my mother's death, I had been corresponding with my grandfather's niece Dana Noreikaite Nausėdienė, who was born in 1934. Her father was Jonas's older brother Pranas. I had periodically sent money in response to her pleas.

When Nijolė and I arrived at her apartment, she was waiting for us outside, wearing a red blouse and a white-and-blue skirt in honor of her American

Aunt Dana Noreikaitė Nausėdienė in Šiauliai.
Photo taken in her apartment in July 2013

guest. As I approached she burst into tears, seizing my hand and kissing it. She had keen blue eyes and was terribly thin. Her apartment, up two flights of stairs, was a small one-room studio containing a bed, a round table covered with a tablecloth, two chairs, and a sink. I sat with her at the table; Nijolė seated herself on the bed.

After a few minutes of conversation, I asked Dana, "Did you ever visit my grandparents' home in Šiauliai?"

"Yes. I was a child then, maybe seven or eight years old."

"Can you describe it?"

"The first floor belonged to the local German administration and had four rooms. The second floor, where your grandparents lived, had six rooms: a living room, a kitchen, a dining room, an office with very big books, and two bedrooms. I remember sleeping in a large double bed with your mother and Teta [Aunt] Antanina."

"How often did you visit?"

"I went for a week or two in the summer, and at Christmas. Once I was there at New Year's. I remember that we danced around a tree as high as the ceiling. I remember parties there. We ran around the apartment with Dalytė. Uncle Jonas would get mad and yell at us.

"This table we are sitting at used to belong to him," she continued. "Do you want to see it?"

"Of course," I answered politely.

She moved a broken white Roadstar radio and lifted the tablecloth to reveal a handsome walnut chess table with etched checkerboard squares of light and dark brown. Impressed, I took a photograph of it.

"Uncle Jonas played chess on this table when he was chief of Šiauliai. I saw him sitting and playing with German soldiers. He was very good at chess."

"What room was this table in?"

She recalled that it had sat prominently in his living room and that he had played with both Lithuanian and German soldiers, as well as with his nephews.

"How did you wind up with the table?" I asked.

"When the Germans took Uncle to Stutthof in 1943, they left only two rooms in the house to your Močiutė. They told her she could get rid of the remaining furniture any way she liked. So she asked her relatives if they wanted any of it. She gave us a sofa, this table, a desk, an armchair, and some doilies. We brought it all home in two trucks. When the neighbors saw the furniture, they became jealous and said that we got rich from killing Jews—but that wasn't true. We took your grandfather's sword and guns, too, but we threw those into the Muša River because we didn't want the Russians to find them. Keeping them would have gotten us in trouble. We had a lot of your grandparents' things, but many of them were burned by the Russians when they came in 1947. When I moved to this apartment, I gave some furniture to the Aušros Museum in Šiauliai."

"Have you heard the rumor that your uncle killed Jews when he was chief of Šiauliai?"

"He was against killing the Jews. Your grandparents even gave Jews some sugar. It was the Germans who did all the killing."

"What was life like here under the German occupation?"

"We didn't feel the war at all during the German occupation. We only felt the war when the Russians came. My father had thirty-nine hectares, and the Russians took that away. In 1947, the Russians started shooting at us. They burned our animals and our beehives. They even shot the storks! They were crazy. Why would they shoot the storks? We love storks!"

She then related how my grandparents had met and spoke of their visit to her home in Pakruojis, when my grandfather had thrown the shin-covering from his military boot at her.

"My parents went to their wedding," she said. "I wasn't there. I saw photos of it, though. Dėdina (Auntie) was so beautiful, like a doll. I never saw such a

The house in Šiauliai where my grandparents lived from 1941 to 1944

beautiful woman. She always wore long skirts to hide her legs, which she was ashamed of because they were a bit plump."

I laughed and replied, "I think I inherited her thighs."

"She was the most beautiful woman I ever saw," Dana repeated, "and so smart. She came to visit once, after Dalytė was born. I remember how Dalytė was chased by our rooster."

After an hour-long visit, Nijolė and I returned to her home. The next day we went to the building where my grandfather had worked as chief of the Šiauliai District. The three-story yellow stucco edifice at 265 Vilnius Street was now the Šiaulių Apskrities Valstybinė Mokesčius Inspekcija, the tax-collection agency. I tried to imagine it as my grandparents' home. Dana had confirmed that the Nazis' offices were located on the first floor, while from August 1941 to July 1944 the Noreika family lived on the second. I walked around the building, counting my steps. It measured forty-three paces long and fourteen paces wide. A balcony overlooked the large yard where my mother had played with her cousins. When I told an agency employee that I was writing a story about my grandfather, who had lived there, she handed me a photograph of the house taken in 1941.[2] It was then only two stories high, and about a third of its present size. I was told that it was among the 11 percent of buildings in Šiauliai that somehow had escaped bombing during the second Soviet invasion.

My relatives thought that Jonas Noreika had initially been appointed to his prominent position as district chair of the Šiauliai region by the Lithuanian provisional government in the belief that the Nazis would allow Lithuanians limited self-rule.[3] Only days later, however, the Germans made it clear that they alone would exert control. Several Lithuanian officials unwilling to serve the Nazis stepped down immediately.[4] Apparently intent upon securing my grandfather's cooperation, the Nazis offered him the best house in town as an incentive, in addition to the highest political office he had ever held. His young family would be able to live in style. My grandfather officially assumed his post on August 4, 1941, with the full understanding that he would be reporting to Gebietskommissar Hans Gewecke.[5]

But, my relatives asserted, my grandfather had accepted the post as district chair of Šiauliai in order to protect Lithuania's interests while only pretending to help the occupiers. Uncle Jonas merely *seemed* to be a willing Nazi collaborator. He intended to play his role cunningly, like a strategic game of chess.

Jadvyga's twin brother, Vladas Budrys, and my grandfather's nephews, Stasys and Antanas Grunskis, all had stories about how Uncle Jonas had let them beat him once at chess when they were children. They had all been exultant at the time, believing that they had genuinely prevailed over him. I wondered whether he had sat at that same chess table with the Gebietskommissar. Perhaps he deliberately lost a game to his boss in order to ingratiate himself with the Nazi official or cause him to relax his guard. He would have had to gauge Gewecke's moods so as to ensure his and his family's safety, as well as that of the homeland that he was helping to render *Judenfrei* (free of Jews).

Having grown up in a nearby village, having attended high school here, and then finding himself ensconced in the highest post available to a Lithuanian under the Nazi thumb, Jonas Noreika almost certainly felt a sense of ownership and authority. He had become empowered to rid the region of the Jews against whom he had railed in more peaceful times.

Anti-Jewish sentiment was strong. A newspaper in Šiauliai called *Tėviškė* (Fatherland) printed several articles attacking Jews.[6] *Shoah Holocaust in Lithuania* describes this publication as the most virulently antisemitic newspaper in Lithuania, similar to Julius Streicher's Nazi tabloid *Der Stürmer*.[7]

At the end of August 1941, *Tėviškė* proclaimed, "The Talmud stipulates that Christians not be tolerated. Jews equate Christians with animals. Jews understand 'loving your neighbor' as hatred for Christians." At the beginning of September 1941, it published an article with the headline "Talmud Secret: Ritual Murder Exists." In October 1941, another long article in *Tėviškė* claimed that "Jews are trying to rule the world." By portraying Jews as Lithuania's mortal enemies, the newspaper fostered a favorable psychological climate for genocide. It urged Lithuanians to assist the Nazis, to thwart any attempts to alleviate Jewish suffering, and to kill Jews.[8] My grandfather undoubtedly read that paper. The views it expressed accorded with those in the brochure he himself had written eight years earlier, when he was stationed in Klaipėda.

At that time, Jews owned most of the businesses in Šiauliai. A survey conducted by the Lithuanian government in 1931 found that 249 of the 330 businesses in the region—75 percent—were owned by Jews. Jews owned 23 of 25 leather and shoe businesses, 25 of 35 grocery stories, and all of the 18 haberdashery and household goods businesses. Šiauliai had 215 small-scale industries, of which 119, or 55 percent, belonged to Jews. And Jewish ownership of so many businesses caused great resentment.[9]

In various books I had found several documents that were signed "Šiauliai District Chief" during the time that my grandfather occupied that post. In July 1941, despite his not yet having officially assumed the position, he issued a proclamation concerning Jews living in the region:

> Šiaulių District
> Regional Head Proclamation Number 6
> July 23, 1941
>
> 1. All Jews who ran from the Šiaulių District to other cities have no right to return. Those who return will be arrested. Owners of homes who allow Jews who returned to stay with them will be punished.
> 2. All Jews, regardless of sex or age, from this date, July 25, will wear the Star of David on their left chest, 10 cm in diameter. They will pay for these symbols with their own funds. Any Jews caught without the star or trying to hide the star under a jacket will be punished.
> 3. Jews are allowed to walk in public from 6:00 a.m. to 8:00 p.m. If they are out outside of this time, they will be punished,

except for those who have special permission from the local administration or mayors.

4. Jews must move their belongings to their assigned places between July 25 and August 15.

5. The organized transfer will be overseen by the local administration along with Jewish representatives:

   All of the police employees will oversee the transfer.

   Those who do not transfer within the assigned time will be punished.

6. Jewish property will be expropriated.

7. Jews cannot use people of other nationalities to work for them.[10]

Močiutė had told me that she gave cookies and bread to her daughter, nieces, and nephews so that they could distribute them to the "poor Jews" walking past their home. Dana said that she remembered handing pancakes with cottage cheese cooked by my grandmother out to them. This story was supposed to prove that they had done all they could to help the Jews. I had always believed them.

I stood in front of my grandparents' stately former home and thought of all the Jews of the Šiauliai District who had been forced to travel to the ghetto in Žagarė, carrying whatever belongings they could fit into one suitcase. They were permitted to take no more than two hundred German marks with them. I now knew that it was my grandfather who had issued the proclamation forcing them on that march to "their assigned places." In the majority of the ghettos to which my grandfather directed local Jews be sent, they were murdered almost immediately upon arrival. Most of the Jews consigned to the Šiauliai ghetto were kept as slave laborers at first, but they, too, were ultimately slaughtered.[11] As I put together the two halves of this story, I felt a dead weight on my heart.

There were other similar documents, issued by my grandfather's office but clearly bearing his signature. The men who had shot Jews into pits were not the only perpetrators with blood on their hands. Even bystanders who did nothing to prevent or to stop the atrocities were complicit in these crimes. But Jonas Noreika was in a different category—what you might call a "desk murderer."

Within days of officially assuming his new position, Jonas Noreika composed a letter instructing that an inventory be taken of all the property that had been owned by Jews. On August 6, 1941, he wrote to the district leaders and the second-in-command city mayors regarding the handling of goods and assets left by "Communist activists" and "Jews"; the two terms were used interchangeably. Three copies were to be made of each list of confiscated possessions—after which parish elders were to wait for orders as to the disposition of the goods. Five days later Noreika notified the district leaders that all Jewish property had to be registered by August 20.[12]

On August 25, the mayor of Žagarė informed Noreika that 715 Jews were living within the 12,135-square-meter ghetto. Jewish and "Bolshevik" property was inventoried and assessed as being worth 5.8 million rubles (equivalent to $18.3 million today). On August 29, another 915 Jews were transferred to Žagarė.[13] This town became a killing ground for the Jews sent there under my grandfather's orders.

Had he been forced to sign all those documents? Perhaps one could venture the argument that these actions were taken under Nazi orders, and that he was afraid of not complying. But it would appear that he also profited from the murders. Documents in the Šiauliai archives signed by my grandfather specified in peculiar detail how the property of murdered Jews should be distributed among Lithuanians. One such directive read:

> 1941 October 9
> To Papilė Village Chieftains
>   Please give Papilė elementary-school teacher Gužauskaitė, a family member of a Bolshevik political prisoner who was tortured, any necessary furniture and clothes for herself from the Jewish property without requiring any compensation.
>   Jonas Noreika
>   District Chief[14]

Did he also help himself to Jewish property? Evidently he did. Historian Andrius Kulikauskas visited the Library of the Academy of Sciences, where my grandfather had worked during the second Communist invasion in 1945.

The archive there houses many records from the Šiauliai municipality during the Nazi occupation. Jonas Noreika's name appears as Nr. 35 on a list of 713 Lithuanians living in Šiauliai who registered the Jewish property that they had purchased during the Nazi-occupation (MAB f.76, a.180, b.28, l.27-63).

He registered the following items:

16 RM	a small cabinet
1.20	a pair of warm shoes
12	a desk
18	a book case
30	2 wooden beds with a mattress
25	a cabinet
18	a buffet
11	a bathroom mirror
3	2 nightcaps

When I picture my grandfather and grandmother wearing nightcaps that had belonged to a Jewish couple sent to a ghetto under his own orders, I'm loath to think how warm and safe they must have felt.

Other letters with my grandfather's signature testify to his authority and autonomy. One such letter secured a teaching job for his wife:

August 5, 1941
To Šiauliai District Elementary School Inspector
If there is an opening for an elementary-school teacher in Šiauliai city, please hire Antanina Noreikiene as a teacher for these responsibilities, and inform me when you do.
Until now, she was a teacher for six years. Her last position was at the Mardosai Grammar School.
Jonas Noreika
District Chief
Tamašauskas
Secretary[15]

On my last day in Šiauliai, Nijolė took me to visit the Hill of Crosses, where Lithuanians had placed crosses since 1831, after a failed uprising against the Russians. Families unable to locate the bodies of loved ones who had perished erected crosses here in their memory. During the last Russian occupation, from 1944 to 1990, Lithuanians had continued this tradition as a gesture of peaceful resistance. In answer, the Communists destroyed the crosses on at least six occasions; in 1961, they used a bulldozer.[16]

Nijolė and I found my grandfather's cross covered in rosaries. Nijolė's late husband had erected an A-frame roof over a crucified Christ and encircled the shrine with rue. A figure of Vytis galloped beneath the crucifix, while above it stood a replica of the Gedimino pillars, a symbol of the grand duke who had founded Lithuania. The plaque read, "To Jonas Noreika, General Storm, from Grateful Lithuania, 1993."

Afterward, Nijolė took me to visit her late husband's younger brother, Antanas Grunskis, who was born in 1934. On the way, we stopped at a grocery store to buy wine and pastries and were surprised to run into Antanas there. He didn't recognize me at first. It had been thirteen years since he'd seen me at my mother's and grandmother's memorial service; since then I had cut my hair and colored it red and had gained weight. He was balder and thinner than I recalled but seemed quite fit.

He took us the couple of blocks to his two-room apartment, which he shared with his common-law wife, Zita. There he showed me the sewing machine that my grandmother had once owned, as well as my grandparents' small wall clock. It had been fashioned of dark wood, but Antanas had painted it over in white and had pasted a sticker of a cat on its side to create a more cheerful effect. My grandparents' walnut buffet was in the kitchen.

"What do you remember of my grandfather?" I asked.

"I went to their home on vacation," Antanas replied. "I must have been eight years old. They had a big house with six rooms. My mother—who was Noreika's sister—would bring eggs and milk from our farm. I remember the son of the guard downstairs. I had to go get some logs for the fire and went out to the woodshed, but then somehow I lost the keys. I blamed the guard's son for stealing them. When I came back, I admitted I'd lost the keys. Your grandfather said he'd have to punish me. He opened a book and told me to read it. I remember the letters just dancing before me. How could I read something like that, at that age?"

The guard must have been a Nazi, I thought. "What else do you remember?"

"There was a war going on, but there were a lot of parties when the Germans were here," Antanas said. "Noreika never drank. He held the same glass of wine or beer the entire evening and lifted it to his lips once in a while, pretending to drink, then set it down to continue a conversation. His German guests would get drunk, but he never did."

"That's interesting," I said. This new detail suggested that my grandfather might have been living a double life, pretending to be a friend of the Germans, pretending to drink with them, pretending to take their orders. *Was there still room for doubt?*

"We played chess together in the living room," Antanas said. "He was very good at chess."

During the winters, Antanas told me, the children played outside: racing, throwing snowballs, and pulling their cousin Dalytė around the yard on a sled. Uncle Jonas would stand on Vilnius Avenue holding a handkerchief; when he dropped it, the boys ran as fast as they could. The winner of the race climbed onto Uncle Jonas's back while he jogged down the street to the Cathedral of Saint Ignatius and back. Sometimes they all built a snowman, which Uncle Jonas high-jumped over to demonstrate his athletic prowess. "The Christmas tree in the living room was the biggest I'd ever seen," Antanas remembered.

"Then there was the time I looked through the keyhole. I remember it was around the end of March 1943, shortly after Uncle Jonas was sent to Stutthof."

"What keyhole?" I queried, intrigued. "What did you see?"

"Your grandmother, Antanina, made a big party for the SS men. They wore uniforms with those double lightning streaks on them. She locked me in a room next to the dining room, so I wouldn't disturb her guests, but I watched the whole party through a keyhole. She served them coffee, tea, biscuits, and schnapps, and she was laughing and joking with them. She was trying to get her husband freed from jail."

"SS men?" I asked.

"Yes. Your mother got angry when I told her about it. But I knew, even back then, what those lightning streaks meant.

"The men listened to Aunt Antanina politely and told her that Jonas Noreika was a lucky man to have such a dedicated wife. Then they left. When she opened the office door to let me out, I took one look at her tears of disappointment and knew I shouldn't ask any questions."

I surmised that Gebietskommissar Hans Gewecke was one of the men my grandmother had invited to her dining room. From Antanas's story, I gathered that she had felt comfortable among those men.

Later I compared this anecdote to one recounted by Vanda Sruoga, the wife of Balys Sruoga, who also had been arrested and taken to the Stutthof concentration camp and whose memoir had been so helpful in understanding my grandfather's time at the camp. According to an article written in a Chicago newspaper by Vanda Sruoga in January 1981, a number of Lithuanians had attempted to secure Jonas Noreika's and Balys Sruoga's release from prison by collecting a large sum of money—evidently to bribe Nazi officials. Damijonas had sent my mother a newspaper clipping that had been republished in Kaunas 1994 about this.

Mrs. Sruoga's letter described her conversation with Karl Jäger, head of the Einsatzkommando, the killing squad that murdered many of Lithuania's Jews. Historians have described Jäger's report cataloguing the atrocities he oversaw as the most chilling document they've seen.

Jäger's agitated response to Mrs. Sruoga's appeal was essentially, *There's a war on, don't you know? The Russians are almost upon us, and how dare Lithuanians stand up to the honorable Germans!* He offered to strike a deal with her: if the Lithuanian youth would join the German Army, the forty-six prisoners of honor would be released. Only then did she understand that her husband and Jonas Noreika and the others were being held hostage in retaliation for Lithuanians' refusing to join the SS.[17]

As my trip to Šiauliai was ending, Mykolas called to ask whether I needed a chauffeur for the trip back to Klaipėda. I told him I'd decided to take the train. It was time I learned the public transportation routes. Nijolė and her son escorted me to the station.

As we waited at the station, Nijolė urged her son to tell me a story. Arturas cleared his throat and said that he remembered visiting his Teta Ona, my grandfather's sister, one summer in Lupaičiai when he was twelve years old. She told him that she had hidden two Jewish girls on her farm for two weeks during the summer of 1941. Her brother Jonas visited and remarked, "I'm glad you're helping Jews, but if anyone finds out about this, I'll be shot. Be careful. You're going to have to find another place for them." According to this account, some Lithuanians arrived about two weeks later to take the two girls into hiding at another farm.

Having become skeptical by that point, I suggested to Arturas that perhaps the story he had been told was not entirely accurate. "Isn't it possible that the girls were transferred to a ghetto?" I asked. "Maybe your Teta didn't want you to know the truth."

He shook his head. "Teta Ona wouldn't have lied."

"Maybe she didn't know," I persisted. "Maybe my grandfather didn't tell her."

Arturas had grown up idolizing Jonas Noreika, as did his father. He had been told that if it hadn't been for his Uncle Jonas, things would have been even worse for Jews. I now knew this myth to be preposterous. Precisely *because of Jonas Noreika*, the Jews' fate could not have been worse. Lithuania had the ugly distinction of having killed a higher percentage of its Jewish population than any other country in Europe. *How much worse could it have been?*

Shortly before my train arrived, Nijolė handed me a small stack of history and poetry books about Siberia, telling me that I might find them useful. We promised to stay in touch.

Seated on the train for my first trip alone in Lithuania, I thought about the choices my grandfather had made during the Nazi occupation. Had he regarded it all as just a clever game of strategy?

I'd heard that he had worked to create a Lithuanian art and science center in Šiauliai during the Nazi occupation. The fact that the Nazis permitted him

to oversee such an endeavor is evidence that they trusted him. His manage-
ment of this cultural project and his directives regarding Jewish relocation
and the disposition of their belongings both demonstrate the tremendous
scope of his authority.

What was he thinking during this time? In his interrogation by the KGB
in 1946, Jonas Noreika was asked if he had used his position as chief of Šiauliai
District to conduct anti-Soviet activities. He responded:

> This I cannot deny. I actively conducted anti-Soviet activity in this
> post. I led the requisition of food products from residents of
> Šiauliai, to feed those fighting against the USSR in the German
> Army. I actively led anti-Soviet propaganda. More than once, I
> gave speeches against the Soviet Union in favor of Hitler's army
> in Šiauliai and surrounding regions.
>
> In 1941 and 1942, I actively led meetings on the Harvest Day
> holiday with the goal of raising active war against the Bolsheviks.
> On these festive occasions, I gave speeches thanking the residents
> for not worrying about their own hardships when giving food
> products to the German Army. I said that, if the Soviet Union
> could be smashed, the Lithuanian nation will help push back the
> wave of Bolshevism threatening to overtake all of Europe.
>
> In 1942, in the summer in Šiauliai, I gave an anti-Soviet speech
> at the exhibition "Red Terror in Lithuania." It was organized as
> propaganda against the Bolsheviks and was taken throughout the
> Lithuanian territory.[18]

Of course, as is demonstrated by his directive of August 6, 1941, among
other documents, "anti-Soviet" could very well mean "anti-Jewish." From June
to December 1941, almost all of the 200,000 Jews living in Lithuania were shot
by Germans and their collaborators. Some Jews—15,000 in Vilnius, 15,000 in
Kaunas, and 4,500 in Šiauliai—were spared initially so that they could be put
to work. Most of the surviving members of this work force, however, were

murdered three years later, when the Nazis went on a killing spree shortly before the Soviets returned in 1944.

In his letters to my grandmother; the three thousand pages of KGB transcripts; the newspaper articles; the book by Ašmenskas; and the novel, articles, and short stories that Jonas Noreika had written I found not a word of remorse or regret for what he had done with regard to the Jews in Šiauliai.

By now, I was angry: with my long-dead grandfather, for his heinous actions; with my grandmother, for feeding me such brazen propaganda; with Damijonas, for his obfuscations and elaborate lies; and with Lithuania itself, for having disingenuously promoted a lying fairy tale for so long. How could Noreika have been declared a hero? All of these documents and witnesses had been available for years.

I had fervently—even forlornly—hoped that my grandfather had been playing a brave double game. Unfortunately, for once, the truth was exactly what it seemed.

Vilnius
March 27, 2019

[T]he [Genocide] Centre acknowledges that the occupational power dragged Noreika into the matter of isolating Jews. In August 1941, Noreika, as the chief of the Šiauliai district, relayed Hans Gewecke's orders to the city and town mayors to transfer Jews to the Žagare ghetto, as well as the order concerning the distribution of the Jews' property. It must be emphasized, however, that the orders were not Noreika's will—he was simply relaying the German administration's orders as the district chief.

"On the Accusation of Jonas Noreika (General Storm),"
Genocide and Resistance Research Centre of Lithuania

Germany's Fifth Column

*For the ideological maturity of the Lithuanian nation it is
necessary to strengthen anti-Communist and anti-Jewish actions
and to unconditionally spread the idea that the Russian-German
armed conflict will truly happen. The Red Army will be quickly
driven from Lithuania, and Lithuania will become a free and
independent state. It is very important at this opportunity to also
shake off the Jews. Therefore, we need to create in the land such
an oppressive atmosphere against the Jews that not a single Jew
would dare to even allow themselves the thought that in New
Lithuania they might still have even minimal rights and or
any possibilities for making a living. The purpose is to force
all Jews to run from Lithuania along with the Red Russians.
The more of them that leave, the easier it will be to finish
ridding ourselves of Jews.*
—Kazys Škirpa, leader of the Lithuanian Activist Front, "Instructions for
Liberating Lithuania," March 24, 1941

B ack in my apartment in Klaipėda, I had a few days to myself to prepare
for the tour of Holocaust sites. I took long baths, washed my clothes,
shopped for food, talked to my husband, went on lengthy walks, and continued sifting through my research and reflecting upon the information I'd
gathered in Šiauliai.

Sitting at the kitchen table piled high with documents, I opened Ašmenskas's book once again. A certain Stepas Kontrimas, associated with the Lietuvos Laisvės Armija (Lithuanian Freedom Army), spoke of Jonas Noreika's arrival in Šiauliai, and of working with him to acquire weapons. According to Ašmenskas, my grandfather asked Kontrimas to act as second-in-command at the Radviliškis fire station so that he could use the fire engine to transport arms. Kontrimas had acquired five radio stations during the German occupation, and also had a contact in the German Army headquarters, as did my grandfather. These contacts enabled them to obtain many weapons from the Germans—weapons that Kontrimas loaded onto the fire trucks and distributed throughout Lithuania, presumably to underground "partisans," which some accounts described as "Germany's fifth column."[1]

I put down my reading glasses and paced the kitchen. Outside my window, the Baltic Sea crashed against the shore. *Why would the German occupiers give weapons to the Lithuanians? The Soviets had already been driven out of the country. Whom did the Germans expect the Lithuanians to kill? Obviously, the Nazis trusted them not to turn the weapons back upon the Nazis themselves. So the Germans must have been enlisting the help of the Lithuanian "partisans" against a common enemy—whether real or imagined. Their target could only have been the Jews.*

Why was this not more widely acknowledged?

I returned to Ašmenskas's book and learned that Jonas Noreika maintained contacts with the Lithuanian Activist Front, while Kontrimas was closely aligned with the Lithuanian Freedom Army; they delivered weapons to both groups.[2] These units were purportedly "fighting Communist activists," including Soviet partisans who had been parachuted in to Lithuania and were hiding in the woods. As I assembled facts gleaned from the many books, newspaper articles, and KGB transcripts, a picture emerged of Lithuanian "partisans" essentially sleeping with the enemy. Although these partisans had many weapons—many of them supplied to them by the Germans—they never once turned those weapons against the Germans occupying their country. Not a single Nazi was killed in Lithuania during the Nazi occupation.[3]

In a book about the Holocaust given to me by Simon Dovidavičius when we met in Kaunas, I came across a letter addressed to my grandfather from the mayor of Žeimelis, a city forty miles north of Šiauliai. It informed him that 180 Jews had been shot and two Jewish women had been brought to Žagarė. I thought the mention of the "two Jewesses" was rather odd, as no other correspondence included any particulars whatsoever regarding the Jewish individuals who were being rounded up, marched to ghettos, and murdered en masse. Yet these two specifically were pointed out, as if they might be of personal interest.

> Lithuanian Republic
> VRM
> Žeimelio district government
> 1941 August 25
> Nr. 268
> Žeimelis
> To the Šiaulių District Chair,
> In Žeimelių village there were 205 Jews. As the Bolshevik army left, 44 Jews ran away. As of today, August 21, 180 have been shot.
> Now two Jewesses have returned, and they have been sent to Žagarė.
> Mayor[4]

Was it possible that these were the two girls of whom Artūras had spoken, the girls hidden by my grandfather's sister? Why else would the mayor think that their fates would be of any concern to Noreika? I knew that Žagarė had been a killing ground in October 1941.

I had always heard that my grandfather was anti-Nazi. But he seemed to have been quite helpful to the occupiers as chief of Šiauliai District. Only after the German defeat at Stalingrad in 1943, generally regarded as a turning point in the war, did Jonas Noreika undertake any anti-Nazi activities, as best I could tell. The record of his conduct during World War II's later years was used to mask his earlier deeds and to absolve him of the role he had apparently played in killing Jews.

I reread the text of my interviews with Damijonas, who had described the beginning of my grandfather's tenure as chief of Šiauliai District immediately following the five-day uprising of June 1941 against the Soviets.

According to Damijonas, on June 26, 1941, five men stood on the balcony of Noreika's new home in Šiauliai. They surveyed his domain and pledged to continue their fight for freedom, even under German rule. They vowed to revive partisan activity—this time against the Nazis—and undertook the creation of the Žemaičiai Legion. The five men were Noreika himself, the group's leader; his newly appointed assistant and the bishop of the Telšiai Diocese, Vincentas Borisevičius; Damijonas himself; and two Ramanauskas brothers, one of whom was Telšiai's district chief, and the other the Kretinga police chief. The Žemaičiai Legion would unite all Lithuanian political organizations into a single entity, to be called Lietuvių Vienybės Sąjunga (The Lithuanian Unity Alliance). The legion would become an underground anti-Nazi group, Damijonas told me, and during the second Soviet occupation it was known as Vanagai (Hawks).[5]

But according to the website of the Genocide and Resistance Research Centre of Lithuania, the Žemaičiai Legion was not very active during the Nazi occupation from June 1941 until 1944, when the second Soviet occupation began.[6] *Why was the legion relatively passive under the Nazis but "aggressive" against the Soviets?*

Damijonas had claimed that his own responsibilities included delivering correspondence between Jonas Noreika, farmers, and other contacts in Plungė, Šiauliai, Telšiai, Kretinga, and Palanga. What was the content of the correspondence between the farmers and my grandfather during the German occupation? Damijonas maintained that he didn't know; perhaps the farmers were being instructed to provide food for the Nazi forces. During the German occupation, my grandfather had travelled around Šiauliai County with his Nazi boss to deliver speeches to farmers, inspiring them to feed the German soldiers who had helped to free Lithuania from the hated Communists. Had he done so under duress, or was he pleased to use his influence to assist the Nazis?

Damijonas had also claimed that one of the Žemaičiai Legion's first acts was to assemble a delegation to go to Kaunas to request that the Germans stop ordering the persecution of Jews.

"Really?" I had asked, curious as to what kind of tale Damijonas would spin.

"Yes, it's true! Your grandfather did everything he could to help the Jews!"

"Do you have any proof of this? Any document, a historical record?"

"No."

This glaring absence from his voluminous archives concerning his hero was telling. Nor did he offer any anecdotes to illustrate his contention—although, leafing through the material he'd given me, I did find an article that Damijonas had written in 1994 describing this alleged mission. It maintained that Jonas Noreika had travelled to Kaunas with ten members of the intelligentsia to demand that the German government stop its genocide against Lithuanians and Jews and restore Lithuania's independence.[7]

I imagined my grandfather storming the government session, demanding that all Jews be spared from that moment onward, proclaiming that they had been part of Lithuania for centuries, that he loved the Jews, and that their slaughter was an unconscionable crime that must be stopped at once. But now I knew this story to be a fiction.

Later, I compared Damijonas's article with an entry in the *Wartime Diary 1941–1944* of Zenonas Blynas, the secretary general of the Lithuanian Nationalist Party. He recounted Jonas Noreika's arriving in Kaunas at the end of July 1941 with a delegation of seven men from Žemaitija, who presented themselves to the Iron Wolf Front, essentially a Lithuanian version of the German "Brownshirts," the Sturmabteilung, or SA. The Iron Wolf was committed to the "closest cooperation with the Great Third Reich."[8] My grandfather and his colleagues also committed themselves to "sincerely and loyally follow the German Nazi pathway."[9]

Damijonas's falsehoods about my grandfather may have been partly motivated by self-preservation, but, in any case, Lithuanian patriots seemed hungry for heroes. In a clipping from a Lithuanian Canadian newspaper, dated 1982, I read this testimony from "A. Kalnis": "I knew [Noreika] well when he was head of the Šiauliai region. He protested even against Gebietskomissar Gewecke, against the Gestapo and the SS. He was an ambitious soldier and a Lithuanian patriot. He helped the youth against the draft, helped [protect] farmers from requisitions. In Šiauliai, not one Jew was hurt. In fact, he helped them. In the Vaiguva foster home, there was an orphanage where seven Jews were hidden. Noreika knew this and took a risk by staying silent. The Jews remained alive here through the end of the war."[10]

I considered my grandfather's actual actions, both during the German occupation and even immediately before it. He had signed papers ordering the Jews into ghettos, no doubt under Nazi instructions. Possibly he would have been killed if he had not complied. Yet I remained puzzled by the fact that one directive was dated July 23, 1941—whereas he officially assumed office only on August 3, 1941.[11] Was his alacrity born of ambition, a desire to please his new masters, or did it fulfill a personal agenda? According to Damijonas, in 1943 Jonas Noreika created a group of anti-Nazi partisans—who, in reality, never turned their guns against any Nazis. And if my grandfather had chosen to defy the Nazis in 1943, why would he not have done so two years earlier? Instead, he had performed their bidding.

Before World War II, Vilnius had one of the largest Jewish populations in all of Europe. (Indeed, Napoleon had referred to the city as "the Jerusalem of the North.") By the end of 1941, most of Lithuania's Jews had been murdered under Nazi orders. The Germans did not use gas chambers in Lithuania; instead, the killings were done one at a time, face to face. Each Jew had to be found, removed from his or her home, and marched to a holding place such as a synagogue, a camp, or a ghetto. The captive Jews then had to be guarded, to prevent escape. Then the Jews had to be marched or driven to a ditch, usually in a forest some distance from a town or city so that local residents would not hear the shooting and the screams— although apparently many did. Altogether, 195,000 Jews were shot into pits and buried; the vast majority—175,000—within a six-month period.[12] There were so many Jews and so few Nazis in Lithuania that the Nazis required help from the Lithuanians.

And my grandfather was a Lithuanian who was willing to help. Perhaps even more disturbing, there were other issues on which Jonas Noreika was willing to resist the Nazis. Ašmenskas cites at least three instances in which he protested against German appropriation of produce from Lithuanian farmers:

On April 17, 1942, Noreika demanded that the Meskučiai police chief return the confiscated flour to Šiauliai resident Jonas Saliūnas.

On July 4, 1942, Noreika sent a handwritten communication to the Vaiguva police chief stating that Ulita Metlevaitė had a case against her for speculation. He defended her, declaring that this was her own food that she had grown. The case was withdrawn, and her products were returned.

On Nov. 11, 1942, he wrote a letter to the Šiauliai police chief asking for the return of animals and inventory to Šarūnas, the manager of the Andrijavas farm.[13]

He had chosen to comply with Nazi orders regarding the relocation of Jews and the plundering of their property—but he chose to resist the Germans when they were seizing food from Lithuanian farmers. Did he simply wish to be on the winning side? Or had he selectively followed Nazi orders when they were to his liking?

In February 1943, my grandfather was invited, with thirty other Lithuanians, on an excursion to view fish farms in Germany. There he learned that the fish were being fed human excrement to conserve resources during wartime. Upon his return he penned a satirical article exposing this practice and saying that the Germans were full of their own shit. It was a parody with a mild political bite. He submitted it to *Tėviškė* in Šiauliai, perhaps in the belief that this was a relatively safe means of expressing his scorn for the occupiers. But when the Nazis learned of the article, they punished him for his mockery and "traitorous" conduct by sending him to Šiauliai Prison, next to the ghetto.[14]

Both then and now, Jonas Noreika was celebrated by his family and by the community for having taken a stand against the Nazis, even at the expense of being jailed. This, too, I had heard repeatedly: what a stalwart anti-Nazi he was, how bravely he'd endangered himself in the name of free speech during an oppressive regime.

The Žemaičiai Legion banded together and secured his release within two weeks. Damijonas wrote, "I, as a Plungė Legionnaire, was sent to Bishop Borisevičius [to ask him to] gather bacon, money and liquor to give to Gebietskomissar Gewecke, so he could free Noreika from jail." Gewecke was a reasonable man, generally well liked, Damijonas opined. Damijonas's brother Liudvikas and Liudvikas Meškauskas brought the money and choice provisions from Bishop Borisevičius in Telšiai to Gebietskomissar Gewecke in Šiauliai. Upon receiving the gifts, Gewecke freed Noreika on March 3, 1943. The legion's members paraded with him on their shoulders, shouting, "Valio! Valio!"[15]

But my grandfather's freedom was short-lived. That was the point at which, desperate to expand their forces, the Nazis had begun pressuring Lithuanians to enlist in an SS unit. My grandfather was among those who staunchly opposed their efforts, instructing the young men to hide. The Germans were frustrated by their inability to conscript able-bodied Lithuanian men, since they had succeeded in drafting Latvians.

This defiance has always been a point of pride for Lithuania. They resisted the Nazis! My grandfather's subsequent incarceration in the Stutthof concentration camp, with the other forty-five Lithuanian leaders, was the Nazis' retaliation.

A man is the sum of his choices. My grandfather had served as chief of Šiauliai District under the command of Geibietskommisar Hans Gewecke for nineteen months. During that time, he signed documents sending thousands of Jews to be sequestered in a ghetto from which they were dispatched to their deaths. His later resistance to the Nazis, I thought, paled in comparison.

Lithuania had become a cemetery for its Jews.

Vilnius
March 27, 2019

Much of the [Lithuanian] self-government became involved in anti-Nazi resistance; nevertheless, there were collaborators.

Jonas Noreika, as Šiauliai district chair, was also active as a leader of the underground Šiauliai District Lithuanian Front, in which he executed instructions given by [anti-Nazi] resistance commanders; in 1942, he was appointed as leader of the Mažeikiai District Lithuanian Front. (Mindaugas Bloznelis, *Lithuanian Front*, Kaunas, 2008, p. 95, 257.)

Self-government employees participating in the Lithuanian anti-Nazi underground were instrumental in foiling demands of the Nazis to mobilize Lithuanians into the German Army, as well as preventing the creation of a Lithuanian SS Legion. (Germans were unable to create SS battalions in Lithuania or Poland—the only countries in all of [Nazi-]occupied Europe.)

"On the Accusation of Jonas Noreika (General Storm),"
Genocide and Resistance Research Centre of Lithuania

CHAPTER TWENTY-NINE

The Death of Denial

I felt as if I were standing at the edge of a whirlpool of mud—the mud that had come crashing through my parents' home in my dream. Lithuanian accounts disclosed very little about my grandfather's duties and activities during his two years as the official in charge in Šiauliai. I found only an occasional paragraph or two, surrounded by text that obfuscated rather than clarified. I hesitated to explore further, but I knew that I must be drawn more deeply into the mire.

Because my grandfather and others had cautioned young Lithuanian men not to join the SS, the country's youth evaded induction into the Nazi ranks. This was a genuine accomplishment. *Jonas Noreika's subsequent incarceration in the Stutthof concentration camp surely was evidence of his anti-Nazi sympathies,* I thought. It also served to demonstrate the danger inherent in opposing the Nazi regime, thus explaining why he had not dared earlier to subvert the German agenda.

As I vacillated between conflicting views of this complex man, I read an account by Šiauliai ghetto survivor Leib Lifshitz, who had researched the mass murder of Jews in Šiauliai. An archive of the evidence he had collected, entitled "The World of the Jews of Šiauliai Murdered in 1941 to 1944," was housed in the city's Aušra Museum. When I asked Lithuanians what they thought of his research, they dismissed it by saying, "He was a Jew. What did you expect?" The fact that his book was printed by a Jewish organization signified to them that it was of no consequence, that it was not "real."

I, too, would have liked to dismiss it—but one journalist's quotation of a particular sentence from these archives riveted my attention. The figure that it cited must be grossly exaggerated, I thought. Lifshitz had written, "Šiauliai municipal and regional head Captain Jonas Noreika is responsible for the murder of 5,100, the entire Jewish population of the Šiauliai region, from July 1941 until April 1943."[1]

The number 5,100 made my head reel. *How could my grandfather possibly have been responsible for the deaths of 5,100 Jews? Was this true?* I felt suddenly faint and began to hyperventilate. I had been taught since childhood that he was an anti-Nazi. My mother said so! He was an anti-Nazi. My grandmother said so! He was an anti-Nazi. Damijonas said so! He was an anti-Nazi. Viktoras Ašmenskas said so!

He was an anti-Nazi.

I tried to cling to my denial. *Could an anti-Nazi also be a Jew-killer?* But the truth had a power of its own. Here was an eyewitness account. Moreover, Lifshitz had corroborated his claim with research. The accumulation of evidence finally forced me to acknowledge it: my grandfather had not merely "relocated" the Jews; he had played a role in their murder by knowingly placing the Jews in the path of a firing squad.

It was too painful a thought to dwell on. Yet I had come this far—intellectually, physically, and emotionally—precisely to determine the veracity of this accusation. If I had to leap into the swirl of mud to gauge its depth, so be it. I'd been prepared to consider that my grandfather had been forced to sequester Jews under Nazi orders; now I needed to ascertain whether he had willingly sent them to their deaths.

Vilnius
March 27, 2019

In the summer of 1941, most of Lithuania's residents, including Jews, did not understand that ghettos were considered as one of the stages in the Jewish massacre. Until the German occupation, Lithuanians had only heard of restrictions against Jews in Germany, of ghettos in Poland; however, they did not know that Jewish isolation would end in mass murder.

**"On the Accusation of Jonas Noreika (General Storm),"
Genocide and Resistance Research Centre of Lithuania**

CHAPTER THIRTY

A Holocaust Map

In July 1941, I came to the city of Telšiai when I joined with the
Commandant of the city, Svilas, and the Telšiai District Chief,
Ramanauskas, and I offered to help them with their work. Svilas
was about 40 years old, a major of the former Lithuanian Army,
and he had his own home in Telšiai. Ramanauskas was about
50 years old and lived near Telšiai. During [President] Smetona's
time, [Ramanauskas] led the police school in Kaunas. Since
the end of 1942, he was the General Inspector in Kaunas on the
question of land farms where foreigners lived. I joined the Telšių
Committee dedicated to freeing Lithuanians from the Bolsheviks.
At the meeting, I gave several strong anti-Soviet speeches to the
partisans urging them to give all their energy against Bolshe-
vism, to not let the Soviet government return to Lithuania ever
again. I took a group of people from this committee to Kaunas to
go to a revolutionary anti-Soviet meeting, where there were 200
Lithuanian leaders led by Dr. Ambrazevičius.
—Jonas Noreika, 1946, KGB interrogation transcripts[1]

Seeking to finally confirm or dispel my worst fears about my grandfather's complicity in the mass murder of Jews, I had hired Simon Dovidavičius as a guide to help me tour various local Holocaust sites. We agreed to meet in Vilnius at a hotel he had recommended. It was a ten-minute walk from the city's Old Town and more modestly priced than those in busier tourist areas. After booking my room there, I found a transportation company that took passengers from Klaipėda to Vilnius in a van designed to accommodate nine people. The other passengers and I were somewhat cramped but—as I kept telling myself during the four-hour drive—this was less expensive than engaging a private chauffeur.

Once I had checked into the hotel, I was pleased to discover that it had a sauna; I immediately made an appointment.

That evening, over a restaurant dinner, Simon and I discussed our ambitious seven-day itinerary. We would visit multiple sites in Vilnius, Kaunas, Plungė, Telšiai, Šiauliai, and Žagarė. For the sake of economy, we agreed that we'd stay at my apartment in Klaipėda for the second half of the trip.

We had eyed each other curiously at the beginning of the meal, in disbelief and perhaps bemusement. Yet, in a situation that should have felt strained, we formed an unlikely alliance. It turned out that we genuinely enjoyed each other's company.

Simon told me that I was the second Lithuanian client who had come to him concerned about a relative's involvement in antisemitic atrocities. As the director of Sugihara House and a tour guide knowledgeable about Holocaust sites, Simon was often confronted with sensitive issues and emotionally challenging circumstances. Most of the people who engaged his services were Jews trying to locate relatives' burial sites.

"Sometimes, all I can do is lead them to a pit and say, 'This is my best guess,'" he said, with a shrug of resignation.

"How sad."

It was evident that he had a personal interest in my case. A year older than me, Simon had an intense nature and exuded tremendous energy. He was perhaps also a bit eccentric, I thought; he had a vaguely academic air and an utter disregard for fashion. He wore black pants with suspenders over a T-shirt, blue Dockers without socks, and he carried a black leather bag from which he was continually pulling one document or another. Two pairs of glasses hung from his T-shirt collar: purple-rimmed reading glasses and sunglasses. Whenever he forgot his reading glasses during our tour, he borrowed mine.

The next morning, after a hotel breakfast of cold cuts, boiled eggs, black bread, and herring, we drove to the Holocaust Exposition in Vilnius.[2] Simon was committed to providing me with as much background information as possible. At the Holocaust Exposition he pointed out the black triangles spread across a huge map of Lithuania. They were congregated in bunches around the cities and scattered throughout the rural areas, indicating the graves of Jews who had been murdered, mainly between June and December 1941. There were more than two hundred triangles, each of them representing hundreds of bodies.

I had looked at maps of Lithuania all my life and was familiar with how the country's contours had changed throughout the various periods of its history. At one time the country's borders had extended from the Baltic Sea to the Black Sea; later, its boundaries were represented merely by a dotted line within the Soviet Union. At another time, Lithuania's bottom eastern third had been chopped off by Poland, which had occupied even the country's beloved capital, Vilnius. I had seen a map with dots signifying the number of Lithuanians sent to Siberia; another in which the dots denoted Lithuanians who had fled the country during the Communist invasion; and yet another showing how many Catholic churches had been converted into atheist museums. But I had never seen a map of Holocaust sites. It was staggering.

Simon introduced me to an entirely new perspective, one blithely ignored by most Lithuanians—who were intent upon avoidance of any reckoning with their history vis à vis the Jews. I understood their position. I myself hadn't given the matter any thought before my mother's deathbed request. Now, after thirteen years of research, skepticism, and agonizing doubt, I was finally prepared to hear the truth.

I noted that Žemaitija occupied nearly a quarter of the Holocaust museum's huge map: its northwest portion. Studying the zones filled with triangles, I was startled to see that Plungė alone had three. Telšiai also had three; Gargždai had four; Mažeikiai had four; Kretinga had three; Rietavas had two; Varniai had two; Šiauliai had two; and Žagarė had four. Kaunas, in the southwest, had nine triangles. Vilnius had too many triangles to count; seventy thousand Jews had been buried there.

"Events in Žemaitija are poorly reported in Holocaust literature," Simon observed. "I keep searching in books for information about the area. And I have a bad feeling that there are no records of it because no Germans were involved. The Germans were meticulous record keepers; they were proud of their efforts. But Lithuanians would have concealed information about the killings."

I agreed that researching the fate of Žemaitija's Jews had been challenging. The information that my research had yielded so far had been gleaned primarily by implication and inference, as I attempted to decode vague or euphemistic terms and read between the lines.[3] I remembered Damijonas's telling me that my grandfather had forbidden any documentation, insisting that all orders be given orally. Nor had he permitted any photographs of himself as leader.

I didn't like the conclusions that I was being compelled to draw. Possibly my mother had known that my journalist's instincts and skills would lead me to the truth she could not admit or divulge herself. *No wonder she had not chosen to write anything after forty years of research!* But if avoidance was a family trait, I was determined to fight it.

Facing the enormous map with its sinister triangles was an enlarged copy of the Jäger Report, the cold-blooded documentation of the genocide of the Jews in Lithuania by none other than Karl Jäger himself, the commander of the Einsatzkommando killing squad that carried out the murders. Reproduced so that its text, wider than my arm span, extended from floor to ceiling, it listed in chronological order the dates and locations of the murders that had begun on July 4, 1941; the numbers of Jews killed; and the totals.

The Commander of the Security Police and the SD Einsatzkommando 3
Kauen [Kaunas]
1 December 1941
=================
Secret Reich Business
=================

Complete list of executions carried out in the EK 3 area up to 1 December 1941

Security police duties in Lithuania taken over by Einsatzkommando 3 on 2 July 1941.

(The Wilna [Vilnius] area was taken over by EK 3 on 9 Aug. 1941, the Schaulen area on 2 Oct. 1941. Up until these dates EK 9 operated in Wilna and EK 2 in Schaulen.)

On my instructions and orders the following executions were conducted by Lithuanian partisans:

4.7.41	Kauen-Fort VII	416 Jews, 47 Jewesses	463
6.7.41	Kauen-Fort VII	Jews	2,514

Following the formation of a raiding squad under the command of SS-Obersturmführer Hamann[4] and 8–10 reliable men from the Einsatzkommando, the following actions were conducted in cooperation with Lithuanian partisans:

This was followed by a grim list of the number of Jews murdered on each of approximately one hundred dates and the cities at which the massacres took place—resulting in a total of 133,346 deaths.

At the bottom of the document, Karl Jäger had added:

Prior to EK 3 taking over security police duties, Jews liquidated by pogroms and executions (including partisans): 4,000

Total 137,346

Today I can confirm that our objective, to solve the Jewish problem for Lithuania, has been achieved by EK 3. In Lithuania there are no more Jews, apart from Jewish workers and their families. The distance between from [sic] the assembly point to the graves was on average 4 to 5 km.

I consider the Jewish action more or less terminated as far as Einsatzkommando 3 is concerned. Those working Jews and Jewesses still available are needed urgently and I can envisage that after the winter this workforce will be required even more urgently. I am of the view that the sterilization programme of the male worker Jews should be started immediately, so that reproduction is prevented. If despite sterilization a Jewess becomes pregnant she will be liquidated.

[signed]

Jäger

SS-Standartenführer[5]

Simon pointed out that Plungė was not even mentioned in this report, yet there were ten burial pits in that city. The most probable scenario, he said, was that Lithuanians had killed the Jews there before the Nazi Einsatzkommando took over from the Lithuanians—that the two thousand Jews massacred at Plungė were part of the four thousand that Karl Jäger listed as having been "liquidated by pogroms and executions (including partisans)" "prior to EK3 taking over security duties." Plungė was the first massacre of Jews in a Lithuanian town of that size in which the entire Jewish population was killed, including the women, children, and elderly.[6] And my grandfather, who played a key role in the "uprising" against the Russians at this time, must surely have played a key role in what Jäger called "pogroms and executions," including those carried out by "partisans."[7]

Lithuanians had figured out how to exterminate Jews with shocking efficiency. Significantly, the Wannsee Conference of January 1942, at which Nazi Germany resolved to make mass murder its state policy, had not yet been convened.

My heart raced as Simon spoke. "But couldn't everything my grandfather did have been done under Nazi orders?" I asked, despite knowing better.

"It's true that the Nazis ordered the Lithuanians to do the killing," Simon conceded, "but why did the Lithuanians have to kill two thousand so swiftly? They could have dragged their feet a little. Why were they so eager, so efficient and zealous?"

It was a good question. I was ashamed and overcome with guilt. I felt like sinking into a hole.

Simon sensed that my own logic would deny me any retreat. He pointed to the relevant paragraph of the Jäger Report: "Prior to EK 3 taking over security police duties, Jews liquidated by pogroms and executions (including partisans): 4,000."

"At the time, the Nazis were hardly concerned with Plungė," he remarked. "Noreika was an antisemite—and being a lawyer, he knew full well what he was doing. Things were happening so fast in the area where he was leading the uprising that the Germans didn't even record events there."

"I see," I said slowly. I struggled to bear up under the new wave of humiliation washing over me.

"The first two weeks of the German occupation were the worst, because that's when the Lithuanians turned against their Jewish neighbors," Simon continued. "The Lithuanians say that the uprising united all parties, but that's not true. The people in Berlin [that is, the Lithuanians leading the Lithuanian Activist Front from Germany] were anti-Jewish, and they set the tone for the rest of the country. They used the pretext that all Jews were Communists. Nobody talks about those first two weeks, because it makes the Lithuanians look bad."

And we all know how much the Lithuanians don't want to look bad, I thought to myself. I had heard that very rationalization growing up, that all Jews were Communists, and all Jews were the enemy. I had come to learn that this was a prima facie excuse for patriots to turn against Jews, to victimize them just as the Communists had victimized Lithuanians.

After considering this appalling report and Simon's conclusions from it, I wondered whether Karl Jäger had known my grandfather. I researched what I could of his life. Jäger had joined the SS in 1932.[8] His career accelerated after he was taken under Heinrich Himmler's wing in 1935. In 1940, Jäger was named the commander of Einsatzkommando 3. He lived in Kaunas from July 1941 to September 1943, submitting reports of the massacres of Jews that he executed throughout that period.

When the war ended, Jäger escaped capture by the Allies, assumed a false identity, and became a farmhand.[9] In March 1959, his report was discovered in the Vilnius archives. Arrested and charged for his crimes, he committed

suicide by hanging himself in prison in Hohenasperg, Germany, while awaiting trial.[10]

Jäger's report has since been the subject of much scrutiny. After studying
the document, Jewish historian Peisachas Friedmanas asked in his book *Second World War*, "What happened in Plungė?" Pointing out that that city is not
mentioned in the report, Friedmanas wrote, "This is why the effort of Jonas
Noreika was so well-honored by the Germans. Having shot 2,000 Jews in
Plungė, the future General Vėtra would continue his bloody work in Telšiai,
and then would be appointed to become the leader of Šiauliai."[11]

No mention was made of Telšiai in the report either, Simon noted.[12]
Telšiai, considered the capital of Žemaitija, was a German center of operations.
Damijonas said that my grandfather had travelled back and forth from Plungė
to Telšiai before, during, and after the uprising. Ašmenskas wrote that Jonas
Noreika was active in Telšiai after the start of the war.[13]

"I've been thinking about the Jews of Žemaitija ever since my youth,"
Simon stated. "According to my relatives, my uncle died in Telšiai—yet that
city doesn't appear in the Jäger Report. I could never figure out why his death
was not documented in any German or Lithuanian records. It's as if it never
even occurred."

I shook my head, at a loss for words. I knew we both suspected that my
grandfather could have played a role in the murder of Simon's uncle. It was
unlikely, but possible. By now, my former proud sense of identity had shriveled
to nothing. I stood there with Simon, thinking that his family members might
have been killed upon my grandfather's orders. Silently, we acknowledged our
ironic, and tragic, ancestral connection. He was the descendant of Holocaust
survivors; I had inherited the wrenching legacy of a Nazi perpetrator.

In Vilnius we visited the Vrublevskis (Wroblewski) Library of the Lithuanian Academy of Sciences, whose exterior sported a plaque honoring my
famous grandfather.[14] The impressive yellow-brick structure at the intersection
of Gediminas, Kosciuszko, and Žygimantų Streets had a red-tile roof and four
white columns. It was here that my grandfather's 1945 rebellion against the
Communists had begun.

I had never been inside the building. Simon and I entered the imposing marble foyer and walked past a life-sized statue of Jogaila, Grand Duke of Lithuania and King of Poland, with his wife, Jadvyga, holding a cross. In 1386, they had converted the Lithuanians to Christianity, laying the foundation for the centuries-long Polish-Lithuanian union.

We climbed the black marble stairs to the second floor, where Jonas Noreika had had an office, possibly in the present-day newsroom.

Zigmas Šerkšnas-Laukaitis, who was with the partisans in the forest during the second Soviet occupation, had met my grandfather in this building to request paper on which to print *Freedom's Bell*. Zigmas's KGB interrogators summarized his activities:

Between June and October 1945, Zigmas Šerkšnas was in a partisan group ("bandits," in the KGB report) in the Alytus District, and after that he became a leader of the battalion. While in the band, he plundered farmers. In October 1945, Zigmas obtained documents with the name Laukaitis and became a teacher in Marcinkonys village in the Vilnius District, but he did not sever ties with the partisans. In December 1945 he connected with Jonas Noreika, asking him to help obtain medicine and paper for the partisans in Alytus.[15]

Zigmas asked a hundred men with a military background from the Marcinkonys village, ages 18 to 45, to join the partisan movement organized by Colonel Juozas Vitkus—the respected figure that my grandfather referred to as the "Old Man" in his KGB interrogation. Colonel Vitkus's code name was "Kazimieraitis" ("Son of Casimir").

I pictured Zigmas with several copies of the partisan newspaper hidden under his coat. During his own interrogation by the KGB, my grandfather described Zigmas thus: "An excellent person, about 25 years old, medium height, average weight, brown hair, oval face, shaven, wears a dark woolen coat, Polish hat, and leather shoes.

"[Zigmas Šerkšnas-]Laukaitis told me he maintains ties with Vitkus and promised to give him my message. He asked me for paper to publish an illegal newspaper, *Freedom's Bell*. I requested he bring me a copy of this newspaper and he promised to obtain it."[16]

Zigmas left five issues of *Freedom's Bell* with my grandfather and, in addition to his repeated request for paper, asked for medicine for the partisans. A few days later, Jonas Noreika gave Zigmas seven pounds of paper.

Intent upon fomenting a rebellion, my grandfather asked Zigmas to form a group of reliable young men in Vilnius. Zigmas agreed, taking the code name "Tiger." He worked with Alfonsas Janulevičius, another student at the University of Vilnius, and K. Valentukevičius, a representative of Colonel Vitkus, to create a group of fit, sharp-witted, and courageous young men willing to dedicate themselves to the cause. My grandfather named them "the Death Squad."

That night, back in my hotel room in Vilnius, I thought about how Jonas Noreika had returned from a concentration camp and instigated a rebellion against the Communists that led to the formation of a death squad. This was the handsome, clever grandfather I had always admired, intrepid as James Bond. But he now seemed to have a Jekyll-and-Hyde nature.

As Simon and I ate breakfast the next day, he spoke of the diary of Zenonas Blynas, the general secretary of the Lithuanian Nationalist Party. In an entry dated July 31, 1941—shortly after the Nazis asserted control over Lithuania—Blynas described Jonas Noreika as wanting to unite the Lithuanian National Party, the Lithuanian Activist Front, and the Iron Wolf Front, which, as we have seen, was a Lithuanian version of the Nazi SA "Brownshirts" in Germany.

The Iron Wolf meetings took place in the Vytautas Magnus War Museum, in Kaunas. Blynas wrote:

> The Žemaičiai land LAF delegation arrived. We spoke nearly two hours. Their leader Capt. Jonas Noreika asked us to make a final resolution. Brunius gave the document. Noreika asked [for] our authorization. The document read:
> The Žemaičiai land representatives met in Telšiai on July 29, 1941, and knowing and understanding the situation, have decided to create the Žemaičiai delegation from these people: 1) Telšiai region LAF leader Captain Jonas Noreika, 2) Telšiai

region police chief and region LAF leader's assistant Juodikis, 3) Telšiai region chief of staff Ramanauskas, 4) Telšiai region TDA commandant Major Svilas, 5) Plungė LAF leader and TDA chief of staff Lieutenant Alimas, 6) Telšiai region hospital director Dr. Plechavicius, 7) Lithuanian Bank Telšiai branch Director Jurkus.

The delegation was quickly sent to Kaunas with the following declaration:

1) The Žemaičiai declare their region's unity and understanding regarding our Nation's destiny in its concerns and invite all Lithuanians with good will to unquestionably find the means to maintain total Lithuanian national unity during this solemn hour....

5) It seems to us that nationwide unity and social justice matters would be more effective in a unified Lithuanian nation. This can and will find a basis of practical common work by sincerely and loyally collaborating with the German Nazi pathway.[17]

This document was possibly the only historical record that revealed where my grandfather stood in the hierarchy of Plungė's and Telšiai's Lithuanian military leaders during the German occupation. The introduction and first full paragraph proved that he was at the top.

I told Simon about Damijonas's claim that Lieutenant Alimas, acting independently, had been responsible for the Jewish murders in Plungė; it was now clear that Lieutenant Alimas reported to Captain Noreika. Major Svilas, whom I had been told was responsible for the Jewish murders in Telšiai, evidently also had reported directly to Captain Noreika, despite the latter's ostensibly lower rank.

"I don't see how these men could have acted independently, without your grandfather's knowledge," Simon agreed.

Reading between the lines, I inferred that the phrases "practical common work" and even "social justice matters" might well be euphemisms for the elimination of Jews. That interpretation seemed supported by the final line: "sincerely and loyally collaborating with the German Nazi pathway."

So my grandfather's collaboration with the Nazis was voluntary! I needed time to digest this.

Later that morning, Simon and I visited the Lithuanian Special Archives to view the KGB's transcripts of their interrogations of my grandfather. Simon indicated a place across the street where a large statue of Lenin had once stood; it had been torn down shortly after Lithuania's independence in 1990.

The massive black doors of the Lithuanian Special Archives in Vilnius—their oval-shaped silver handle set at eye-level, as if designed for giants—did not yield to my first attempt. I reached up a second time to turn the knob, leaning into the door with all my might. Simon threw his weight into the effort. Eventually the door swung open. I felt that we had earned our way in.

We ascended the stairs to the second floor, turned left, and then turned right at the end of the corridor, until we succeeded in finding the librarian. I told her that my grandfather was Jonas Noreika, and that I'd like to read the transcripts of his KGB interrogations. She said that they would be ready the next day.

As we strolled around the building, Simon and I glanced at the names engraved on its gray marble walls: names of the prisoners interrogated and executed by the KGB. Soon enough we located my grandfather's name. I pressed my fingers against the carved letters. This very building had been the KGB prison where he was tortured and had confessed to instigating a plan to reclaim Lithuania. The records pertaining to the most renowned period of his life resided here, in the place of his execution.

Simon and I ate lunch at the archives' café, ordering fish soup, mushroom *kibinai*, Lithuanian-style empanadas, and zucchini pancakes.

"Have you ever had cold beet soup?" Simon asked.

"Yes, I love it! Especially in the summer. My husband calls it 'Pepto-Bismol soup.'" We both laughed, thinking of the bright pink color of beets and buttermilk combined.

"When we get to your apartment in Klaipėda, we should make cold beet soup together," Simon pronounced.

"Sounds like a good idea."

The next day, we returned to the Special Archives to read the transcripts. The librarian gave us only a portion of the material and informed us that each page would cost one litas. Had I chosen to read all three thousand pages on a compact CD, it would have cost me $1,200. I replied that I only needed to see part of the file.

Simon and I found a computer and popped the disc I'd been handed into it. The file was entirely in Russian; I couldn't understand a word. Simon began translating. "Let's see: After his arrest, Noreika was vaccinated."

"Wow, that was nice of the Russians to vaccinate him just before torturing and executing him," I said. "A vaccination! Unbelievable!"

The absurdity of Russian protocol had us both laughing, until a librarian instructed us to be quiet. We apologized for causing a disturbance. Simon spent another half-hour translating KGB text, but I learned nothing that I didn't already know from the Lithuanian translation I had studied.

While still in Vilnius, I decided to interview Viktoras Ašmenskas. I made inquiries and discovered that he was now 101 years old and living in a local nursing home. I took a taxi there, alone, excited to see him again. When I told the receptionist whom I had come to visit, she seemed surprised. Evidently he had not had many visitors recently.

A nurse escorted him to the lobby. He looked frail, his blue eyes dimmer. It took him several minutes to recognize me.

I was sad to find him so diminished. "Hello! Do you remember my grandfather, Jonas Noreika?"

He brightened at the sound of the familiar name, and the fog of Alzheimer's lifted. "Yes, he was a great man. A great man!" Viktoras eyed me curiously. "It's like a mirage you're here, a dream. I can't believe you're here!"

"I know. I'm still working on that book about my grandfather, and I wanted to ask you a few questions."

"Of course. Follow me." He shuffled slowly down the hall in his pajamas, leading me to his room.

I asked if he would allow me to take a picture of him. He agreed, but only on the condition that he wear his blue air force jacket. He took it out of the closet and put it on, then posed near the window overlooking the woods. After

Viktoras Ašmenskas, who participated in the rebellion against the Soviets and was jailed along with my grandfather, pictured here at the age of 101 years, in a nursing home in Vilnius, August 2013

I had snapped some photographs, we conversed for a few minutes about each other's families. When I tried to broach the subject of his time with my grandfather, he became disoriented. I wanted to ask about his involvement with the KGB, how he had met my grandfather, and whether he'd informed the KGB about the rebellion. I wanted to throw him a hardball question: "Did you inform the KGB about my grandfather's activities?" After a number of none-too-subtle attempts, however, I concluded that Viktoras was simply unable to answer questions about the past. Instead he gazed repeatedly at the forest outside the window. Whatever he knew, whatever he remembered, was contained in his book; it and the KGB transcripts that had served as his source material would have to suffice.

After a while, we embraced and said goodbye.

I would have to return to the written record.

Simon, for his part, remained preoccupied with the deaths of his relatives in Telšiai. Since Lithuanian Nationalist Party secretary Zenonas Blynas's wartime diary had placed Jonas Noreika firmly at the head of Telšiai's hierarchy, the Jews who had lived in that city were of interest to me, as well. Simon had assembled various bits of information, but I needed a clear chronology. After some searching, I found an account on Jewishgen.org, written by Yosef Rosin, chronicling events in Telšiai from June 23, 1941, onward: "The Germans bombed Telšiai on June 23, 1941, and occupied it June 26, 1941."

Damijonas had said that my grandfather went to Telšiai on June 26, 1941.

I read on:

On Friday, June 27, its Jews were ordered to leave their houses unlocked and [were] directed to the shore of Lake Mastis. Armed Lithuanians under German command encircled them.

During the night, women and children were allowed to return home, where they found their houses emptied, while the men were left by the lake. The next day, Saturday, June 28, armed Lithuanians appeared at the Jewish homes again, evicting the women and children. They led them to a farm in Rainiai about four kilometers away. Here they found the Jewish men waiting. For several days, they were all held in the open, then the men were separated from the women and imprisoned in barns and stalls full of manure.

The Jewish men were taken to work. Their first task was to dig up the corpses of 73 political prisoners murdered by the Soviets. Accused of taking part in the murder of these political prisoners, the Jews were forced to wash the corpses, kiss them and lick the decayed wounds. During the funeral of the murdered prisoners, thirty Jewish men who had washed the corpses were forced to kneel in the street. The Catholic Bishop Staugaitis proclaimed the day of the funeral, July 13, as Holy Sunday, to symbolize victory over Soviet rule. All the guards in the camp and in the working places were Lithuanians.

On July 15, the Jewish men were taken out of the camp, led to a grove and murdered. They were forced to undress and stand on a plank put across the pit, then shot. Many fell unhurt and were buried alive. Several days later, the thin layer of soil which covered the corpses cracked and a terrible stench arose. This may be why, on July 22, Lithuanians appeared in the Rainiai camp to order that all Jewish women and children go to the Geruliai camp, 10 km away.

Altogether about 4,000 Jews, mostly women and children, were crowded into the Geruliai camp. Jews from several surrounding towns were brought from Alsėdziai, Rietuva [Rietavas], Varniai, Luokė, Laukuva, Zarėnai and Navarėnai. Farmers took Jewish women from the camp for [help with] harvesting because of a shortage of workers. Some farmers exploited them ruthlessly, even raping them, while others were kinder. Jews were allowed to walk to the town for several hours in the evenings, going door to door for some food. On August 30, 1941, Lithuanian police expelled all women and children from the shacks and selected about 600 of them to walk to the ghetto in Telšiai. The rest were ordered to take off their dresses and shoes, then form into lines and go to the prepared pits. The 600 Jews in Telšiai were killed December 30 and 31.

Several hundred Jewish women, however, managed to escape; only 64 survived until liberation day.[18]

Simon's mother, eight years old at the time, had been sent to Geruliai from another camp in Varniai. She told him that many of the Jewish women had tried to disfigure themselves so as to avoid being raped by Lithuanian farmers.

"Raped?" I asked, horrified.

"Yes," he affirmed.

Such bestial, opportunistic behavior had nothing to do with following military orders. And the ransacking of Jewish homes to steal property was simple greed. Unbridled greed and lust: man's basest instincts.

Simon's grandmother and her four children were saved by a German soldier from being shot at the Geruliai camp. They must have been among the six hundred Jews sent to the Telšiai ghetto. His mother and her sisters went into town in the evenings to beg for food from Lithuanian citizens. She and one of her sisters were among the sixty-four who survived until liberation.

The more I thought about it, the more likely it seemed that my grandfather was complicit in the killing of Simon's family members in Telšiai. I shuddered. *Why don't I just go back to Chicago, as several people have urged me to do? But can I pretend not to know what happened?*

From Vilnius, Simon and I drove to Kaunas, where I stayed in a hotel and he returned to his home, near Sugihara House. He gave me several more books about the Holocaust in Lithuania, and we visited the Ninth Fort. As is documented in the Jäger Report, this fortress was the site of the largest massacre of Lithuanian Jews; 9,200 men, women, and children were murdered there on a single day—October 29, 1941.[19]

Although Jonas Noreika was not thought to have been involved in the Holocaust in Kaunas, an exhibit at the Ninth Fort Museum included photos of the forty-six "prisoners of honor" held at the Stutthof concentration camp, and we quickly identified my grandfather's picture.

We strode alongside lush expanses of green grass. "These are the sites of mass graves," Simon told me. "Some Lithuanians hold weddings here."

"Where Jews are buried?" I exclaimed, aghast.

"It's a pretty setting. They all pretend not to know," he responded.

The next day we drove to Telšiai, where Simon took me to a stately green house, the Petrauskas Manor. It once was considered opulent, he said. Kipras Petrauskas was a famous operatic tenor. While he travelled around Europe performing concerts, Nazis and their Lithuanian collaborators held Jews captive in the sheds—built for housing animals and storing food—on his property.[20]

Simon and I forged an unusual bond during the course of our time together. Despite being on opposite sides of history, we harbored no suspicion of or resentment toward one other. He did not blame me for my grandfather's deeds. He even seemed to respect me for my search; we shared a passion for truth. I found his generosity remarkable—and his perspective invaluable. I had monuments and plaques and a school named after my grandfather to point out across the country; Simon had ghettos and pits to show me. How was it possible that both of us were speaking of the same man?

After spending a day in Telšiai, we drove to my apartment in Klaipėda. We were hungry and decided to make the cold beet soup. We had been comparing recipes throughout our trip, and now we were ready to try cooking in tandem. At an IKI grocery store, Simon chose fresh beets. I shook my head: I had always bought pickled ones. But these were fresher, he said. As he was from Lithuania, I reasoned that he must know how to make cold beet soup better than I did. He bought some buttermilk; I bought eggs and potatoes. He bought dill; I bought cucumbers.

In the kitchen, he instructed me to boil the potatoes. Once they had softened, I began peeling them.

"Don't peel them," he said. I left a few unpeeled.

When we tasted the soup, it was all but flavorless, a complete failure.

"I told you it needs pickled beets," I said.

Sheepishly, he agreed.

He ran down four flights of stairs and back to the store to buy pickled beets. I prepared the potatoes and sprinkled more salt, pepper, and dill into the pot. The addition of pickled beets transformed the mixture. Yes, this was very good cold beet soup. We slurped it down. Delicious!

Vilnius
March 27, 2019

"Let's keep in mind, that at that time people did not know about the Holocaust. We knew about it only after viewing the entire picture of World War II." (Zigmas Vitkus, "Vilnius Ghetto— When People Tried to Imagine Life," *Journey,* 2013)

"On the Accusation of Jonas Noreika (General Storm),"
Genocide and Resistance Research Centre of Lithuania

CHAPTER THIRTY-ONE

Interview at the Museum of Genocide Victims

On the morning of July 17, 2013, Simon and I met with Teresė Birutė Burauskaitė, director general of the Genocide and Resistance Research Centre of Lithuania, at the Museum of Genocide Victims in Vilnius. I had requested the interview a few days earlier at Simon's urging, in order to learn more about my grandfather's military career. Initially I had made excuses to avoid speaking with the director of an institution that had exonerated my grandfather of participation in Jew-killing, telling Simon that she would be too busy to respond, that I didn't see how this connected to the Holocaust tour, and that talking to her really wasn't necessary for my book. But Simon persisted, and, finally, wanting to please him, I made the phone call. To my surprise, we were connected immediately; she sounded welcoming and friendly on the phone, and we set up the interview for the next morning.

Before entering her office, Simon and I noticed a display case in the hall that exhibited eight books. Seven large volumes profiled Lithuanians who had fought for the country's independence, while the smallest book concerned the Holocaust. It seemed eclipsed by the others. Simon was indignant that there was only a single Holocaust title, physically the slightest of the volumes, at a museum purportedly dedicated to genocide victims.

"They just can't stand the whole subject of the Holocaust!" he fumed. I hadn't considered how this display might look to a Jew—that it might seem a grave affront. I pointed out that the Holocaust title had been placed at the center of the arrangement, but Simon countered that it was so small as to be overwhelmed by the larger tomes. Moreover, the exhibit suggested that Jews were not the primary victims of genocide; the term that specifically denoted their annihilation evidently had been usurped to describe Lithuanian suffering at Soviet hands.

We were ushered into Ms. Burauskaitė's office. She was slim and blonde with green eyes, and she was wearing a navy-and-white striped dress. Her manner was cordial. A picture of the Vytis hung on the wall behind her desk. On a table sat a photograph of a soldier with a bird perched on his left shoulder.

She asked if we had visited the Library of the Lithuanian Academy of Sciences, where Jonas Noreika, working as a lawyer, had forged connections important to the underground. I told her that we had recently toured the building housing the Lithuanian Academy of Sciences, and had stood on its balcony. Figuring that she must have been wondering whether we had seen the bronze plaque with his image that graced the academy's front wall, I said that I was familiar with it.

The director explained that after having led the rebellion against the Communists from November 1945 until March 1946, my grandfather was captured by the KGB and tortured in its prison, which had been converted into the museum in which we were now sitting.

She told us that she was nearing retirement and had been given this job because of her familiarity with both the Nazi occupation, from 1941 to 1943, and the two Communist occupations, from 1940 to 1941 and from 1944 to 1990. During the Communist era she had been subjected to surveillance by the KGB, and her experience had given her a thorough understanding of the ordeal that her country had endured.

I asked her what she thought of the accusations that my grandfather had killed Jews. She replied that, based on the KGB file and transcripts, she believed he was innocent. She asked whether I was aware of the file. I replied that my mother had left me three thousand pages of transcripts, which I had read.

I asked her opinion of the documents replicated in the book *Masinės Žudynės Lietuvoje 1941–1944* (Mass Slaughter in Lithuania 1941–1944), published in Vilnius in 1973.[1] The book contained reproductions of my grandfather's signature at the bottom of several letters directing that the Jews be sequestered in Šiauliai and then sent to Žagarė, where they were killed. I told the genocide museum director that I regarded these documents as irrefutable proof that Jonas Noreika had played a role in the mass murder of Jews and that I could not understand how, forty years after their publication, they still were not considered sufficient to incriminate him.

She answered, "All the Jews were sent to Žagarė. It's difficult to know what he was thinking. But the result, of course, is that the Jews were killed."

I found her answer evasive. The documents bore his signature, yet she was trying to exonerate him by stating that she couldn't read his mind or his heart. She was offering the justification that I commonly heard from Lithuanians: he could not really have wanted to kill Jews; he must have been forced to do so. They dismissed any evidence that besmirched the reputation of their hero.

She claimed that one of the killers of Jews in Žagarė later committed suicide, and that one of his teenaged children developed epilepsy. She was trying to suggest that any Lithuanians involved in the atrocities regretted their deeds and that retribution would be visited upon the next generation, a dreaded curse. Then she mentioned a man recruited to kill Jews who had crawled away and hidden when the shooting started. "You can't say all of Lithuania was involved in the Jewish killings. We still don't know how to live with our history, in many respects."

I was ready to end our interview when Simon asked whether Lithuanian authorities would publicize the names of those who had murdered Jews. She answered that no action would be taken in cases that had not been proven, out of consideration for the families of alleged perpetrators. "We cannot be the ones to deliver a verdict regarding these individuals. There has to be a case filed against each of them to be proven one way or the other."

The Museum of Genocide Victims was founded in 1992, shortly after Lithuania's independence, ostensibly to proclaim to the world that Lithuanian nationalists had suffered under Communism as greatly as the Jews had under Nazism.
Criticized for having misappropriated the word "genocide," the institution
changed its name to the "Museum of Occupations and Freedom Fights" in 2018.[2]

The International Commission for the Evaluation of the Crimes of the Nazi and Soviet Occupation Regimes in Lithuania
April 10, 2019

The Centre has explained that on 22 August 1941 and 10 September
1941, Jonas Noreika, following the directives of the German Commissar of Šiauliai District, Hans Gewecke, issued orders for the
ghettoization and expropriation of the Jews of the district, and
followed up the process with additional detailed instructions.
Nearly all victims rounded up under these orders were subsequently murdered as part of the killing operations carried out by
the Nazis and their collaborators during the summer and fall of
1941, by far the bloodiest page in Lithuania's modern history. This
is the historical reality supported by unequivocal documentary
evidence. If this is not participation in the process of the genocide
of Lithuania's Jewish citizens, then what is?

> **A Response to the Statement of the Genocide and Resis-
> tance Research Centre of Lithuania of 27 March 2019,"On
> the Accusations against Jonas Noreika (General Vėtra)."
> The Sub-Commission for Evaluation of the Crimes of the
> Nazi Occupation Regime and the Holocaust (a sub-com-
> mission of the International Commission for the Evalua-
> tion of the Crimes of the Nazi and Soviet Occupation
> Regimes in Lithuania)**

The Mud Pits

In those terrible days, there were no Germans in Plungė. In the
first war days, their army came and left. Only two weary, short
German men who looked miserable and had no rank were there.
They walked through the street and only the gods knew what
they did. Two unimportant men. At that time, a group of
Lithuanian army officers was in power in Plungė, with the
commandant Captain Noreika at the head.
—Aleksandras Pakalniškis[1]

This third Sunday in July Simon had invited me to attend the annual Holocaust memorial service in Kaušėnai. Situated in the forest about two miles from Plungė, Kaušėnai's three burial pits contained the remains of more than 90 percent of the city's murdered Jews.

I stood among a group of nearly thirty people, gazing down at an elongated gray rectangle sunk into the terrain. This scar in the earth, surrounded by a border of smooth cobblestones, indicated one of the approximately 229 such killing sites throughout Lithuania.[2] There were 11 of these in and around Plungė alone. A marble plaque at this mass gravesite unreservedly denounced the massacre and its perpetrators: "The Nazi assassins and their local collaborators brutally murdered about 1,800 Jews from Plungė: children, women, and men."[3] Behind us a newly constructed wall composed of bricks from a destroyed synagogue in Plungė enumerated 1,800 names.

An elderly Jewish man recited a prayer commemorating those slaughtered here in June and July 1941, at the very beginning of the German occupation. Then a Lutheran minister spoke about the far-reaching effects of the
Jewish tragedy.

I noticed a few people in the crowd snapping photos of me; Simon had
told them who my grandfather was. Everyone present seemed to believe that
General Storm was one of the local collaborators to whom the plaque referred.
I considered uttering some words of apology, but I couldn't summon them.
Instead, I placed two candles near the plaque, to acknowledge and to atone in
some small way for the 1,800 lives so ruthlessly cut short.

Jakovas Bunka, the elderly Jew who had spoken the words of prayer, had
fled to Russia with his family on the second day of the uprising. Upon returning to his hometown in 1948, he learned how few Jews had survived.[4] He vowed
not to allow the people of Plungė to forget the annihilation of half the town's
population during the German occupation. He had held a memorial ceremony
at Kaušėnai every year since the late 1980s.

After retiring from his job in a furniture factory in 1983, he spent his time
creating wood carvings depicting the Jewish tragedy. Each of his slender,
poignant statues towered about fifteen feet over a site of mass execution. Paths
and stairs leading to the three gravesites here in Kaušėnai, and the fences surrounding them, had been added by the Plungė municipality.

After the commemoration ceremony, Simon and I drove to the Bunkas'
home in Plateliai, a quiet village on the outskirts of Plungė, to hear his account
of the uprising. Jakovas and his wife Dalia lived in a spacious home owned by
their son. Jakovas had celebrated his ninetieth birthday a week before. Outside
his bedroom stood nearly thirty of the wooden figures for which he had
become famous; he was known as Lithuania's only Jewish folk artist. I admired
his portrayals of a cellist, a blacksmith, a woman reading as she spun linen,
and a Jewish scholar wearing side-curls, as well as a huge representation of
Moses carrying a tablet of the Ten Commandments.[5] Several photographs
hung on Jakovas's bedroom wall, including one of him—"The Last Jew in
Plungė," sometimes also called "Plungė's Moses"—presenting one of his sculp-
tures to Lithuanian president Adamkus.

Jakovas showed me a few of the items stored in his closet. These included photographs, newspaper articles, and books about his town's pre-war Jewish population. When I asked for permission to photograph him, he proudly displayed his Soviet-Lithuanian army uniform.[6]

The majority of his archive was now in the hands of his son, Eugenijus, who apparently had been appointed to pass down the family's traditions. I compared his role ironically with my own.

Jakovas handed me a recently published book entitled simply *Jakovas Bunka*, whose cover featured a dramatic image of his Moses sculpture. He was proud of his heritage,

Jakovas Bunka, a Jewish man who fled to Russia on the second day of the uprising, proudly showing me his Soviet Army uniform

and fiercely nostalgic.[7] He deemed it essential to serve as a witness to history: both to memorialize the lives lost and to ensure that the crimes of the past were never forgotten and never repeated. His story was an important element in my reconstruction of my grandfather's role in the 1941 uprising.

On the first night of the uprising, Jakovas recounted, he was awakened by noise in the streets. The city's Jews were anxiously asking one another whether to stay or escape. A Jew who had just arrived from Kretinga was telling a wild tale, warning that they would all be killed if they didn't leave immediately. It was difficult to comprehend his account. Then a German plane flew overhead and shot at them. The terrified Jews immediately dispersed.

On the second day of the uprising, seventeen-year-old Jakovas and his family marched toward Russia with three hundred other Jews. At the time no one knew that this would be the sole opportunity for escape. The road was jammed with Russians, who were retreating in the face of the German Army's advance from Klaipėda. German pilots fired repeatedly into the throngs below them, causing the Jews to scramble into roadside trenches. Jakovas saw a four-year-old girl get fatally shot. Her mother, holding two other children, stared at her fallen daughter, desperately willing her to live—not realizing it was already too late. As the crowd moved on, she refused to leave the girl's side. Eventually, someone persuaded the distraught mother to resume her journey.

Bunka and his family settled onto a wagon train that, over the next two months, carried them to the Novosibirsk station in Siberia, about 3,500 kilometers from Plungė. There they joined a collective farm. About a year later, he, his brother, and his father joined the Sixteenth Lithuanian Division of the Communist army. Of the seventy-two Jews from Plungė who served in the military, forty-two died in combat—Bunka's father and brother among them.

Less than 10 percent of Plungė's Jews fled to Russia when the uprising broke out. The rest were killed by Lithuanians, led by Jonas Noreika. Under my grandfather's direction, the Jews' homes and their contents were stolen. By the time the bloodletting had ended a month later, 2,234 Jews from Plungė had been shot, Bunka asserted. Only six Jews, sheltered by their Lithuanian neighbors, had survived.

On June 24, the third day of the uprising, the Germans assumed full control over Kaunas, Lithuania's capital. They had marched through Plungė, but left only two German soldiers in the town, with Captain Noreika in charge—evidently confident that the Lithuanians under his command would "maintain order."

Five days later, all the Jews of Plungė were ordered to gather at the Great Synagogue. Those who did not go voluntarily were rounded up by "White-banders"—Lithuanian soldiers wearing white armbands—and local police.

Aunt Rūta told me that her family remembered two Jewish girls who had run to her home, beseeching her mother for help in evading the Whitebanders. Her mother, then pregnant with Rūta and her twin brother, turned them away—troubled, said my aunt, at not being able to provide assistance.[8]

Most Lithuanians claimed not to know who had issued the order to confine all of Plungė's Jews in the Great Synagogue. Aleksander Pakalniškis's 1980 memoir, *Plungė*, stated unequivocally that the order to kill them had come from the regional commandant, Captain Jonas Noreika. Pakalniškis was in a position to know; he had been working as a secretary in the commandant's headquarters at the time.

He confirmed that the German Army's presence then consisted of "two miserable German soldiers" who watched the town. One of them approached Captain Noreika and asked, "What do you plan to do with the Jews locked up in the synagogue?"

My grandfather replied, "I've already given the order to shoot every single one."

In 1988, Pakalniškis published a book of letters written by Leonas Olšvangas, a Jew who had returned to Plungė after the war. Olšvangas sought to determine who had been responsible for ordering the Jews to be led into the forest to be killed. The results of his investigation corroborated Pakalniškis's account: the directive had come from Captain Jonas Noreika.

During my visit to Plungė, teacher and historian Bronius Pocius told me that his mother, Stanislava Bieliauskitė Pocienė, had also named Captain Jonas Noreika as the commandant of Plungė.[9] "Noreika came to Plungė on the night of June 23," he affirmed. "Arnold Pabrėža was the executor, but he had to get orders from someone." Pocius's mother had told him that when she had gone to repay her debts to local Jews—scant days before they were rounded up and sent to the Great Synagogue—they had spoken to her of their urgent need to hide from men who were acting upon orders from Captain Noreika.

My journalism classes had taught me that any story required at least three sources of corroboration. I now had three sources.

How had my grandfather's crucial role remained hidden for so long? Pocius told me that he had presented his mother's information to Lithuania's Museum of Genocide Victims several years before, only to receive the reply that it was "*another* Jonas Noreika," not my grandfather, who had committed the alleged actions. I asked Pocius if he had retained a copy of that letter. He said he'd been so enraged by it that he'd thrown it away.

I assessed the facts. Captain Noreika had led the uprising in Mardosai, and probably others throughout Žemaitija. He was both ambitious and virulently antisemitic. He was the commander of the Lithuanian forces in the region at the time that the Jews were forcibly confined in the Great Synagogue. Sickened by this accumulation of evidence, I began to weep.

The single remaining shred of hope—of possible refutation—was Damijonas's insistence that my grandfather had moved to another town at the time of these events in Plungė.

Jakovas Bunka wrote that one of the Jews rounded up was Jankelis Garba, who had married a Lithuanian Catholic and converted. When he, too, was forced into the synagogue, his wife successfully implored the Reverend Povilas Pukys, the local priest who had presided at my grandparents' wedding, to get her husband released. Garba lived to tell Bunka what had befallen the rest of the town's Jews.[10]

Whitebanders guarded each of the synagogue's four entrances. The Jews were not given any food or drink, and many died of hunger and thirst. The children's crying could be heard from several blocks away. The guards fenced in the yard. Those who tried to throw food over the fence to the Jews were warned that they, too, would end up in the synagogue if they continued to help the captives. When some of those imprisoned banged on a door to beg their captors for water, the guards opened the door and gunned them down. The victims' bodies were left inside to decompose. The stench became so unbearable that some of the captives lost their minds. Others resorted to prayer.[11]

The guards commanded their prisoners to dig a hole in the synagogue's yard and to throw in all the prayer books and the Holy Ark housing the Torah: an unthinkable act of sacrilege for a Jew. Mendelis Berkovičius, Plungė's photographer, was ordered to pour gas onto the books and the sacred Torah scroll and to light the fire. The guards pushed him dangerously close to the flames, laughing mockingly. Then they selected two old Jewish men of unequal height, placed a log on their shoulders, and ordered them to walk around the bonfire. Each time the log rolled off their shoulders, they were beaten with sticks. A Jewish woman became so incensed at their mistreatment that she attacked the Whitebanders. One of them drew his pistol and shot her.

Every night another group of captive Jews was taken from the synagogue into the nearby woods and slaughtered.[12]

One Lithuanian witness to whom I spoke had been a young girl when these events transpired. She recalled having run to the woods one morning to play with her brother, and seeing clothes scattered on the ground. Among them lay a red velvet shoe, its laces untied. She assumed that the elegant shoe had belonged to a rich Jewish girl. If even a girl so young understood that Jews were being undressed, killed, and buried in the forest, clearly this was common knowledge among the townspeople.

On the first night of the mass-murder operation, the Whitebanders told the Jews that they would be transported to a hospital to recover from the effects of their captivity. So many Jews climbed into the truck that the Whitebanders had to hold some back. When no one had returned from the "hospital" by the second week, those in the synagogue suspected what had happened and resisted being put into the trucks. The Whitebanders had to devise another way to get Jews into the woods.[13]

On July 12 a fire broke out in the center of Plungė. Orė Gilisas and his son, Jewish blacksmiths who had been permitted to continue working in town, were blamed for the blaze and sent to be held in the synagogue with the others. Whitebanders ordered them to dance around the bonfire. When they tripped, they were kicked and shot.[14]

As "punishment" for the Jews' allegedly having set fire to the town, an order was given to kill all the remaining 1,800 Jews at once.

Aleksander Pakalniškis wrote that Arnoldas Pabrėža—who reported to my grandfather during the uprising—had dispatched a group of men to the Great Synagogue, where they commanded the captive Jews to march down the smoke-filled road. The prisoners proceeded down Vytautas Street and past the Catholic church to the Kaušėnai forest. Those who were too exhausted to walk were shoved into trucks and driven to their final destination. Many Lithuanians lined the streets to watch the spectacle of Jewish men, women, and children led to their deaths.[15] I can only imagine myself standing, watching as a bystander, perhaps horrified, but terrified of intervening. Or perhaps I would have thought the Jews deserved it for setting the town on fire. I don't know.

Pakalniškis recounted, "When I saw the first group of Jews led down the smoky street, I became so scared I grabbed my bike and rode out of Plungė."[16]

A teenager named Juozas Mineikis, who was hiding in the forest, witnessed the massacre. The murderers had been drinking while awaiting their victims' arrival. When the Jews saw the deep ditches that had been prepared, they panicked. Pabreža, whose grandmother was Jewish, callously addressed them in Yiddish, instructing them to remove their clothing and stand quietly in front of the ditches.[17] How unnerving it must have been to hear their murderer speaking their own language.

To save bullets, the killers snatched babies from their mothers, grabbed them by their ankles, and swung them against the trees before tossing their corpses into the pit. Some of the naked Jews who were shot fell into the ditches still alive.

When all of the Jews were dead or presumed dead, the murderers sat down to eat and resume their drinking before staggering home. A new round of killers dispatched the next round of Jews. Jews about to be shot were ordered to throw dirt over the bodies already in the pit. Each new layer of earth pitched and heaved with the last frantic struggles of individuals who had been buried alive.[18]

As it was Sunday, Pabrėža went to St. John the Baptist Church and waited for the Mass to end before directing ten congregants to accompany him to Kaušėnai. He needed their help to complete the digging. Later, these men told Bunka what they had seen.[19]

Afterward several Lithuanian men in civilian clothes rounded up hundreds of women from the synagogue and forced them three miles westward into the Kaušėnai forest. When they arrived about an hour later, they could not have failed to notice the large open graves, filled with rows of those already massacred.

The chaplain of Plunge's school, Father Petras Lygnugaris, drove up, out of breath. An eyewitness claimed that he tried to calm the Jewish women by offering to baptize them. He purportedly told them that, although he was powerless to reverse the decree against them, baptism would free them of sin and permit them to go straight to heaven. The older women did not respond. Many of the younger ones, however, seemed eager to accept this suggestion, perhaps believing they might thus be spared. Seventy-six young women stepped forward. One of them is alleged to have claimed, "We want to see Christ."

Father Lygnugaris drove to a nearby farm and returned with a bucket. After praying and making the sign of the cross, he sprinkled holy water over five or six young women at a time.

As soon as they had been baptized, the young women sank to their knees. They were ordered to crawl to a nearby pit, as the Lithuanian men trained their guns on them. One of the girls facing the pit may have declared, "We are not afraid. We will see Christ." In the next moment, she was shot in the back and fell into the grave.[20]

In 1951 Father Lygnugaris was tried for anti-Soviet speech and for "participation" in the massacre of Jews. He was sentenced to deportation to Siberia for ten years.

Aleksander Pakalniškis's *Plungė* and his other memoirs describing the atrocities were dismissed by many in Chicago's Marquette Park community.[21] After the publication of *Plungė*, Pakalniškis was generally shunned. Was this how Holocaust denial worked, I wondered?

I found a copy of Pakalniškis's book in my mother's archives—with my grandfather's name underlined in it, presumably by her.

I was struck by the contrast between Damijonas and Jakovas, two ninety-year-old Lithuanian men from the same region whose accounts could hardly have been more divergent. One saw Jonas Noreika as a hero; the other as a war criminal. An invisible barrier had separated their two worlds, whose people lived entirely separate lives; neither could fathom the other's reality.

I was haunted by the three mud pits I'd seen at Kaušėnai, and by the other burial pits in the Plungė region that I hadn't had time to see: at Šateikiai, Laumalenka, Plateliai, Vieštovėnai, Milašaičiai, Jovaišiškė, Purvaičiai, and Alsėdžiai. In the area administered by my grandfather, there were simply too many burial sites to visit. It was beyond comprehension.

I thought of all those bodies in all that mud—and of the more than two hundred other mass gravesites throughout the country. How many mass murders had been perpetrated with ruthless efficiency under Nazi orders?

Couldn't Lithuanians have dragged their feet and created delays? *And how many mass murders had been zealously committed on Lithuanian initiative?*

No wonder I dreamt of mud rising so high that, when it finally swooped down, it had the force of an avalanche.

The International Commission for the Evaluation of the Crimes of the Nazi and Soviet Occupation Regimes in Lithuania
April 10, 2019

The notion that the establishment of the ghettos created, albeit temporarily, some sort of haven for the Jews not only recycles the Nazi argument of 1941, but is deeply offensive to the memory of the inmates who perished, and also to the handful of remaining elderly survivors who suffered this unspeakable horror. The statement that "the Vilnius Jews themselves wanted to live together in the ghetto" based on the memoir of a single person, an outlier, is astonishing in its dismissal of what life in the ghetto entailed, described in numerous diaries and historical studies: death by starvation and disease, constant harassment, overcrowding and, ultimately, death at Paneriai. The Jews were the only group destined for total annihilation by the Nazis. This is what makes the Holocaust a unique event in European history and distinguishes it from other crimes against humanity during World War II.

> **A Response to the Statement of the Genocide and Resistance Research Centre of Lithuania of 27 March 2019,"On the Accusations against Jonas Noreika (General Vėtra)." The Sub-Commission for Evaluation of the Crimes of the Nazi Occupation Regime and the Holocaust (a sub-commission of the International Commission for the**

Evaluation of the Crimes of the Nazi and Soviet Occupation Regimes in Lithuania)

CHAPTER THIRTY-THREE

Killing Ground

Simon's windshield wipers swiped across the glass as we sped toward Šiauliai in a relentless downpour. He was driving one of the country's few automatic-transmission vehicles, a gray Toyota station wagon that had zig-zagged across the nation in the service of Jewish families exploring their histories. We'd resolved to visit the remains of ghettos and Jewish cemeteries, in addition to mass burial sites. Today we planned to drive three hundred miles. By now we had established a comfortable rapport, and we would have hours of uninterrupted time to talk.

We were a strange pair: a Jew whose family had suffered under the Nazi occupation escorting the granddaughter of a Nazi collaborator—and travel-ling to sites where that collaborator had probably played a role in the massacre of Jews. The road was poor, as was visibility in the persistent rain. Simon gripped the wheel with both hands.

Although his English was excellent, we spoke mostly in Lithuanian. I finally mustered the nerve to ask him how it felt to be driving around the country with the granddaughter of a man who may have orchestrated the killing of Simon's own family.

"I might not have been able to do it ten or fifteen years ago, but now I look at it more philosophically," he replied. "We can't be held responsible for our grandparents' actions."

I was relieved by his answer, but I couldn't shake my own sense of culpability—which drove my search for truth.

We spent less than an hour in Šiauliai, visiting the two sites in Kaukazas and Ežero-Trakų that had been combined to create the Šiauliai ghetto, west and south of the Frenkelis leather factory, where many of the Jews had worked. Had Simon not known exactly where to look, it would have been easy to miss. When the Soviets invaded Lithuania in 1944, their air force bombed the city, leaving widespread devastation. Only a granite memorial stone in Trakų Street now marked where the ghetto entrance had been. Standing under umbrellas in the rain, we read the inscription on a marble plaque affixed to the thigh-high stone: "On this spot July 18, 1941–July 24, 1944 stood the gates of the Šiauliai Ghetto Trakų-Ežero District."

I wished that I had a candle to place near it. Simon informed me of the Jewish custom of leaving a stone as a token of one's visit to a gravesite, to honor it. I found a small jagged rock, placed it near the marker, and stroked the granite boulder. I felt a bewildering torrent of emotions: acute sorrow; fury at the blind, ignorant hatred; and horror at the ugly realization that my grandfather was a Jew-killer.

I took a deep breath. All I could do was to honor the real past: not a whitewashed version, not a fairy tale.

I pictured the German soldiers entering the city on June 26, 1941, accompanied by local collaborators. According to Damijonas, this was the very date on which my grandfather had arrived to take up his job as the chief government official in the county. As in Plungė, hundreds of Jews immediately fled to the Soviet Union, saving their lives. At first a number of those who remained were incarcerated in the Šiauliai prison, including rabbis and the head of the Hebrew high school. Within two weeks about one thousand Jews, including their intelligentsia, had been murdered: taken ten miles away to the woods of Kužiai and forced to dig their own graves.[1] There were ten pits.

The German occupation authorities ordered the rest of Šiauliai's Jewish population to register between July 19 and 22 at the office of the civil government, the building that now displayed yet another bronze plaque as a tribute to Jonas Noreika. Preparations began that month for the establishment of a main ghetto. The project had been assigned to Gebietskommissar Hans Gewecke, who allowed my grandfather to decide which Jews could go in and out of the ghetto to work. The ghetto itself was under the jurisdiction of the Šiauliai mayor. It was determined that two hundred dilapidated houses in Kaukazas—a neighborhood facetiously named "the Caucasus" because it was situated on a mound—would serve as the ghetto.[2]

Thousands of Jews were forced to cram themselves into these confines, and the accommodations were grossly inadequate. In response to continued protests, a second location was found, 500 meters away, along Ežero and Trakų Streets. It comprised 110 houses, with a lake bordering one side. Together the two ghetto areas contained 8,000 square meters of living space: 1.5 meters per person. Many were compelled to live in attics, storerooms, stables, or cowsheds. Lithuanians guarded the ghetto's perimeter.[3]

Despite the deplorable conditions in the ghetto, Jews were desperate to enter it because those outside would be shot. Germans, along with Lithuanian collaborators who provided lists of Jews to be killed, conducted frequent *Akcijas*, massive killing sprees intended to eliminate "useless" Jews. The first victims were 47 children, 150 elderly and ill people, and 50 members of the intelligentsia. They were most likely part of the first group to be taken from the ghetto on September 11, 1941, and slaughtered in the Gubernijos forest.[4]

When the two ghettos each housed about three thousand residents, the Jews petitioned that a third ghetto be created. The Lithuanian authorities promised them an area in the Kalniukas neighborhood but demanded that a thousand Jews assemble in two synagogues and a nursing home until the new site's preparation was complete. When homeowners protested having the proposed ghetto in their neighborhood, a more convenient solution was found: the Jews were marched to Kužiai in groups of five hundred and shot. The final group of five hundred were killed in Bubiai.

By September 8, 1941, the ghetto area had been fenced in and its inhabitants forbidden to enter or to leave for work without a certificate. The city beyond the ghetto's walls had virtually been cleared of Jews; all the others had been killed in Kužiai or sent to Žagarė.[5]

We drove forty miles north to Žagarė, heading into the storm. A larger ghetto had been established there, between Daukanto, Vilniaus, Malūno, and Pakalnio and Gedimino Streets. It was surrounded by barbed wire and guarded by local activists and police. Jonas Noreika had ordered that all Jews and half-Jews in the region be transferred to Žagarė by August 29. They were brought in from Šiauliai, Joniškės, Kuršėnai, Plateliai, Žeimelis, and other towns. The Jews of Žagarė had already moved to the ghetto between July 26 and August 2.[6]

On August 25, 1941, my grandfather received a reply to his order that all remaining Jews be sent to Žagarė from the mayor of Žeimelis—this is the letter that we have already seen, in chapter 28. As it serves as proof that Jonas Noreika was meticulously informed of the mass murder of Jews, I also include it here:

Lithuanian Republic
VRM
Žeimelio district government
1941 August 25
Nr. 268
Žeimelis
     To the Šiaulių District Chair,
     In Žemelių village there were 205 Jews. As the Bolshevik army left, 44 Jews ran away. As of today, August 21, 180 have been shot.
     Now two Jewesses have returned, and they have been sent to Žagarė.
     Mayor[7]

In that same month, the Fourteenth Lithuanian Police Battalion was formed to guard warehouses, industries, and railroads in Šiauliai, Telšiai, and Plungė. This unit was also responsible for transferring Jews to Žagarė and for maintaining order and control. By September 20, there were 5,566 people living in Žagarė, 2,402 of whom were Jewish.[8]

During the last days of September, the police ordered local residents to dig a ditch in the shape of the letter *L* in the city's Naryškinas Manor Park. Perhaps the *L* shape was chosen for its patriotic significance, to denote "Lithuania." The ditch was 120 meters long, 3 meters wide, and 2 meters deep.[9]

On October 2, the German commandant ordered the Jews to assemble in the market square. There they were lined up and the men separated from the women, children, and elderly, as if to be sent off to work. When the commandant blew his whistle, partisans and police appeared and surrounded the square. The Jews attempted to escape and were shot. Wagons arrived in the marketplace and were loaded with bodies, then driven to the L-shaped ditch. The clothing and any money were taken from the victims' bodies, after which the corpses were buried in the pit. Two thousand two hundred thirty-six Jews were slaughtered in Žagarė that day: 633 men, 1,107 women, and 496 children.[10] Žagarė's mayor informed the Šiauliai District leaders that no Jewish property remained; six synagogues, the Jewish library, and all Jewish stores had been confiscated.[11]

The Žagarė ghetto was no more.

Simon had shown me a Holocaust film by Vaidas Reivytis entitled *Sunset in Lithuania*.[12] Reivytis maintained that a Nazi with a gun had sat on a balcony overlooking the market square shooting Jews who tried to flee. A witness who sat in a bakery, also overlooking the square, had noted that the belongings of the murdered Jews were loaded onto wagons and sent to Šiauliai to be distributed as gifts to the townspeople.

The drenching rain continued as we approached Žagarė. Simon and I noticed fair tents and a stage being erected. This area was renowned for its cherries, and, heedless of the weather, the residents were preparing for the annual cherry festival. We drove on, passing an unattended barricade and veering onto a dirt road, until we found the place for which we'd been searching, inside Naryškinas Manor Park.

Worried about getting stuck in the mud if he drove any farther, Simon stopped the car and pointed through the windshield. I grabbed my umbrella

The author at the gravesite of the Žagare genocide

and picked my way through the mud to the spot he had indicated, about fifty yards away. It was fenced in, the ground covered with hostas and moss, and surrounded by willow trees. My feet sank into the mud up to my ankles as I gazed at the large patch of ground. I was unable to discern an *L* shape; it appeared to be simply a long rectangle.

This is where my grandfather sent the Jews, I told myself; *2,236 bodies lie buried in this unmarked grave.* I contemplated that number. Standing there, soaked to the skin despite my umbrella, I endeavored to pray. *I have no words. I do not know what to say. But I have come. Is it enough to bear witness? What else can I do? I cannot undo the past, or redress my grandfather's actions, but I am willing to face what was done. I am sorry, so sorry, for the unimaginable loss.*

I returned to the car and wiped the mud from my feet. Simon suggested we drive into town to view the market square where the massacre had taken place.

The clouds parted for the first time that day as we passed horse stables and scarecrows perched on fences or posed on chairs in front of homes, baskets of cherries in their arms. We accidentally drove into Latvia, but quickly turned around.

After finding our way again and remarking at Žagare's colorfully painted traditional wooden houses, we parked near the infamous town square. The very sunshine felt odd—a small, welcome reprieve. Simon gestured toward the balcony from which the Nazi sniper had targeted fleeing Jews.

All around us, people clad in traditional costume thronged the square. One man stepped up and began playing an accordion, and those around him burst into song. Another group performed a spirited dance. Simon and I strolled among the booths and sampled cherry dumplings, cherry chocolate, cherry blintzes, and, best of all, cherry wine.

Vilnius
March 27, 2019

Throughout his life, Jonas Noreika placed the well-being of other citizens and the Fatherland above his own interests. He actively resisted the Nazi and Soviet occupations—for which he was imprisoned by both regimes—and [was] executed by the Soviets. Once freed from the Stutthof concentration camp, he had the opportunity to escape to the West, where his wife and young daughter waited; however, he returned to Soviet-occupied Lithuania in an attempt to unify the country's armed forces in a resistance movement that would lead to an uprising [against the Communists] for Lithuania's freedom.

"On the Accusation of Jonas Noreika (General Storm),"
Genocide and Resistance Research Centre of Lithuania

CHAPTER THIRTY-FOUR

A Stolen House

Having conducted most of my planned interviews with the surviving witnesses and completed my tour of Holocaust sites, I returned to my writing headquarters in Klaipėda to review my notes. After a long refreshing walk, I phoned my cousin Rasa, who told me that her mother, Aldona, urgently wanted to speak to me. Rasa said that her mother was known to have a remarkably keen memory, and that she wished to divulge key particulars regarding Noreika.

Fortunately, Aunt Aldona, my grandmother's niece, lived within walking distance of my current apartment. Because of her poor health, we agreed that she would throw a key down to me from her third-story window so that I could let myself in.

When I arrived, she embraced me and led me to the table. Within a few minutes her sister Rūta arrived. We shared sandwiches and discussed my impressions of Lithuania and what I'd learned about Noreika. Then, during dessert, Aldona disclosed information that changed everything I'd thought about my grandparents.

In 1941, Aldona Budrytė Bužienė was ten years old and living in Plungė in the large family home at Telšiai 65 where my grandparents' wedding reception

Aunt Rūta Budrytė and Aunt Aldona Budrytė Bužienė in Klaipeda. Photo taken in July 2013 at the home of Aunt Aldona.

was held. She remembered visiting the Noreikas at the Mardosai schoolhouse in the months before the uprising against the Soviets. Uncle Jonas was usually not present, she said, but she played with her two-year-old cousin Dalytė (my mother).

A few days before the uprising, my grandfather advised Aldona's family to leave Plungė temporarily. They travelled in a horse-drawn carriage to Barstyčiai, where they stayed with Aldona's grandparents.

A few days later, Aldona's family returned to Plungė, and the Noreikas lived with them for about a week, until a house in the center of Plungė "became suddenly free." Uncle Jonas moved his family into the newly vacated house, settling there for "not long," before relocating with his family to Šiauliai.

I choked on my crumble cake. "What do you mean by 'suddenly free'?" I asked.

"The Jews were gone, so the house was free. Many Lithuanians were moving into the new, free houses."

I took a deep breath. "Do you mean the houses became free because the Jews who lived in them were killed?"

She nodded, with pain showing in her eyes.

I sat stunned for a moment. "But Damijonas said my grandparents stayed in Barstyčiai and Telšiai the whole time," I told her. "Nobody said anything about moving into a house in Plungė."

"I was *there*, and I happen to have a very good memory," she responded.

"She most definitely does," her sister Rūta affirmed.

"Which house did they move into?" I managed to ask.

"It was a two-story building, two doors away from a prominent corner. My mother took me there often. We climbed a staircase to the second floor, where we could view the Kromas, a large marketplace. My mother spent most of her time speaking to your grandmother, while I spent most of my time playing with Dalytė and Teta Antanina."

My heart was pounding. *A prominent corner?* The whereabouts of my grandfather and his family during the June 1941 uprising had become a critical issue because it could determine the extent of his involvement in the murder of Jews. Damijonas had reassured me that my grandfather couldn't possibly have been killing Jews in Plungė in late June and July of 1941 because he was nowhere near there during the massacres; he was in Telšiai at that time. Aldona's assertions entirely contradicted Damijonas's claims. The fact that Damijonas had lied about my grandfather's movements during the uprising indicated that he knew about my grandfather's deeds. Jonas Noreika, later to become General Storm, had been at the very center of the repugnant events.

Aldona remembered seeing Uncle Jonas in a military uniform and recalled his having met many times with other soldiers—including his messenger, Damijonas.

"Damijonas said he only became his messenger in Šiauliai," I countered.

"That's not true. He was Uncle's messenger in Plungė, as well. He came almost every day. There was always a big fuss when he arrived. Everybody would say, 'Damijonas is here! Damijonas is here!'"

"Aren't you confusing this with Šiauliai?"

"We didn't visit them very often in Šiauliai," answered Aldona. "No, this was in Plungė."

Damijonas had said nothing about his serving as Noreika's messenger during and immediately after the uprising in Plungė.

"But Damijonas said my grandfather did not live in Plungė—that he lived in Telšiai after the uprising," I protested weakly.

Aldona crossed her arms, stiffened her back, leaned forward, and looked me straight in the eyes. "I'm sorry, but I'm a Žemaitė, and I have to tell it the way it happened. Damijonas is a liar!"

People from Žemaitija are known for speaking bluntly, a trait upon which they pride themselves. I sat back in my chair, stunned.

Nevertheless, I felt compelled to pursue the matter. "Who ordered the Jews to be killed?"

"The Jews brought it upon themselves by setting the fire," replied Aldona. "I don't believe the killings were Uncle Jonas's initiative. He was a Lithuanian officer. He was so talented, so smart. He fought for our independence. He was a true Lithuanian patriot. I still bow my head to him."

Despite myself, I persisted. "But if he was living right there at the time, as you said, and if he was the head of the uprising, as Damijonas and many others have told me, wouldn't he have been the one to give the order? Who else would have had the authority?"

For a minute or two, Aldona did not respond. She must have been piecing together the events, as I had been doing during the past several weeks. Then she shook her head and began to weep. "I can't believe it! I just can't believe it! Maybe he had no choice. Nobody really knows how that fire started. It's still a mystery. And he had to maintain order. If the Jews hadn't started the fire, they might still be alive. I don't know. I don't know what to think anymore! I suppose it's possible."

I sat quietly. I knew that realization and acknowledgment would come to her slowly, over time.

After a long moment, I asked, "So which was his house, exactly?"

"I don't know the address, but I can describe where it is and what it looks like. It's still there, near the Kromas. If you look out the window from the second floor, you can see the marketplace. The house is on a major corner."

"Good. We're going to figure this out. What did the house look like inside?"

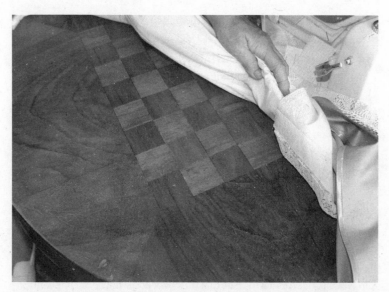

The chess table at Aunt Dana's house in Šiauliai. It was taken from a house in Plungė that had belonged to Jews.

Aldona recalled the fine furniture, especially a round table engraved with a chessboard pattern. "Uncle Jonas loved to play chess. Everyone who visited admired that chess table and the handsome chess pieces sitting on top."

Remembering the table that my Aunt Dana had shown me in Šiauliai, I took my camera from my purse and scrolled through my digital photos to find the picture of it. I showed it to Aunt Aldona. "Was it *this* table?"

"Yes! That's the one! Where did you get that picture?"

I told her about my trip to Šiauliai a few weeks earlier and repeated Dana's story about how she had acquired the table. "So the furniture travelled from that house in Plungė to my grandfather's new home in Šiauliai!" I concluded.

The house in which he had lived in Plungė, and his very furniture—which he must have transported to his next residence—would have been stolen Jewish property.

Later that evening, back in my borrowed apartment, I reflected on my good fortune in having been offered this place by my friend's sister. Otherwise I would never have found myself in Klaipėda, which I had considered irrelevant to my grandfather's life. And yet here I had stumbled on an important witness whose testimony destroyed the last of the excuses that could be made for him.

The next day I contacted the librarian in Plungė, Zita Palauskaitė, whom I had met during a previous trip. She told me that many houses in the vicinity belonged to Jews who had escaped or had been slaughtered during and after the uprising. Surprisingly and serendipitously, she had been compiling a catalogue of the houses formerly owned by Jews to honor the memory of the town's Jewish residents. Elated, incredulous, I described the house Aldona had told me my grandparents lived in to her, reading from my notes: "On Kulių Street, right on the corner.... It was a big apartment. All the furniture was originally from Jews."

Zita promised to send me a photo of the house that she thought might be the right one. I forwarded the picture that she emailed me to Rasa, who showed it to Aldona. But Aldona told me that this was not the house she'd meant. She offered more identifying details. "It was a former Jewish house that became free. It was on the side of town that had brick houses. Uncle and his family lived on the second floor. On the other side were all the wooden Jewish houses."

I related the new details to Zita by phone and email. She sent another picture, then a third and a fourth, each of which Rasa showed to her mother— only to have Aldona reject each one. But when she saw a picture of the fifth possibility, she instantly exclaimed, "Yes, that's it!"

The grainy photograph, taken in the 1950s, shows a two-story wooden structure with a slanted roof with a chimney and two or three windows on each floor facing the street. Its address, Vaižganto 11, was utterly damning.[1]

The Great Synagogue of Plungė was one house away from my grandparents' house.

The Great Synagogue had been built in 1814, a plastered-brick edifice measuring ninety-five by seventy-two feet with a gently sloping roof. Its stately prayer hall featured arches, flat classical columns, and fourteen windows. At the center of its southeastern wall was the Holy Ark containing the Torah scrolls.[2] This is where Plungė's Jews were imprisoned in horrific conditions— denied food and water for days, their children's cries audible blocks away, the

The house into which my grandparents moved, formerly owned by Leibas and Rocha Orlanskis, on Vaižganto 11. The Great Synagogue of Plungė, which served as a ghetto in 1941, is seen to the left. My grandparents would have lived there during the month of July 1941 before moving to Šiauliai in August 1941.

smell of decaying bodies driving people out of their minds—before they were marched into the woods and shot.

It was impossible for my grandmother not to have known what was happening in that synagogue.

And why otherwise would she have asked me not to pursue this story? I was incensed at the magnitude of the cover-up, the lies I had been told by my own family.

Zita told me that the home in which my grandparents had lived in Plungė belonged to Leibas and Rocha Orlanskis, who were believed to have fled the town just before the uprising. Leibas was later sent to a Siberian prison, where he languished for fifteen years. Upon his release, he and his wife moved to Israel.

I spent days staring at the photograph of his former home.[3] As my old naïveté and denial were replaced by dread certainty and a devastating awareness of betrayal, I began to vibrate with anger. A peculiar icicle formed in my throat and extended into my belly. All of my uncertainty about writing this story vanished, and I vowed to finish it if it was the last thing I did.

Damijonas's duplicity was finally exposed. Having doubted him for some time, I now knew him to have been a willing accomplice in the monstrous crimes perpetrated by Jonas Noreika—my grandfather.

I confronted Damijonas. "I spoke with my Aunt Aldona, who was ten at the time, and she said my grandfather lived in the center of Plungė, in a home left by a Jew, across the street from the police station. He was *right there* during the uprising. What do you have to say to that?"

"Aldona is lying," he replied. "She was too young to remember anything. Your grandfather was in Telšiai when everything happened. He did not live in Plungė. He had nothing to do with it. It was the Germans."

It took all my powers of restraint not to throttle him.

Vilnius

October 1, 2018

The prosecution, depending on S. Foti's witness, includes a photograph of a home seized from Jews in Plungė on Vaižganto Street to indicate where J. Noreika lived. However, her witness cannot be considered historically reliable because, at that time, S. Foti was not born. In addition, according to the Lithuanian Central Archives of 1942 residencies, nobody by the name of J. Noreika ever lived in Plungė on Vaižganto Street. J. Noreika, as a home owner, does not exist.

Vilnius Regional Administrative Court

File No. el-4215-281/2018

Response from the Genocide Resistance and Research Centre to the prosecution's claim against the Genocide Centre's refusal to change its historical conclusion on Jonas Noreika

CHAPTER THIRTY-FIVE

Acts of Remembrance

Lithuanian tradition dictates that a gravesite include a headstone and a small garden, filled with colorful flowers during the spring and summer and with lit candles in the fall and winter. Its borders should be marked with stones, bricks, or a low fence. Family members are expected to visit often to tend the garden and pray.

Anyone unable to fulfill these devotional duties commonly asks a close friend to perform them. Of course, this request represents an imposition, as frequent visits are time-consuming. Therefore, it is customary to repay one's friend with a bottle of vodka, gifts for the children, and Easter and Christmas presents. If one does not have a close friend to undertake the task, a distant acquaintance, a friend of a friend, or even a stranger must be sought. The arrangement usually entails a payment plan. A neglected gravesite that goes to weed is likely to become an eyesore, signaling that the family must not love its deceased member. Such disgrace must be avoided.

When my brother and I buried our mother and grandmother in Vilnius, we had no idea how challenging the care of their gravesite would become. Initially our relatives agreed to maintain it, but all were nearly eighty years old or else lived far from the cemetery. They had to make the trip by bus, laden

The gravesite of my mother Dalia Kučėnienė and grandmother Antanina Noreikienė, who were buried in October 2000 in Antakalniai, Vilnius. This photo was taken in July 2013.

with a bucket, broom, rags, and candles. Because we lived five thousand miles away, Ray and I had designed the memorial site to be as maintenance-free as possible, with granite all around instead of earth and greenery. Nonetheless, our relatives were required to pay at least two visits a year: to dust and clean the marble, to pull the weeds, and to leave flowers or a wreath and burning candles at Easter and on All Souls' Day.

My relatives in Vilnius graciously obliged me for a few years before phoning me in Chicago one day, in tears, to tell me that they could no longer carry out the task; they could barely walk. Although I understood, I hung up almost in tears myself. Who would maintain my mother's and grandmother's gravesite?

Unexpectedly, my father's second wife offered to have her adult children in Kaunas assume this responsibility. Twice a year, they travelled from Kaunas to Vilnius, sometimes by bus, sometimes with friends or in their own cars. But after nearly a decade, it became clear that this duty was becoming too onerous for them.

On this trip, I had visited all of my relatives' graves, sometimes escorted by Simon. I asked almost everyone I knew—my family, Simon, even Damijonas—whether they could recommend someone to care for my mother's and grandmother's gravesite. No one seemed able to do so.

In Rainiai, Simon took me to a chapel expressly built to honor seventy-four Lithuanians killed by the Communists on June 24, 1941. They were politicians, teachers, lawyers, landowners, farmers, businessmen, and high school students whom the Communists had captured and held as political prisoners in the Telšiai prison. Some were thought to have been arrested for owning a tri-colored Lithuanian flag or literature advocating national independence. When the Nazis invaded, the Communists decided to kill these captives rather than releasing them. On the night of the feast day of Saint John the Baptist, they loaded the prisoners into trucks, drove two miles southeast to a forest in Rainiai, murdered them, and then disfigured some of them before burying them.[1] The Nazi propaganda machine proclaimed that several of the massacre's organizers were Russian Jews, accompanied by "local collaborators"—a term that most Lithuanians would interpret as yet another reference to Jews. Thus, the seventy-four men came to be regarded as martyrs who had defended their country against the Communists and Jews. This allowed local Lithuanians to claim that their uprising against the Communists, during which so many Jews were slaughtered, had been instigated in self-defense.[2] Years later, Lithuanians alleged that the Communists were perpetrators of a "genocide," and demanded their extradition for trial. Calculatingly, their claim mirrored that of Jews seeking to bring to justice the Lithuanians who had collaborated in the Holocaust. Many responsible for the carnage had gone to the United States, Canada, South America, or Australia.

The Rainiai Chapel of Torment was built in 1991 to commemorate the fiftieth anniversary of the Communists' murder of the seventy-four Lithuanians. It was a small white-and-gray building whose mainly white stained-glass windows were flecked with red, signifying drops of blood. When Simon and I arrived late on a Monday afternoon, the chapel was closed. I admired its design and noted its prominent setting next to the highway. I read the names of the martyrs and prayed.

Simon then led me across the highway to a shabby sign informing the reader that five hundred Jewish women and children had been massacred in the forest there; an arrow indicated the location of the mass grave. I recalled with disgust how on June 27, 1941, Nazis and Lithuanian collaborators had ordered Jewish men to exhume the Lithuanian martyrs, wash their bodies, and lick their decayed wounds.[3]

I compared the relevant dates with my grandfather's June 24, 1941, arrival in Telšiai. He had arrived on the day the martyrs were killed there, four days before the Jews were ordered to dig up their bodies.[4] Who had issued that revolting order? *My grandfather had been right there.*

During the martyrs' funeral procession on Tuesday, July 1, 1941, thirty Jewish men were forced to kneel on the street facing the cemetery. Five hundred Jewish women and children were marched to a camp in Geruliai. Some months later they were brought back to a camp in Telšiai, and on December 23 they were taken two miles southeast to the forest in Rainiai and told to undress in front of a burial pit.[5]

Simon and I, exhausted from a long day spent visiting Holocaust sites, decided to forgo hiking into the forest to see the Jewish memorial. As many as 7,500 Jews had been murdered in the region surrounding Telšiai,[6] but the 500-yard walk on an uneven trail would have afforded us only a view of a small rock with a plaque. The next day, feeling rested, I regretted not having made that effort.

The harsh contrast between the two memorials—the dignified Chapel of Torment honoring seventy-four Lithuanian men and the simple stone marking the burial site of 7,500 Jews from the same area—could not have been more telling.[7] This was a country of gravesites, where everyone compared their family members' headstones and cemetery-plot maintenance to that of their neighbors. Simon wondered aloud, "Why does our government spend so much money for seventy-four Lithuanians and so little for 7,500 Jews?" The question went straight to the heart of the matter. And the answer was self-evident: Lithuanians refused to recognize their role in the deaths of Jews, and they refused to accord Jews—in death as in life—the same honor and dignity shown to their "own" dead. The Jews, despite having been Lithuanian, were eternally "the other." The lack of will even to acknowledge this obdurate antisemitism meant that there was no guilt or shame, either—without which there could be no self-knowledge, no remorse, and no atonement. Without an admission of guilt there was no way to tell the truth about the complex fabric of Lithuania's history— just as it was impossible for me to see the reality about my own family until I had given up the fairy tales that I had been told all my life about my grandfather the hero. Ironically, the truth about Jonas Noreika and Lithuania not only made me more broken. It also made me more whole, connected me more deeply to my heritage.

At Paneriai, the site of the second-largest massacre in all of Eastern Europe—after Babi Yar in the Ukraine—70,000 Jews were buried in mass graves. In 1940, when the Russians invaded Lithuania, they dug seven pits in Paneriai Woods, about seven miles outside of Vilnius.[8] The ditches, measuring 112 feet wide and five feet deep, were originally intended to store fuel tanks. When the Germans marched in, however, they recognized that the pits, conveniently prepared in advance, would be useful for burying Jews. Within four months, the Nazis' Einsatzkommando 9, their elite killing unit, had massacred about half of Vilnius's Jewish population. They were greatly assisted by local Lithuanians.[9]

Three years later, when the Soviets invaded Lithuania once again, the Nazis resolved to eradicate all evidence of the bloodbath. They commanded that the bodies be dug up and burned.

I approached the Soviet-era memorial there and read the inscription. It noted the 70,000 "Soviet citizens" killed at the site. I stared at the phrase: "Soviet citizens." The fact that the Russians hadn't even used the word "Jew" when describing the deaths in Paneriai rendered the loss of Jewish lives invisible. Everyone killed, without distinction, had simply been deemed a Soviet citizen. If there was no evidence of Jews' ever having been in Lithuania, the country could hardly have known a Holocaust! The memorial itself was intended to mislead.

Of course, I was not the only one to regard this erasure as unconscionable. To recognize and honor the dead appropriately, a second monument had been

At the Paneriai Memorial with Simon Dovidavičius, a Holocaust guide who was the director of Sugihara House in Kaunas

brought from Tel Aviv in July 1991, displaying a Star of David at the top and a menorah at the bottom. On its face was a Hebrew inscription, while on the back was the text that was translated into Russian, Lithuanian, and English:

> Eternal memory of 70,000 Jews of Vilnius
> and its environs who were murdered and
> burnt, here in Paneriai, by Nazi executioners
> and their accomplices

Because Israeli president Shimon Peres was visiting Lithuania that day—August 1, 2013—a number of Lithuanian Jews had gathered at the foot of this impressive marker for a commemoration ceremony. Men wearing kippas (skullcaps) milled about, as did Lithuanian soldiers in green uniforms. They affixed yellow crime-scene tape marked "Caution" to a number of trees to create a secure perimeter.

While waiting for the event to begin, Simon and I viewed the place where the Nazis had shot up to four thousand Jews at a time into pits, in layers.

The ceremony began with mournful violin music and a Yiddish song about Vilnius. Lithuanian president Dalia Grybauskaitė addressed those assembled:

> We are standing on the land where the blood of thousands of innocent people was spilled. Most probably, the right thing to do would be to stand in silence, because it is hard to find the words that describe the evil of the Holocaust. One hundred thousand people, mostly Jews, were mass-murdered here during World War II. All of them had names, families, home, and occupation. They were our friends and neighbors who lived and worked in Lithuania and for Lithuania.

Then Israeli president Peres, who would turn ninety years old the following day, intoned solemnly,

> I meet the trees of Ponar and I can hear the words and cries of the murdered brothers and sisters.... The pastoral scenery is misleading. The grass remains green, but the ground is red. Screams emanate from the damp soil, and are a disgrace to humanity.... There were no gas chambers here, just murder. Soldiers pressing the trigger, one after the other, day in and day out, five hundred a day, no interruptions, no second thoughts. These were killers. So few survived. From their scorched bodies, we hear their eternal spirit, which has faced evil. In Vilnius, there were 200 churches and 110 synagogues, but there is one Lord for all of us. Let us convert souls into friendship. Let us pray for peace.
>
> One and a half million children were murdered. Always teach children to withstand the darkness. Lithuania has begun to take on this duty with responsibility. Educate its youth about the

shameful stain so it will never happen again. The key to raising a new, tolerant generation is to face the horrors of history. Painful memories are etched into our hearts, yet high hopes beat in our souls—not to forget, not to forgive, but to pray.

I visited my mother's and grandmother's gravesite in Vilnius three times during my trip. On one occasion, I told Simon that my grandfather was also to have been interred there. My mother had acquired this gravesite for him, but—because his body never was identified—she was unable to bury his remains. She died only four years later.

As I spoke, I dusted and then polished the marble headstone. The eight-foot square covered in granite depicted the Columns of Gediminas, an early symbol of Lithuania and one of its coats of arms. The headstone had the same theme. On the horizontal pillar was inscribed:

"My God, I remain the way you called me…
Allow me to be near, allow the tired to be warmed
In Your Love's fire, O God."
From Jonas Noreika's prayer in Stutthof

I visited again with a friend of my mother's, who thought that the gravesite looked too austere. She suggested that several bushes be planted on one side. I considered this suggestion for weeks. She was willing to purchase and plant the bushes and to care for them. It was a generous offer. But I eventually felt compelled to decline. She was over seventy years old and would have had to enlist the help of her younger relatives to ensure that the bushes did not become unruly, overtaking the gravesite. It was better to have it look stark than neglected.

On my third visit to the cemetery, I was accompanied by Sakalas Goro-deckis, whose father, Stasys, had been my grandfather's right-hand man in the resistance movement. Stasys had died in 2002; his gravesite was in the same cemetery. I was greatly relieved when Sakalas agreed to look after my mother's and grandmother's gravesite. He, his wife, one of their sons, and I set to work cleaning it. When we finished, I left two candles in glass lanterns, to protect the flames from the wind—symbolizing prayers that would burn for days. So many memories wavered and burned in my heart.

The last gravesite that I visited was my grandfather's. His still unidentified remains reposed somewhere in the Memorial Complex of the Tuskulėnai Peace Park in Vilnius, built on twelve acres in 2008. Many of the prisoners who had been killed by the KGB were laid to rest there, beneath a hill near the Neris River, in an underground burial chamber resembling a mausoleum. At the top of the hill danced a circle of orange and red flames fashioned of steel, an eternal bonfire for the prisoners who were nameless in death. Several of them were believed to have murdered Jews. A lot of people thought that no Jew-killer—like my grandfather—should have his bones accorded such dignity. But how to separate the unidentified heroes from the Jew-killers?

Nearby, the Tuskulėnai Manor Museum displayed shoes, buttons, fragments of combs, and prayer books that had belonged to KGB prison inmates. A soundtrack of beating drums accompanied by the tapping of old typewriter keys played. I found my grandfather's file: "He was sentenced to death on November 20–22, 1946, by the FSSR Vilnius Garrison Military Tribunal according to Article 58-1a of the RSFSR penal code.... He was arrested for voluntarily working for the Germans between 1941 and 1946.... He was shot on February 26, 1947."

Major Vasily Dolgiev, a notorious drunkard who personally killed 650 people, may have been the one to execute my grandfather. Once the men had been shot, the bodies were stripped, loaded onto a truck at night, covered by a tarpaulin, and buried on the grounds of Tuskulėnai Manor under the watch of NKGB–MGB soldiers. Trenches were used repeatedly, with new bodies thrown on top of the old ones. The burials were referred to as the "disposal of the contingent."

Entering the burial chamber, I passed a cement gate in the shape of a double cross. At first the interior was pitch black, but my steps evidently activated a series of light switches. A tall circular set of shelves stood in the center of the room. Each square in every row held a numbered steel box. Inside each box lay the bones of an unidentified prisoner. There were 717 boxes. I walked around the entire structure, wondering which box contained my grandfather's bones. I looked for the containers numbered 550 and 551, which the archaeologists had originally believed to be his. There I stopped, bewildered. Despite two attempts, my grandfather's DNA had never been identified. Perhaps this was fitting, some kind of cosmic justice. After all, his victims had been no more than numbers to him. All those thousands of Jews had been innocent of any crime. I paused for a moment in the artificial light—not to forget, not to forgive, but to pray.

CHAPTER THIRTY-SIX

Storm in the Fatherland

For many years I assumed that I was the only one willing to expose my grandfather's role in the Holocaust. The weight of this undertaking seemed unbearable: I felt like I was carrying the whole reputation of my ancestral country on my shoulders. But eventually I learned of others who were also investigating Jonas Noreika's acts during the Nazi occupation. Prominent among them was Grant Gochin, an American Jew of Lithuanian descent who had lost more than one hundred relatives in the Holocaust in Lithuania. In early 2018 he engaged the services of Lithuanian researchers Andrius Kulikauskas and Evaldas Balčiūnas.

Balčiūnas was the first to disclose my grandfather's true wartime record to the English-speaking world. The web journal Defending History, which is edited by Vilnius-based Dovid Katz but is in English, published Balčiūnas's article in 2012.[1] I had read it several times in the year before my summer trip to Lithuania; it strengthened my conviction to persevere. Balčiūnas and Katz had both endured harassment by the Lithuanian government, lost their jobs, and been followed and interrogated by the police. Eventually, they were declared "enemies of the state." These men are true heroes of Lithuania who took enormous risks to publicize the story in spite of the nation's determination to maintain its tale of innocence at all costs.

After my return from Lithuania in 2013, it took another five years for me to complete my book. I was facing another tremendous psychological battle at home, with my daughter's heroin addiction. Our family's anxiety and anguish over her inability to stop her self-destructive behavior absorbed most of our energy. But our struggle was to no avail. On October 22, 2015, Alessandra Foti succumbed to an overdose. She was twenty-one years old. Our family collapsed in grief, the loss so acute I questioned the meaning of every aspect of my life.

For a long time I was unable to return to my manuscript. At last I resolved to resume writing, perhaps with a new sense of clarity about what truly matters: using one's time to do what is right. At that point the worst had already happened to me.

In March of 2018, having completed a draft of my manuscript, I created a related website, hoping to attract media attention. Andrius Kulikauskas, who at that point had been conducting research for some weeks, got in touch with me almost immediately. It was he who informed me of Grant Gochin's lawsuit against the Genocide and Resistance Research Centre of Lithuania, requesting that it cease honoring Jonas Noreika. I was stunned. *A lawsuit about my grandfather against a Lithuanian government agency? How many others were aware of this issue? How big would this story get?*

Andrius also related how Evaldas Balčiūnas had visited Plungė, where he had learned from Zita Paulauskaitė that my aunt had identified the house, formerly owned by Jews, into which my grandparents had moved. Similar details were becoming public knowledge.

When Andrius asked whether I wanted to communicate with Gochin, at first I was distressed. *What would this Jew, whose relatives may have been killed by my own grandfather, have to say to me?* I imagined his lashing out, vowing vengeance against me and my family.

It took me weeks to muster the courage to email Grant. *Having spent the last twenty years investigating my grandfather's past, shouldn't I attempt to get in touch with the descendants of those he had harmed?* And so, with trepidation, on April 19, 2018, I sent him a message:

Dear Mr. Grant Gochin,

I believe you know who I am, the granddaughter of Jonas Noreika.

After nearly two decades of research, I have come to the same conclusion as you have about my grandfather. For me, this is heartbreaking, but I am finally ready to begin speaking about this more publicly.

As you know, Andrius Kulikauskas has been in touch with me, and ever since I have been thinking about our strange connection. I have promised to write him a letter about my findings.

In the meantime, I was hoping that we could begin to talk to each other, perhaps initially by phone, and perhaps eventually in person.

Within days, we spoke on the phone. To my relief, Gochin was understanding; he did not blame me for Jonas Noreika's actions. Once we had compared notes, our independent investigations revealed that some of Gochin's relatives must indeed have been murdered by my grandfather. Many of Gochin's family members had lived in Papilė, a small town under Noreika's jurisdiction during the Nazi occupation. They were rounded up upon his direction and transported to the Žagarė ghetto, where they were murdered in October 1941. These victims included Grant's grandfather's first cousin, Meyer Simon Gochin; Meyer's wife, Rochel Reiza (née Gittelson); their daughter, Miriam; Miriam's son, Raymond; his uncle Mones and aunt Tsipa; and Grant's grandfather's first cousin Tsile, along with her five children.

Grant said that his cousin Sonia Beder, a Holocaust survivor, had testified that, three days before the Nazi occupation, armed Lithuanians had prevented the six thousand Jews in Biržai from escaping to the Soviet Union. Eighth-grade boys from the local school were recruited to shoot Jews. Armed Lithuanian men plundered Jewish homes, fatally beating their residents and humiliating, raping, and killing girls. They set Rabbi Bernshteyn's beard on fire and branded his body with hot irons before shooting him. Sonia endured a series of perils in Telšiai, Geruliai, and Tryškiai, ending up in the Šiauliai ghetto. She would go on to survive the Dachau concentration camp.

It did not take long for me and Grant to decide to join forces. We had no idea how effective our partnership would become. It generated so much media attention that we soon found ourselves embroiled in a disinformation campaign by the Genocide and Resistance Research Centre. The resulting publicity caused an international scandal and a public-relations disaster for the Lithuanian government.

While I had concentrated my efforts on verifying my grandfather's collaboration with the Nazis and his responsibility for thousands of Jewish deaths, Gochin had catalyzed an initiative in Lithuania to expose a number of men who had played roles in the Holocaust and who were being lauded as heroes by the Genocide and Resistance Research Centre. In 2015 he had embarked on a campaign to have my grandfather's plaque removed from the Wroblewski Library of the Lithuanian Academy of Sciences in Vilnius. Despite widespread media coverage and a petition signed by nineteen prominent Lithuanian politicians, writers, and historians, the government refused to get rid of the plaque.[2]

In June of 2018, Gochin presented to the Genocide and Resistance Research Centre Andrius Kulikauskas's extensively researched challenge of its denial of Noreika's crimes against humanity. I submitted an affidavit of support that detailed the results of my investigation.

And in an effort to promote public awareness of this subject, I published an article on Salon.com in July 2018. To my surprise, it caused a political and cultural earthquake, followed by several aftershocks. The article received extensive coverage in Lithuania for weeks. I was still more surprised when the *New York Times* accorded the findings of my investigation front-page coverage on September 11, 2018, and when the *Chicago Tribune* featured the story on its front page on January 14, 2019.

After the Salon article, the effort to remove the plaque honoring General Storm was taken up by the Lithuanian Jewish Community. The American Jewish Committee joined in shortly thereafter. In September 2018, amid growing international attention, Lithuania's foreign minister urged the relevant authorities to discard the plaque. This was the first time a Lithuanian government official had taken such a stand.

Yet despite the international media attention, the fairy tale of the heroic Jonas Noreika prevailed in Lithuania. The mayor of Vilnius declared that his hands were tied by the Genocide and Resistance Research Centre's conclusions. Everyone in the country seemed to have the same rationale; their position was "informed" by the centre's decisions.

Grant Gochin's case was heard by the Vilnius Regional Administrative Court on March 5, 2019. The Genocide and Resistance Research Centre argued that Gochin had no material interest in its certificate regarding Noreika. On March 27, 2019, the court rendered its verdict. It dismissed the lawsuit, declining to judge the truthfulness of the centre's answers but declaring that the centre had answered Gochin's query completely, objectively, and without abuse of power. The court demanded that Grant pay the centre's expenses in defending the case. Gochin called the court costs "a Jew tax."

Andrius Kulikauskas had been scheduled to give a press conference and lead a discussion entitled "How Can We Take Responsibility for Lithuania's Past, Present and Future?" at the Vilnius County Adomas Mickevičius Public Library on the day after the verdict. The event was to be filmed. Hours after the verdict, the centre successfully pressured the library to cancel the event, raising the question: How much control does the Genocide and Resistance Research Centre exert in this country?

The centre misrepresented its court victory as a validation of its rosy view of Jonas Noreika. On the day of the verdict it posted a series of over-the-top assertions: that "the Nazi occupation regime in Lithuania operated differently than in other countries," that "residents of occupied Lithuania in 1941 didn't understand ghettos as part of the Holocaust," and that Noreika was not a collaborator but rather a member of the anti-Nazi underground which rescued Jews.

The Simon Wiesenthal Center's chief Nazi-hunter, American-born Israeli historian Dr. Efraim Zuroff, described the court's decision as "absolutely ludicrous and an insult to victims of the Nazis [and to] survivors the world over. In Lithuania, Nazi killers are glorified and their bloody past ignored, as if the Jewish citizens murdered there are of no concern to the country."

The Lithuanian Jewish Community also expressed profound disappointment, demanding that "representatives of the Lithuanian executive and legislative branches respond appropriately and in a timely manner by condemning this incident of institutional antisemitism, and that the Centre take responsibility and publicly retract the text, apologise to the [Lithuanian Jewish Community] for the gross belittlement of the scope of the Holocaust, and apologise to the Lithuanian public for misinforming [the public]."

On April 8, 2019, Stanislovas Tomas, a Lithuanian running for election to the European Union Parliament, was filmed smashing the Jonas Noreika commemorative plaque with a sledgehammer. He called the police and was duly arrested. Vilnius mayor Remigijus Šimašius denounced the act as hooliganism but said he would not replace the plaque—it was not his administration's responsibility. The illegal destruction of the plaque demonstrated the frustration many feel at the Lithuanian government's failure to take a stand against Holocaust perpetrators. The verdict vindicating Jonas Noreika still stands, as do several street signs, the school named after him, and the marble block bearing his name on the wall of the Museum of Genocide Victims. The posthumously conferred Cross of the Vytis medal has not been revoked.

On April 11, 2019, the International Commission for the Evaluation of the Crimes of the Nazi and Soviet Occupation Regimes in Lithuania also weighed in, condemning the lawsuit's verdict. The International Holocaust Remembrance Alliance followed suit.

Then the Vilnius mayor changed his mind about the plaque and ordered city workers to reassemble and rehang it within ten days. Meanwhile flowers, candles, and photographs of Jonas Noreika were placed where the plaque had hung, and round-the-clock vigils were held there.

That is when I wrote a petition and letter, with Andrius's and Grant's help, calling the nation to revoke honors given to my grandfather. Since then, about a thousand people have signed it.

Petition
Remove all honors awarded to
my grandfather Jonas Noreika

I am Silvia Foti, granddaughter of Jonas Noreika. The facts about my Grandfather have been clearly established. The convoluted gymnastics of the Genocide and Resistance Research Centre of Lithuania to deny his culpability is a stain on the nation and an abuse of the memory and dignity of my Grandfather's victims.

I cannot stand by and watch the deceptive distortions and revisionism by the Government of Lithuania in order to validate its conduct in reforming my Grandfather into a national hero. He was not. My Grandfather was a Holocaust perpetrator, and he was not alone. Lithuania has the freedom—and responsibility—to look at the actions of Lithuanians during the Holocaust. We must face our grandparents' misdeeds. It is time.

I urge the Government of Lithuania to tell the truth, and to remove all honors awarded to my Grandfather. Simply as a matter of respect to his victims. I ask all freedom and peace-loving Lithuanians to sign this petition in the name of regret, sorrow, and respect for Jonas Noreika's victims.

Letter
It is Time for Lithuania to Acknowledge
Its Role in the Holocaust

The plaque honoring my grandfather, Jonas Noreika, on the Wroblewski Library in Vilnius has turned into a flashpoint between those who believe he should continue to be honored as a hero and those who believe he is guilty of willingly participating in the Holocaust.

For much too long, the discussion of Lithuania's role in the killing of 200,000 Jews in 1941 has been buried because it has been too painful to work through the collective guilt.

It has been too easy to cast blame on everyone else but the Lithuanians—it was the Germans who "forced" the Lithuanians into killing Jews, or the victims themselves deserved it. They were Communists after all, including the babies and grandmothers. The Jews stole from Lithuanians who had no choice but to defend their country and honor. Killing Jews meant killing Communists, end of story.

This form of denial and obfuscation worked during the Soviet occupation when Lithuanians were not allowed to analyze their history, when it was forbidden to discuss anything except what they were told to evaluate.

But now that the country has been free for nearly 30 years, Lithuania has the freedom—and responsibility—to look at its actions during the Holocaust squarely in the eye.

We must face our grandparents' misdeeds. It is time.

My grandfather agreed to be the head of the Šiauliai district during the Nazi occupation. Nobody "forced" him into that position. It was a huge promotion for him. He was only 30 years old. Nobody "dragged" him into living in the best house in Šiauliai or into accepting a salary of 1,000 rubles/month. For him it was an honor and his family lived in style.

In fact, he tried to convince other Lithuanians into taking leadership roles in the government during the Nazi occupation. Documents prove this. Several Lithuanians refused. They knew what it meant to be a leader during that time period. And yet my grandfather didn't?

Nobody "coerced" him into signing a document on August 22, 1941 to send Jews into a ghetto in Žagarė. My grandfather was a brilliant lawyer, a captain in the Army, who was also a creative writer. He certainly had the imagination to understand what would happen to those Jews once they were rounded up into the ghetto.

Two months earlier, he led the uprising in Żemaitija, with his headquarters based in Mardosai, just outside of Plungė. By mid-July 1941, 1,800 Jews were rounded up into a Synagogue, which served as a ghetto, and then marched into the woods and shot, one by one. Plungė has the unfortunate distinction of being the first city in Europe where Jews were killed on a massive scale during World War II. My grandfather was in the middle of all this—before the Nazis had arrived in any substantial numbers, and it was no accident.

Yes, the Nazis started it. Yes, the Nazis "ordered" the Lithuanians to kill Jews. But why couldn't the Lithuanians drag their feet? Make excuses? Create obstacles? Instead, they "followed orders"—worked as fast and furiously as they could to help the Nazis exterminate Jews.

I have always heard how my grandfather resisted the Nazis when they wanted Lithuania to join the SS. He was sent to a Nazi concentration camp in March 1943 for taking such a stand. Here is some more information: Heinrich Himmler made him an "honorable prisoner." This means he had his own bed with sheets, did not have to work, and could walk freely around the camp. He did not experience what Jews did. Why do you think he survived this camp?

Please go deeper into history and think about these questions:

• Why didn't he take a stand 18 months earlier, in the summer and fall of 1941, when all the Jews were being killed?

• Why did he stay silent in the second half of 1941?

• Why didn't he refuse to sign documents sending Jews to a ghetto in 1941?

• Why didn't he refuse to sign documents calling for the distribution of Jewish property once they were taken to the ghetto?

• If he could resist the Nazis to have Lithuanians join the SS, why didn't he resist the Nazis when he was "ordered" to participate in the killing of Jews?

• Why did Himmler make him an honorable prisoner? What did my grandfather do that was so "honorable" in Himmler's eyes?

• He lived for another six years after all those Jews were killed. If he was so sorry about what happened to the Jews, if he was "forced" or "dragged into it," why didn't he write at least one article expressing his remorse?

When my mother, on her deathbed, asked me to write a book about her father, I thought I would be writing about a hero. But once I started researching the Nazi occupation, particularly my grandfather's role during that "complicated" time period, I realized my grandfather was no hero.

How should I view my own grandfather? As his granddaughter, I have decided to love him because he is still my grandfather. But I hate his sins, and I am willing to bear witness to them in their full horror so that others understand that his actions were wrong.

Just because Lithuanians were victimized by the Russians did not give Lithuanians the right to victimize Jews.

This "tragic figure" does not deserve to have a plaque to honor him. We should weep over what he did and express our sorrow over his actions, vowing to do all we can to make sure there are no other "tragic figures" like this in the future of our beloved Lithuania.

Respectfully,

Silvia Foti, Chicago

Grant Gochin plans to appeal the Lithuanian court's verdict and to take his case to the European Court of Human Rights.

It has been eloquently pointed out by several Jewish writers and Lithuanian academics that the Jews were innocent, and that the hate heaped upon them was out of all proportion to the reality of their place in Lithuanian society. On the spectrum of victimhood, I would contend that the Jews were the greatest victims in Lithuania, and that fact must be acknowledged by Christians. Some movement has been made in this direction.

This account of Jonas Noreika, I would hope, will be seen as a contribution to this discussion. As so many authors have pointed out before me—Ellen Cassedy in *We are Here: Memories of the Lithuanian Holocaust*, Rūta Vanagaitė and Efraim Zuroff in *Mūsiškiai (Our People)*, Christoph Dieckmann and Rūta Vanagaitė in *How Did It Happen?*—the time period was complicated, and even today the discussion is difficult. But there is so much hope, now that more people are willing to look more deeply into this complicated history.

Jonas Noreika's Unfinished Fairy Tale, 1944

D ear child, I want to tell you a story.

I. Once upon a time, there lived a little girl. She was as beautiful as a rose. She was dressed nicely and had a wonderful, childlike smell. She lived in the most splendid mansion because her father was a duke and her mother a duchess. Everyone noticed her and praised her. Under the love and guidance of her parents and others, she bloomed.

When she was six years old, a terrible storm occurred. The world had never seen such a storm. Lightning struck the mansion, leaving only rubble. The little girl was kidnapped by a witch, who had transformed herself from the storm's wind. The witch shrieked, "Come with me, Elytė! You have been happy, but you haven't learned about hardship and misery. Come, come! Ha, ha, ha, ha!" Cackling, she flew away with Elytė in her arms. She flew like the fastest airplane. Farther and farther. No one could hear Elytė's cries.

Then suddenly, it became very quiet, and Elytė found herself standing on the ground. "What's this?" she wondered. All around her were gigantic frogs crying, "Kvar, kvar, kvar. We know where your father and mother are! We can tell you. But you can't understand us. Do you want to learn our language?"

Elytė didn't understand a word. But she saw the witch standing right next to her. She looked angrily at Elytė and said, "You will stay here until you learn the language of the frogs. If you don't study, you will never see your mother or your father again! You will stay here forever, among the frogs."

(Be brave, my daughter!)

II. After the dreadful storm, Elytė's parents could not find her anywhere. Their pain and worry knew no bounds. In a rage, the duke ordered, "Go through the ruins of the mansion, and search for our daughter under every stone!" But Elytė still could not be found. Her poor mother, the duchess, could not even see through her tears. Elytė's nanny didn't know what to do, either. In vain, the duke howled; in vain, the duchess cried; in vain, the nanny shook with worry. Nothing helped. Elytė was gone.

The duke called upon the most famous thinkers in the world and asked for their best advice. He promised to pay as much as they wanted. When all of the best minds of the world had gathered at his fallen mansion, he asked, "Who can tell me where my beloved daughter is?" Everyone was silent. The duke repeated his question, but no one could help him.

The duke became so sad that his heart almost stopped beating. Then he heard his lovely wife's voice: "My heart feels something. It's saying something. I hear a dove's voice. It's flying around us! Yes, I hear it! I have to follow the dove."

III. The duke and all those around him looked up and saw a white dove flying. It was flying extraordinarily high, but suddenly landed on the duchess's shoulder. She extended her hands, and the dove flew into them. Holding the bird, she began to question him. And she understood his answers very clearly. "I know where your one and only daughter is," said the dove. "A witch took her away from your home. You have to go after her right away, because she's very far away. I'll show you the way!"

As the duchess listened, her hands shook, and her heart beat very quickly. The duke ordered that twelve horses be harnessed for the duchess, the nanny, and their escorts. Everything was prepared with great haste. The duke wanted to go himself, but he had to stay behind to govern the country.

IV. The twelve horses were divided among four carriages that stood in the yard, ready for the unknown road ahead. The nanny waited in a carriage while the duchess prepared for the journey. When she returned, she found her husband sitting on a chair that he'd found in the rubble. He was so lost in thought that he didn't even see her.

"What are you thinking, my love?" she asked. The dove was resting on her shoulder.

"Oh, you're ready," said the duke. "I'm sorry. I was thinking about our daughter's fate and your road into the unknown. Beloved! What should I do? I can't imagine my life without you. How can I leave you in the hands of fate? No, I love you too much! Life will be without meaning if I'm left without my one and only daughter and without my beloved wife! I'm going with you! We'll find our daughter or we'll die together."

The duchess cried. She knew how deeply her husband loved her. Her lips trembled, but she couldn't utter a word.

V. The duke saw his wife's tears and was filled with pain. The tears fell like pearls down her cheeks, which he had kissed so often.

His head was spinning. It was as if he heard his daughter's voice saying to him, "Father, Father, why won't you let Mother leave? I'm all by myself. There's no one to talk to. I've been waiting so long, and you are delaying Mother's trip because you don't know what to do! I know you won't forget me. Don't worry that I'm still so young. I'm brave enough to wait for the days of freedom. But dear Father, please hurry!"

Suddenly the duke stood up. He had decided not to wait a minute longer. He took the duchess by the hand, kissed her, and said, "I'm going with you. Let's go!"

They went out into the yard, where the nanny was waiting impatiently. The escorts were amazed that the duke had decided to go. No one dared point out to him that the kingdom shouldn't be left alone. The escorts took hold of the horses' reins, and the travelers were on their way.

But when they arrived at the town's gates, they met a breathless rider covered in dust. "Your Grace, the enemy has crossed the wall and is invading our country!"

The duke jumped out of the carriage.

VI. The duke was wild with rage and frustration, but no one was able to tell him anything about the enemy invasion. The rider who had brought the awful news had collapsed from fatigue. The duke set out to wage war. He had to meet and defeat this enemy, to free his country.

What was his life without his homeland? What would his people say if he deserted them in the country's moment of need? No, he had to fulfill his responsibility; he was sure of that. But how could he risk letting his wife go on such a journey by herself during this dangerous time? He looked at her and wondered what to do. The duchess said, "We have to share the responsibility. I understand your duty, and I see your pain. God is testing our love for our country and our daughter. We have required sacrifices from others; now our hour has come. You belong to your country, where you will live or die. I must go to our daughter."

As she spoke, the dove bent its head. When she finished, the dove chirped, "Yes, yes, yes!" The duchess and the nanny left, while the duke led his troops into battle. The loving family now was separated.

VII. Elytė was imprisoned by the witch. On a small island in the middle of a deep, wide sea, the witch had built an underground mansion. Its enormous halls were covered with gold and silver and decorated with diamonds. Some of the halls were so bright that they seemed to be illuminated by the sun. Other halls seemed to be lit by moonbeams. In some rooms, the stars shone brightly, while other chambers were always velvety black. Elytė had walked through these halls only once, when she was first brought to the witch's home. Since then she had been in the basement, where it was very dark. She had been crying.

Suddenly, the room became very bright, and a beautiful young girl stood in front of Elytė, smiling. "From now on, you will live in this basement," she said. "Beyond those doors is a huge swamp, with a lot of frogs. You will be free only when you learn the frogs' language. Until that day, one frog will take care of you and feed you."

The girl left, and the basement became dark once again. Elytė looked around, and suddenly the door opened. On the threshold, there was a giant frog.

VIII. Elytė began to tremble. She flew into a corner and waited to see what the frog would do. It was so huge that when it stood on its hind legs it could reach the doorknob. Its eyes shone in the darkness like two wet, black prunes. Their eyes met: the zealous eyes of the frog and the frightened eyes of the young duchess.

The frog tried to let Elytė know that he didn't want to harm her and that nothing bad would happen to her. Just the opposite. His goal was to calm her because he liked her from the very first glance. He said, "Kvar, kvar, kvar."

Elytė didn't understand a word. The frog jumped, turned around, and left, but he returned quickly with two small frogs. Each frog carried a dishful of food. Elytė noticed that the big frog was the leader. When he gave orders, the small frogs carried them out right away. Standing on their hind legs, they placed a white tablecloth on the table, followed by the dishes and soup. When the table was set for two, the two small frogs stood behind the chairs, while the big frog turned to Elytė, inviting her to the table. She understood from his movements what he was trying to say. Although she was still afraid and trembling, her hunger was so strong, and the steaming hot soup smelled so good, that she ran to the table. In front of her sat the big frog. The two little frogs served dinner.

IX. After dinner, the frogs left. Elytė was very tired. She lay down on the room's small bed and fell asleep right away. While she was sleeping, she heard the witch's terrifying voice. "Your mother is on her way with the dove, to free you. I cannot abide this. I must transform you into a frog."

Elytė woke up in fear. It was dark all around her. She jumped out of bed and ran outside. She could still hear the witch's words in her ears. In the yard, she saw thousands of frogs croaking, "Kvar, kvar, kvar."

X. All of the frogs lay piled on top of each other, not moving. Although they could not open their eyes, they were not sleeping; the witch had cast a spell on them. From the sun's setting to its rising, the frogs could not see.

The frogs knew that they could turn back into people again if an innocent girl would kiss them on the dawn of March 4, St. Casimir's Day. That was the very day that the witch had brought Elytė to her mansion. But Elytė didn't know that secret. She had no idea that, at sunrise, she could have changed thousands of frogs into beautiful boys and girls, releasing them from the witch's tragic spell. She was good and innocent, but she simply didn't know about the power she had. And the sun already had risen.

She stood at the door and her heart quivered because of what the witch had said in her dream. The frogs wailed so loudly and mournfully that Elytė was alarmed. The sun's first rays shone into the witch's yard. The rays seemed as bright and as loving as her mother's eyes.

All at once, Elytė understood that she was still alive on a glorious earth, and that her mother and father and nanny would come to free her. She remembered the command to learn the language of the frogs. She bent down next to a little frog, and rubbed her cheek and ear against him, trying to hear what he was saying. Oh! Suddenly, in the frog's place, stood an unusually handsome young man. But he was only a man from the waist up. His bottom half was still a frog's, because Elytė had only stroked him with her cheek, and this was like only half a kiss. "Beautiful girl, don't worry. I am a person, like you," he told her.

XI. The young man explained that, a long time ago, he had been snatched away from his parents and changed into a frog because he hadn't listened to the witch's commands. "Some of the frogs are real frogs, but some of them are children, like you and me."

"Can the witch change me into a frog?" asked Elytė.

"Yes, she can, if within ten days you haven't learned at least one word of the frogs' language, or if you forget your mother's and your father's and your nanny's names. Every ten days, the witch will come by and question you. If you don't answer her, she might get so angry that she will do what she threatens. She could change you, a lovely girl, into the most awful frog. Be careful. Be brave. Learn the frogs' language and keep repeating those three most important names. This work will give you courage and energy. Then the witch will not harm you."

"But how can I learn the language?" asked Elytė. "Who will help me?"

"Be calm and don't be afraid," said the young frog-man. "See that gigantic frog? He's the oldest son of King Vilnadon. For ten years the richest and most powerful king searched in vain for his son. And during that time the son tried to escape from here, without any luck. Maybe he has already forgotten who he really is, because the witch trusts him completely. He will be your teacher.

"Now the sun has risen, and all the frogs can see again. They are crying because you didn't know the secret that could change them from frogs back into people. But they are not angry. They love you. You will be their princess.

"I'm sorry," he continued. "I have told you everything now. I can't remain as half a man. I must die."

ACKNOWLEDGMENTS

To the witnesses of my grandfather's life: May They Rest in Peace.

Viktoras Ašmenskas, Jadvyga Budrytė Bivainienė, Aldona Budrytė Bužienė, Jakovas Bunka, Simonas Dovidavičius, Dalia Noreikaitė Kučėnienė, Antanina Krapavičiūtė Noreikienė, Antanina Noreikaitė Misiūnienė, Damijonas Riauka

I have so many to thank: my mother Dalia Kučėnas who bequeathed her lifelong mission to me; my grandmother Antanina Noreika who spent hours telling me stories of the fatherland, filling my mind and heart with valuable memories, a deposit of the faith, if you will; my aunt Antanina Noreika Misiun, the sister of Jonas Noreika, who spent hours telling stories of her brother's childhood; Franco Foti, who shared his knowledge of World War II history; my brother, Rimas Kucenas, who accompanied me on so much of the physical and emotional journey; and my father, Jonas Kucenas, whom I have come to understand better.

I thank all involved in running the creative writing program at Murray State University, especially my mentors Karen McElmurray, Chris Hale, and Elena Passarello, who helped draw out parts of the tale I didn't even know existed.

I thank all those who helped me during my research trip to Lithuania, as well as those I contacted before and after for advice: Simonas Dovidavičius, Rasa Kovalenkienė, Eva and Viktoras Kovalenko, Rūta Budrytė, Jadvyga Budrytė Bivainienė, Aldona Budrytė Bružienė, Nijolė Grunskienė, Arturas Grunskis, Antanas Grunskis, Dana Noreikaitė Nausėdienė, Ina Budrytė, Damijonas Riauka, Pranas Abelkis, Albinas Kijauskas, Mikolas Mičiudas, Maria Lisinskienė, Dalia Sruoga, Sakalas and Ona Gorodeckis, Teresė Birutė Burauskaitė, Arūnas Bubnys, Edmundas Balčiūnas, Jakovas and Dalia Bunka,

Zita Palauskaitė, Danutė Serapinienė, Bronius Pocius, Ina Navazelskis, Elona Limantienė, Vytautas Damasevičius, Viktoras Ašmenskas, Saulius Sužiedėlis.

I thank friends who have read and commented upon portions of the book: Gail Lukasik, Dalia Vitkus, Svajonė Kerelis, Shoshana Gray, Daiva Markelis, Neal Rutstein, Jill Sherer, and especially Dr. Salvador Morote. I thank Rūta Vanagaitė for her encouragement and support. A distinct thanks goes to Hanley Kanar who has been a witness to the unfolding of this story from the beginning and has helped with several drafts. A writer needs good readers, and they are the best.

I thank Andrius Kulikauskas for his diligent fact-checking of the manuscript and for becoming the curator of my website's online museum on Jonas Noreika, and Evaldas Balčiūnas for helping with research and citations. I thank Lisa Ferdman for her incisiveness, doggedness, and going the extra mile with editing the manuscript, as well as a fair amount of fact-checking and researching. Lisa truly poured her heart and soul into this. I thank Michele Wallace for her developmental suggestions and Rita Gabis for her recommendations. I thank Mark Malatesta for his invaluable advice on all aspects of shaping and pitching the project. For helping me get the story out into the world, I thank the Op-Ed Project, especially my mentor Michael Massing, and Salon.com for being the first to feature an article on my findings.

I'd also like to thank Regnery History for taking on this story—Alex Novak for acquiring it, Elizabeth Kantor for editing, and all those behind the scenes quietly helping. This book would not exist were it not for my agent Helen Zimmerman, whom I greatly appreciate and admire for her sound sense, reassurance, and persistence.

I'd also like to give a special thanks to the Simon Wiesenthal Center, and especially to Alison Slovin, Liebe Geft, and Efraim Zuroff for embracing the project.

Finally, I'd like to thank Grant Gochin, who has had an indelible impact on the final story, as well as on me. His friendship, partnership, and inspiration have meant the world.

SELECTED BIBLIOGRAPHY

Archival Source

KGB transcripts. March 16, 1946–February 1947. Lithuanian Special Archives. Translated from Russian to Lithuanian by Damijonas Riauka in 1997 and from Lithuanian to English by the author.

Books and Essays

Ašmenskas, Viktoras. *Generolas Vėtra* [General Storm]. Vilnius, Lithuania: Lietuvos Gyventojų Genocido ir Rezistencijos Tyrimo Centras [Lithuanian Genocide and Resistance Research Centre], 1997.

Bubnys, Arūnas. "The Holocaust in Lithuania: An Outline of the Major Stages and their Result" in *The Vanished World of Lithuanian Jews*, edited by Alvydas Nikzentaitis, Stefan Schreiner, and Darius Staliūnas, pp. 203–219. Amsterdam, Netherlands: Rodopi, 2004.

Buchaveckas, Stanislovas. "Jonas Noreika—Generolas Vėtra" in *Lietuvos Valščiai: Lyguma, Stačiūnai*, edited by Robertas Jurgaitis, pp. 817–35. Vilnius, Lithuania: Versmė, 2001.

Bunka, Jakovas. *Jakovas Bunka. Plungė: Viešoji Įstaiga Tautodailininkų Sąjungos Fondas.* Public Institution Fund of Folk Artists Union, 2013.

Cicėnienė, Rima et al. *Lietuvos Mokslų Akademijos Vrublevskių Biblioteka: 1912–2012* [*Wroblewski Library of the Lithuanian Academy of Sciences, 1912–2012*]. Vilnius, Lithuania: Vrublevskis Library, Lithuanian Science Academy, 2012.

Cohen-Mushlin, Aliza et al. *Synagogues in Lithuania: A Catalogue.* Vilnius, Lithuania: Academy of Arts Press, 2016.

Eidintas, Alfonsas. *Jews, Lithuanians and the Holocaust.* Vilnius, Lithuania: Institute of International Relations and Political Science, Vilnius University, 2012.

Eidintas, Alfonas et al. *Lithuania in European Politics: The Years of the First Republic, 1918–1940.* New York, New York: St. Martin's Press, 1997.

Erslavaitė, G., E. Rozauskas, Kazys Rukšnas, and Boleslovas Baranauskas. *Masinės Žudynės Lietuvoje 1941–1944* [Mass Slaughter in Lithuania, 1941–1944]. Vilnius, Lithuania: Mintis, 1973.

Freidhamas, Peisachas. *Lietuva Antrajame Pasauliniame Kare 1935–1945* [Lithuania in the Second World War, 1935–1945]. Vilnius, Lithuania: Politika, 2008.

Gervydas, A. *Beyond the Barbed Wire.* Chicago, Illinois: Lithuanian Catholic Press Association, 1950.

Greenbaum, Marsha. *The Jews of Lithuania, A History of a Remarkable Community 1316–1945.* Jerusalem: Gefen Publishing House, 1995.

Hoffman, Eva. *After Such Knowledge: Memory, History and the Legacy of the Holocaust.* New York, New York: Public Affairs, 2004.

Jankauskas, Juozas. *1941 m Birželio Sukilimas Lietuvoje: Pagrindiniai sukilimo organizatoriai, vadovai, ryšininkai ir pasiuntiniai* [June 1941 Uprising in Lithuania: Principal Organizers, Leaders, Liaisons and Messengers]. Vilnius, Lithuania: Gyventojų Genocido ir Rezistencijos Tyrimo Centras [Lithuanian Genocide and Resistance Research Centre], 2010.

Kijauskas, Albinas and Damijonas Riauka. *Sukilėliai, Mardosų Kuopa: 1941 Metų Birželio 21–25 dienų* [Uprisers, Mardosu Troop: June 21–25, 1941]. Kaunas, Lithuania: Atmintis, 1998. Reprinted in 2005.

Levinsonas, Josifas. *ŠOA Holokaustas Lietuvoje: Skaitiniai I dalis* [Shoah Holocaust in Lithuania: Essays, Part I]. Vilnius, Lithuania: Valstybinis Vilniaus Gaono Žydu Muziejus [Vilna Gaon Jewish State Museum], 2001.

Lietuvių Enciklopedija. Boston: Lithuanian Encyclopedia Press, 1960.

Melamed, Joseph, ed. *Lithuania, Crime and Punishment.* Tel Aviv: The Association of Lithuanian Jews in Israel, 1999.

Narutis, Pilypas. *Lithuanian Uprising 1941: Struggle for Independence: Caught between Nazi-German and Soviet Empire.* Saline, Michigan: McNaughton & Gunn, 1994.

Noreika, Jonas. *Penki Broliai* [Five Brothers]. Vilnius, Lithuania: Versmė, 2013. (In my translation of the original text, I replaced the third-person voice with first person; otherwise, the text is unchanged.)

Pakalniškis, Aleksandras. *Plungė*. Chicago, Illinois: M. Morkūno spaustuvė, 1980.

Pakalniškis, Aleksandras, Jr. *Praeities Atgarsiai* [Echoes from the Past]. Chicago, Illinois: M. Morkūno spaustuvė, 1988.

Prunskis, Juozas. *Lietuviai Sibire* [Lithuanians in Siberia]. Chicago, Illinois: Lithuanian Library Press, 1981.

Pūkelis, Kestutis. *Leiskitį Tėvyne: Tremtinių Atsiminimai* [Let Us into the Fatherland: Memories of the Exiled]. Kaunas, Lithuania: Šviesa, 1989.

Riauka, Damijonas. *Iškilmės Žemaitijoje Minint Jono Noreikos—Generolo Vėtros 85-ąjį Gimtadienį 1995: Jis Taip Mylėjo Lietuvą* [Celebrations in Žemaitija Remembering Jonas Noreika—General Storm on his 85th Birthday, 1995: He So Loved Lithuania]. Kaunas, Lithuania: Atmintis, 1975.

———. *Pasakojimai apie Generola Vėtra, Lietuvos Radijo ir Televizijos Laidos* [Stories about General Vėtra, Lithuanian Radio and TV Broadcasts]. Kaunas, Lithuania: Atmintis, 1994.

Rudis, Gediminas. *Zenonas Blynas Karo Metų Dienoraštis 1941–1944* [Zenonas Blynas's Wartime Diary, 1941–1944]. Vilnius, Lithuania: Lietuvos Istorijos Institutas [Lithuanian Institute of History], 2007.

Rupšienė, Alisa. *Hell's Gates—Stutthof*. Vilnius, Lithuania: Lithuanian Genocide and Resistance Research Centre, 1998.

Sruoga, Balys. *Forest of the Gods*. Vilnius, Lithuania: Vaga, 1996. (Translated into English by his granddaughter, Aušrinė Byla.)

Sutton, Karen. *The Massacre of the Jews of Lithuania: Lithuanian Collaboration in the Final Solution, 1941–1944*. Jerusalem: Gefen Publishing House, 2008.

Vilna Gaon Jewish State Museum. *Šiaulių getas: kalinių sarašai 1942* [The Šiaulių Ghetto: Lists of Prisoners, 1942]. Vilnius, Lithuania: Valstybines Vilniaus Gaonožydų muziejus, 2002.

Yla, Stasys. *A Priest in Stutthof: Human Experiences in the World of Subhuman* [sic]. New York, New York: Manyland Books, 1971.

———. *Žmonės ir Žvėrys* [Men and Monsters]. Putnam: Putnam Sisters Press, 1951.

Zwi, Rose. *Last Walk in Naryshkin Park*. North Melbourne, Australia: Spinifex, 1997.

Film

Reivytis, Vaidas. *Saulėleidis Lietuvoje* [Sunset in Lithuania]. 2000.

Interviews

Bosas, Aleksandras. Personal interview. July 18, 2013.

Bubnys, Arūnas. Personal interview. August 2013.

Budrytė, Aldona Bužienė. Personal interviews. July and August 2013.

Budrytė, Ina. Personal interview. August 2013.

Budrytė, Jadvyga Bivainienė. Personal interview. July 2013.

Budrytė, Rūta. Personal interview. July 2013.

Bunka, Jakovas. Personal interview. July 2013.

Burauskaitė, Birutė. Personal interview. July 17, 2013.

Dovidavičius, Simon. Holocaust-related tour. July 14–22, 2013.

———. Personal interviews, July–August 2013.

Grunskis, Antanas. Personal interview. July 2013.

Grunskis, Arturas. Personal interview. July 2013.

Grunskis, Nijolė. Personal interview. July 2013.

Limantienė, Ilona. Personal interview. July 2013.

Misiūn, Antanina Noreika. Personal interviews: 1984, 1985, 2001, and 2002.

Nausėdas, Dana. Personal interview. July 2013.

Navickas, Povilas. Personal interview. June 2013.

Noreikaitė, Danutė Nausėdienė. Personal interview. July 2013.

Paulauskaitė, Zita. Personal interview. July 2013.

Pocius, Bronislovas. Personal interview. July 2013.

Riauka, Damijonas. Personal Interview. June 2013.

———. "1941 Sukilimas" (pictogram).

Newspaper and Periodical Articles

Blazevičius, Kazys. "Lithuanians in the Stutthof Hell." *Kaunas Atmintis*, no. 24. March 28, 2001.

Buchaveckas, Stanislovas. "Lyguma, Stačiunai." *Kaunas Atmintis*, no. 49. June 7, 2001.

———. "Nazi Prison." *Kaunas Atmintis*, no. 51. July 4, 2001.

Kalnis, A. *Teviškės Žiburiai*. June 3, 1982.

Kijauskas, Albinas. "Kazys Kijauskas." *Kauno Diena*, no. 46. February 25, 1997.

Lukauskienė, Dana. "Esu žydas, bet jaučiuosi esas tikras žemaitis" [I am a Jew, but I feel like a true Žemaitis]. *Vakarų Lietuva*. July 16–22, 2013.

Masaitytė, Bronė. "Ištrauka Iš V. Sruogienės Laiško 1981 m. kovo 12 d." [Excerpt from V. Sruogienė's letter of March 12, 1981]. *Kauno Diena*, no. 7. March 28, 1994.

Pocius, Bronislovas. "Plungės Žydų Bendruomenė [The Plungė Jewish Community]." *Plungės Žinios*. July 12, 2013.

Riauka, Damijonas. "Karas Prasidės Rytoj" [The War Will Start Tomorrow]. *Kauno Tiesa*. June 22, 1991.

Sužiedelis, Saulius. "The Burden of 1941." *Lituanus* [Lithuanian Quarterly Journal]. Winter 2001.

"The Soviet Government, the Chronicle, and the Church in Lithuania." *Chronicle of the Catholic Church in Lithuania*, no. 44. July 30, 1980.

Veruitienė, Aldona. "Nuomonė: Žmonės išgąsdino ne tiek Generolo Vėtros atminimas, kiek savi…politikai ir politikieriai [Opinion: People were scared not by General Vėtra's memorial, but by their own…politicians and leaders]. *Šiaulių kraštas*. October 11, 1995.

Online Sources and Articles

"Around the Jewish World Lone Jew in Lithuanian Town Spends Life Preserving the Past." Jewish Telegraphic Agency. June 13, 2002. https://www.jta.org /2002/06/13/archive/around-the-jewish-world-lone-jew-in-lithuanian-town-spends-life-preserving-the-past.

Balčiūnas, Evaldas. "The Posthumous Remaking of a Holocaust Perpetrator in Lithuania: Why is Jonas Noreika a National Hero?" Defending History. June 13, 2014. https://defendinghistory.com/posthumous-remaking-of-a-holocaust-perpetrator-in-lithuania-why-is-jonas-noreika-a-national-hero-by-evaldas-balciunas/31531.

Bubnys, Arūnas. "Lietuvių saugumo policija ir holokaustas (1941–1944)" [Lithuanian Security Police and the Holocaust (1941–1944)]. January 30, 2004. http://www.genocid.lt/Leidyba/13/bubnys.htm.

Dumčius, Arimantas. "Tautos Sovietinis Genocidas—Kasmetinis Altajaus Krašto ir Šiaurės Jakutijos tremtinių susitikimas" [The Nation's Soviet Genocide—Annual Meeting of the Altajaus Region and Northern Jakutijos Exiles]. Partizanai. December 23, 2011. http://partizanai.org/failai/html/antikomunistinis-kongresas-II.htm.

Edeiken, Yale F. "Historical Note on the Jaeger Report." Holocaust History. November 23, 2013. https://phdn.org/archives/holocaust-history.org/works/jaeger-report/htm/intro001.htm.

Ellick, Adam B. "The Last Jew in the Lithuanian Village of Plunge Has Made It His Life's Work to Commemorate the Jews Killed There in War World II [sic]—and to Remind Locals of Their Past Deeds." JBFund. http://jbfund.lt/the-last-jew-in-the-lithuanian-village-of-plunge-has-made-it-his-lifes-work-to-commemorate-the-jews-killed-there-in-war-world-ii-and-to-remind-locals-of-their-past-deeds/.

"Holocaust Atlas of Lithuania." Vilna Gaon State Jewish Museum. http://www.holocaustatlas.lt/EN/.

HuntleyFilmArchives, "Nazi Germany Invades Memel in 1939. Archive Film 91545," YouTube, July 30, 2018, https://www.youtube.com/watch?v=LtQIcRDqoz4.

"Šiauliai." International Jewish Cemetery Project. http://iajgscemetery.org/eastern-europe/lithuania/siauliai.

Jager, Karl. "The Jager Report." A Teacher's Guide to the Holocaust. Florida Center for Instructional Technology. https://fcit.usf.edu/holocaust/resource/document/DocJager.htm.

Joffe, Shimon, trans. "S) Under the Nazi Occupation–Destruction of Lithuanian Jewry." Translation from *Encyclopedia of Jewish Communities, Lithuania*. Edited by Dov Levin and Josef Rosin. Jerusalem: Yad Vashem. https://www.jewishgen.org/yizkor/pinkas_lita/lit_00090.html.

Lietuvos gyventojų genocido ir rezistencijos tyrimo centras [Lithuanian Genocide and Resistance Research Centre]. http://genocid.lt/centras/.

Lietuvos Žydų Bendruomenė [Lithuanian Jewish Organization]. https://www.lzb.lt.

Perna, Tom. "Mondays with Mary—Our Lady of Šiluva." https://tomperna.org/2017/11/13/mondays-with-mary-our-lady-of-siluva/.

Rabinowitz, Eli. "Jewish Community of Telz." JewishGen KehilaLinks. https://kehilalinks.jewishgen.org/telz/Home.html.

Rosin, Josef. "Plungė" in *Encyclopedia of Jewish Communities in Lithuania*. Jerusalem: Yad Vashem, 1996. https://www.jewishgen.org/yizkor/pinkas_lita/lit_00484.html.

——— "Šiauliai" in *Encyclopedia of Jewish Communities in Lithuania*. Jerusalem: Yad Vashem, 1996. https://www.jewishgen.org/yizkor/pinkas_lita/lit_00658c.html.

Pamphlets

Danta, Tadas. "Don't Slander Captain Noreika, Sir!" Reprinted in *Kraštis Aušros Alėja* 13, no. 32. April 2–9, 1993.

Dumčius, Arimantas. "Tautos Sovietinis Genocidas—Kasmetinis Altajaus Krašto ir Šiaurės Jakutijos tremtinių susitikimas" [The Nation's Soviet Genocide—Annual Meeting of the Altajaus Region and Northern Jakutijos Exiles]. Partizanai. December 23, 2011. http://partizanai.org/failai/html/antikomunistinis-kongresas-II.htm.

Noreika, Jonas. *Pakelk galva, Lietuvi!!!* [Hold Your Head High, Lithuanian!!!] Kaunas, Lithuania: V. Atkočiūnų spaustuvė [Atkočiūnai Printing House], 1933.

Šiauliai Aušros Muziejus [Sauliai Dawn Museum]. "Jewish Heritage in Šiauliai: The Merchant Frenkelis."

Personal Correspondence

Čiakas, Antanas. Personal correspondence to Dalia Kučėnienė. 1976.

Gorodeckis, Ona Jaskelevičiūtė. Obituary of Stasys Gorodeckis. Personal correspondence. Vilnius, 2002.

Gorodeckis, Sakalas. Personal correspondence. February 18, 2014.

Grunskis, Nijolė. Personal correspondence. May 9, 2011, and February 2012.

Noreika, Jonas. Personal correspondence: Letters from Stutthof. 1943–1945.

———. Personal correspondence to Stasys Noreika. November 1, 1925.

Noreika, Pranas. Personal correspondence to Antanina Noreika Misiūn. March 2, 1976.

Paulauskaitė, Zita. Personal email correspondence. July, August, and September 2013.

NOTES

Chapter Three: The Imprisonment and Trial of Jonas Noreika

1. Jonas Noreika interrogation, Case #9792, KGB transcripts, March 16, 1946–February 1947, Lithuanian Special Archives, vol. 1, pp. 304–6, translated from Russian to Lithuanian by Damijonas Riauka in 1997 and from Lithuanian to English by the author.
2. "Jonas Noreika," in *Lietuvių Enciklopedija* 20 (Boston: Lithuanian Encyclopedia Press, 1960).
3. Viktoras Ašmenskas, *Generolas Vėtra* (Vilnius: Lietuvos Gyventojų Genocido ir Rezistencijos Tyrimo Centras [Lithuanian Genocide and Resistance Research Centre], 1997).
4. Ibid.
5. Ibid.
6. Ibid.
7. Ibid.
8. KGB transcripts, Case #9792.
9. Ašmenskas, *Generolas Vėtra*.

Chapter Four: The Last Letter

1. Jonas Noreika's last letter to his daughter (written from the KGB prison).

Chapter Seven: Fatherless

1. Republic of Lithuania Law on the Organization of the National Defense System and Military Service May 5, 1998, No. VIII-723 Vilnius (as amended by January 14, 1999, No. VIII-1027 and July 7, 1999, No. VIII-1289), https://e-seimas.lrs.lt/rs/legalact/TAD/TAIS.90344/format/ISO_PDF/#:~:text=upon%20being%20assigned%20as%20the,out%20my%20duties%2C%20to%20the.
2. Antanas Čiakas, personal correspondence to Dalia Kučėnienė, 1976.
3. Antanina Noreika Misiūn, personal interviews with the author, 1984, 1985, 2001, and 2002.
4. Čiakas correspondence.
5. Misiūn interviews.
6. Čiakas correspondence.

7. Ibid.
8. Misiūn interviews.
9. Jonas Noreika, personal correspondence to Stasys Noreika, November 1, 1925.
10. Čiakas correspondence.

Chapter Nine: The Arrest of Jonas Noreika

1. Dana Noreika Nausėdas, personal interview with the author, July 2013.
2. See "Bendron kovon su bolševizmu" ["Join in the Fight against Bolshevism," urging Lithuanians to enlist in the German Army], *Ateitis*, February 24, 1943, http://www.epaveldas.lt/recordImageSmall/LNB/C1B0 004111267?exId=397311&seqNr=1. References to "Tėvynės legionas" ("Homeland legion") and to "Lietuvių legionas" ("Lithuanian legion," or "legion of Lithuanians") can be found on that site, and also at *Ateitis*, December 9, 1943, http://www.epaveldas.lt/object/recordDescription/ LNB/C1B0004111267.
3. In fact, the Poles also refused.

Chapter Ten: Tender Letters and a Dark Fairy Tale

1. Jonas Noreika, personal correspondence to Antanina Noreika, seventy-seven letters dated from 1943–1945.
2. Janina Grabowski-Chalka, *Guide: Historical Information* (Gdansk and Sztutowo, Poland: Muzeum Stutthof w Sztutowie, 2011).
3. Jonas Noreika correspondence to Antanina Noreika.
4. Ibid.
5. Ibid.
6. Ibid.
7. Ibid.
8. Stasys Yla, *A Priest in Stutthof: Human Experiences in the World of Subhuman* [sic] (New York: Maryland Books, 1971).
9. Josifas Levinsonas, *OA Holokaustas Lietuvoje: Skaitiniai I dalis* [Shoah Holocaust in Lithuania: Essays, Part I] (Vilnius: Valstybinis Vilniaus Gaono Žydu Muziejus [Vilnius Gaon Jewish State Museum], 2001).
10. This was the area of Šiauliai District during the Nazi occupation; it is somewhat different today.
11. Silvia Foti, "The Dove and the Webbed Witch of the Wind," *Lituanus* 43, no. 4 (Winter 1997), http://www.lituanus.org/1997/97_4_02.htm.

Chapter Eleven: The KGB Transcripts

1. Jonas Noreika interrogation, Case #9792, KGB transcripts, March 16, 1946–February 1947, Lithuanian Special Archives, vol. 1, 304–6, translated from Russian to Lithuanian by Damijonas Riauka in 1997 and from Lithuanian to English by the author.

2. "Guziavičius (Gudaitis-Guziavičius) Alexander Avgustovich," Shield and Sword, http://shieldandsword.mozohin.ru/personnel/guzevicius_a_a.htm. An account of Markulis's activities with Jonas Noreika can be found in A. Anušauskas, *Išdavystė* [Treachery] (Versus Aureus, 2017). See also Vaidas Saldžiūnas, "Garsiausias Lietuvos išdavikas, pražudęs šimtus žmonių: mano sąžinė rami (845)," Delfi, February 24, 2017, https://www.delfi.lt/news/daily/medijos-karas-propaganda/garsiausias-lietuvos-isdavikas-prazudes-simtus-zmoniu-mano-sazine-rami.d?id=73860064.

3. Viktoras Ašmenskas, *Generolas Vėtra* [General Storm] (Vilnius, Lithuania: Lietuvos Gyventojų Genocido ir Rezistencijos Tyrimo Centras [Lithuanian Genocide and Resistance Research Centre], 1997.

4. While accounts differ, probably at least 118,000 Lithuanians were deported from 1944 to 1952; the total number may be as high as 155,796. Of these, 12,304 were deported, primarily for having supported partisans, between 1945 and 1948. Most of the later deportees were farmers deemed to be too well-off. Although it is difficult to establish the exact number of those deported to Siberia and to gulags (forced-labor camps), the best source appears to be this research data base: "Research Database," The Secretariat of the International Commission for the Evaluation of the Nazi and Soviet Occupation Regimes in Lithuania, https://www.komisija.lt/tyrimai/. Lithuanian-language Wikipedia states that 30,000 partisans were killed: "Lietuvos partizanai," Vikipedija, https://lt.wikipedia.org/wiki/Lietuvos_partizanai. It is likely that most of these deaths occurred in the field.

5. Elena Jurgutytė, personal correspondence, 1990.

6. Noreika interrogation, vol. 1, pp. 304–6, describing the plan to steal the paper from the newspaper *Žaibas*.

7. The bell was made in 1919 but traveled around the United States for a year. It was presented to Lithuania's representative in Chicago in 1920 and arrived in Lithuania in 1922. "The Liberty Bell of Lithuania," Bulletin of Lithuanian Societies, The Newberry, https://flps.newberry.org/article/5423970_3_1207.

8. Ona Poškienė interrogation, case #9792, KGB transcripts, March 18, 1946, Lithuanian Special Archives, vol. 2, p. 32, translated from Russian to

Lithuanian by Damijonas Riauka in 1997 and from Lithuanian to English by the author.

9. "Lithuanian Partisans," Wikipedia, https://en.wikipedia.org/wiki/ Lithuanian_partisans.

10. Arūnas Latišenka, *Lietuvos istorijos atlasas* (Briedis, 2001),p. 25.

11. Noreika interrogation, vol. 1, p. 17.

12. Ašmenskas, *Generolas Vėtra*, p. 425.

13. Noreika interrogation, vol. 1, p. 17.

14. Arvydas Anušauskas. "M. Rinkimai į Sovietų Sąjungos Aukščiausiąją Tarybą," 1946, http://www.xn--altiniai-4wb.info/files/istorija/IIoo/A._ Anu%C5%A1auskas._ 1946_m._rinkimai_%C4%AF_Soviet%C5%B3_S%C4%85jungos_Auk%C5 %A1%C4%8Diausi%C4%85j%C4%85_Taryb%C4%85.II1503.pdf.

15. Arvydas Anušauskas, *Lietuvių tautos sovietinis naikinimas 1940–1958 metais* (Vilnius, Lithuania: Mintis, 1996), 80.

16. Noreika interrogation, vol. 1, pp. 240–43.

17. Noreika interrogation, vol 1., p. 243.

18. Gorodeckis interrogation, KGB Transcripts, Case #9792. March 16, 1946– February 1947, Lithuanian Special Archives, vol. 1, p. 281, as translated from Russian to Lithuanian by Damijonas Riauka in 1997 and from Lithuanian to English by the author.

19. Gorodeckis interrogation, vol. 1, p. 280.

20. Ašmenskas, *Generolas Vėtra*.

21. Poškienė interrogation, vol. 2, p. 55.

22. Noreika interrogation, vol. 1, p. 95.

23. Ašmenskas, *Generolas Vėtra*.

24. Noreika interrogation, vol. 1, p. 95.

25. Ašmenskas, *Generolas Vėtra*.

26. Ibid., p. 429.

27. While this figure is commonly cited, the United States Holocaust Memorial Museum recently posted online that 130,000 of the 153,000 Jews living in Lithuania in 1937, constituting 85 percent, were killed in the Holocaust. This is comparable to the percentage of Polish Jews murdered and less than the percentage of Jews from Serbia, Macedonia, and Montenegro who were killed. But as the Jewish population in Lithuania was tallied only in 1937 (rather than in 1939) and since the Vilnius region was not included in the census, the true number of deaths was higher; 95 percent is probably more accurate. See "Jewish Losses during the Holocaust: By Country," Holocaust Encyclopedia, United States Holocaust Memorial Museum, https://encyclopedia.ushmm.org/content/

en/article/jewish-losses-during-the-
holocaust-by-country.

Chapter Twelve: Beginning the Dreaded Search

1. Jonas Noreika, *Pakelk galva, lietuvi!!!* [Hold Your Head High, Lithuanian!!!] (Kaunas, Lithuania: V. Atkočiūnos spaustuvė, 1933).
2. Ibid.
3. Jonas Noreika, *Penki Broliai* [Five Brothers] (Vilnius, Lithuania: Versmė, 2013).
4. Ibid.
5. Ibid.
6. G. Erslavaite, *Masinės Žudynės Lietuvoje 1941–1944* [Mass Murders in Lithuania 1941–1944] (Vilnius, Lithuania: Mintis, 1973).
7. Ibid.
8. Viktoras Ašmenskas, *Generolas Vėtra* [General Storm] (Vilnius, Lithuania: Lietuvos Gyventojų Genocido ir Rezistencijos Tyrimo Centras [Lithuanian Genocide and Resistance Research Centre], 1997).
9. Ibid.
10. Josifas Levinsonas, *ŠOA Holokaustas Lietuvoje: Skaitiniai I dalis* [Shoah Holocaust in Lithuania: Essays, Part I] (Vilnius, Lithuania: Valstybinis Vilniaus Gaono Žydu Muziejus [Vilnius Gaon Jewish State Museum], 2001).
11. Tadas Danta, "Don't Slander Captain Noreika, Sir!", *Kraštas "Aušros Alėja"* 13, no. 32 (April 2–9, 1993).

Chapter Fourteen: An Unreliable Witness

1. Damijonas Riauka, "1941 Sukilimas" [1941 Uprising] (pictogram).
2. Kazys Škirpa, *Uprising for the Restoration of Lithuania's Sovereignty: A Documentary Survey* (Washington, D.C.: Franciscan Fathers Press, 1973).
3. Ibid.

Chapter Fifteen: Groundwork for a Rebellion

1. Kazys Škirpa, *Uprising for the Restoration of Lithuania's Sovereignty: A Documentary Survey* (Washington, D.C.: Franciscan Fathers Press, 1973).
2. Viktoras Ašmenskas, *Generolas Vėtra* [General Storm] (Vilnius, Lithuania: Lietuvos Gyventojų Genocido ir Rezistencijos Tyrimo Centras [Lithuanian Genocide and Resistance Research Centre], 1997), p. 74. For more information about the army during the occupation, see Stasys Knezys, "Lietuvos kariuomenės likvidavimas 1940–1941 m." [The Liquidation of

Lithuanian Army in 1940–1941], Tarptautinė Komisija Nacių ir Sovietinio Okupacinių Rezimų Nusikaltimams Lietuvoje Įvertinti [The Secretariat of the International Commission for the Evaluation of the Nazi and Soviet RegimesinLithuania]https://www.komisija.lt/tyrimai/ii-pirmoji-sovietine-okupacija-1940-1941-m/2-nusikalstamos-okupacines-politikos-sistema-okupaciniu-politiniu-policiniu-kariniu-visuomeniniu-bei-juridiniu-strukturu-vaidmuo-ir-kolaboravimas-su-jomis/2-1-lietuvos-kariuomenes-likvidavimas-1940-1941-m/.

3.   Albinas Kijauskas and Damijonas Riauka, *Sukilėliai, Mardosų Kuopa: 1941 Metų Birželio 21–25 Dienų* [Uprisers, Mardosu Troop: June 21–25, 1941] (Kaunas, Lithuania: Atmintis, 1998, reprinted 2005).

4.   Damijonas Riauka, personal interview, June 2013.

5.   Josef Rosin, "Plungė," *Encyclopedia of Jewish Communities in Lithuania* (Jerusalem: Yad Vashem, 1996).

6.   Albinas Kijauskas, "Kazys Kijauskas," *Kauno Diena* 46:15073 (February 25, 1997).

7.   Andrius Kulikauskas, email correspondence with the author, December 23, 2018.

8.   Škirpa, *Uprising*.

9.   Alfonas Zaldokas et al., *Lietuvių tautos sukilimas 1941m birželio 22–28 d.* [Lithuania's Uprising June 22–28, 1941] (Vilnius, Lithuania: Lietuvos Gyventojų Genocidas ir Rezistencijos Tyrimo Centras [Lithuanian Genocide and Resistance Research Centre], 2011).

Chapter Sixteen: A Slaughter of Innocents

1.   Damijonas Riauka, personal interview, June 2013.

2.   Damijonas Riauka, "Karas Prasidės Rytoj" [The War Will Start Tomorrow], *Kauno Tiesa* [Kaunas Truth], June 22, 1991.

3.   Riauka personal interview.

Chapter Seventeen: A Maze of Alibis

1.   Damijonas Riauka, "Karas Prasidės Rytoj" [The War Will Start Tomorrow], *Kauno Tiesa* [Kaunas Truth], June 22, 1991.

2.   Ibid.

3.   Pilypas Narutis, *Lithuanian Uprising 1941, Struggle for Independence, Caught between Nazi-German and Soviet Empire* (Saline, Michigan: McNaughton & Gunn, 1994), 335–36.

4. Joseph Levinson, *ŠOA Holokaustas Lietuvoje: Skaitiniai I dalis* [Shoah Holocaust in Lithuania: Essays Part I] (Vilnius, Lithuania: Valstybinis Vilniaus Gaono Žydu Muziejus [Vilna Gaon Jewish State Museum], 2001).
5. Damijonas Riauka, personal interview, June 2013.

Chapter Eighteen: Lost Credit
1. Joseph Levinson, *ŠOA Holokaustas Lietuvoje: Skaitiniai I dalis* [Shoah Holocaust in Lithuania: Essays Part I] (Vilnius, Lithuania: Valstybinis Vilniaus Gaono Žydu Muziejus [Vilna Gaon Jewish State Museum], 2001).

Chapter Nineteen: Murder and Celebration
1. Damijonas Riauka, *Pasakojimai apie Generola Vėtra, Lietuvos Radijo ir Televizijos Laidos* [Stories about General Vėtra, Lithuanian Radio and TV Broadcasts] (Kaunas, Lithuania: Atmintis, 1994).
2. Damijonas Riauka, "Karas Prasidės Rytoj" [The War Will Start Tomorrow], *Kauno Tiesa* [Kaunas Truth], June 22, 1991.
3. Albinas Kijauskas and Damijonas Riauka, *Sukilėliai, Mardosų Kuopa: 1941 Metų Birželio 21–25 Dienų* [Uprisers, Mardosu Troop: June 21–25, 1941] (Kaunas, Lithuania: Atmintis, 1998, reprinted 2005).
4. Damijonas Riauka, *Iškilmės Žemaitijoje Minint Jonas Noreikos—Generolo Vėtros 85-ąjį Gimtadienį 1995: Jis Taip Mylėjo Lietuvą* [Celebrations in Žemaitija Remembering Jonas Noreika—General Storm on his 85th Birthday 1995: He So Loved Lithuania] (Kaunas, Lithuania: Atmintis, 1975).

Chapter Twenty: The Blood Libel
1. HuntleyFilmArchives, "Nazi Germany Invades Memel in 1939. Archive Film 91545," YouTube, July 30, 2018, https://www.youtube.com/watch?v=LtQIcRDqoz4.
2. "The Jewish Community of Klaipeda," The Museum of the Jewish People at Beit Hatfutsot, https://dbs.bh.org.il/place/memel-klaipeda.

Chapter Twenty-One: A Privileged Status in Hell
1. Balys Sruoga, *Forest of the Gods* (Vilnius, Lithuania: Vaga, 1996), translated into English by the author's granddaughter, Aušrinė Byla.
2. Stasys Yla, *A Priest in Stutthof: Human Experiences in the World of Subhuman* [sic] (New York: Manyland Books. 1971).
3. Sruoga, *Forest of the Gods*.
4. Ibid.

5. Stasys Yla, *Žmonės ir Žvėrys* [Men and Monsters] (Mahopac, New York: Putnam Sisters Press, 1951).
6. Jonas Noreika, personal correspondence, letters from Stutthof 1943–1945.
7. Yla, *Žmonės ir Žvėrys.*
8. Sruoga, *Forest of the Gods.*
9. Ibid.
10. Alisa Rupšienė, *Hell's Gates—Stutthof* (Vilnius, Lithuania: Lithuanian Genocide and Resistance Research Centre, 1998).
11. Sruoga, *Forest of the Gods.*
12. Ibid.
13. Ibid.
14. Yla, *A Priest in Stutthof.*
15. Sruoga, *Forest of the Gods.*
16. A. Gervydas, *Beyond the Barbed Wire* (Chicago: Lithuanian Catholic Press Association, 1950).
17. Sruoga, *Forest of the Gods.*
18. Ibid.
19. Yla, *Žmonės ir Žvėrys.*
20. Ibid.
21. Noreika, personal correspondence.
22. Sruoga, *Forest of the Gods.*
23. Yla, *A Priest in Stutthof.*
24. Ibid.
25. Noreika, personal correspondence.
26. Ibid.

Chapter Twenty-Two: A Torrent of Questions

1. Jonas Noreika, personal correspondence, letters from Stutthof, 1943–1945.
2. Ibid.
3. Ibid.
4. Viktoras Ašmenskas, *Generolas Vėtra* [General Storm] (Vilnius, Lithuania: Lietuvos Gyventojų Genocido ir Rezistencijos Tyrimo Centras [Lithuanian Genocide and Resistance Research Centre], 1997).
5. Noreika, personal correspondence.
6. Janina Grabowska-Chalka, *Guide Historical Information Stutthof* (Muzeum Stutthof w Sztutowie, 2011).
7. Ibid.
8. Ašmenskas, *Generolas Vėtra.*
9. Noreika, personal correspondence.

10. Pilypas Narutis, *Tautos Sukilimas 1941* [Nation's Uprising 1941] (Saline, Michigan: McNaughton & Gunn, Inc., 1994).
11. Ašmenskas, *Generolas Vėtra*.
12. Noreika, personal correspondence.
13. Viktoras, *Generolas Vėtra*.
14. Balys Sruoga, *Forest of the Gods* (Vilnius, Lithuania: Vaga, 1996), translated into English by his granddaughter, Aušrinė Byla.
15. Stasys Yla, *A Priest in Stutthof: Human Experiences in the World of Subhuman* [sic] (New York: Manyland Books, 1971).
16. Sruoga, *Forest of the Gods*.
17. Grabowska-Chalka, *Guide*.
18. Ibid.

Chapter Twenty-Three: The Candle That Went Out

1. Jacob Yosef Bunka, "Historical Beginnings of Jewish Settlement in Plungyan (Plunge)," JewishGen website, www.jewishgen.org/yizkor/ plunge/plu001.html. See also the information about the 1923 census in "Plungė," Vikipedija (Lithuanian-language Wikipedia), https:// lt.wikipedia.org/wiki/Plung%C4%97.
2. Yet other Lithuanians were grateful to receive credit. And, while Jewish moneylenders often refused to conduct further business with delinquent borrowers, they rarely, if ever, foreclosed.
3. Aledsandras Pakalniškis, *Plungė* (Chicago: M. Morkūno Spaustuvė, 1980), 35–49, available online at https://silviafoticom.files.wordpress.com/2018/12/ PakalniskisPlunge.pdf.
4. Dana Nausėdas, personal interview, July 2013.

Chapter Twenty-Four: Pilgrimage

1. The Knights of Lithuania, Our Lady of Šiluva website, https://www. ourladyofsiluva.org/our_lady/Web.
2. Jonas Noreika, *Pakelk galva, lietuvi!!!* [Raise your head, Lithuanian!!!] (Kaunas, Lithuania: V. Atkočiūnos paustuvė, 1933).
3. G. Erslavaitė, *Masinės Žudynės Lietuvoje 1941–1944* [Mass Slaughter in Lithuania 1941–1944] (Vilnius, Lithuania: Mintis, 1973).

Chapter Twenty-Five: A Desperate Rationale

1. Jonas Noreika interrogation, Case #9792, KGB transcripts, March 16, 1946– February 1947, Lithuanian Special Archives, vol. 1, pp. 125–29, translated

from Russian to Lithuanian by Damijonas Riauka in 1997 and from Lithuanian to English by the author.

2. "Lietuvos okupacija (1940 m. birzelio 15 d.)" [Lithuania's Occupation June 15, 1940], Lietuvos Respublikos Seimas [Lithuanian Republic Parliament], https://www.lrs.lt/sip/portal.show?p_r=7365&p_k=1.

3. See *The Chronicle of the Catholic Church in Lithuania* 44 (July 30, 1980), http://www.lkbkronika.lt/index.php/en/issue-no-44.

4. Of these, 2,000 were Jews and 1,500 were Poles. Juozas Prunskis, *Lietuviai Sibire* [Lithuanians in Siberia] (Chicago: Lithuanian Library Press, 1981); A. Anusauskas, "International Commission on Nazi and Soviet Occupational Regimes' Victims of Crime in Lithuania Estimates. June 14–18 1941: Banishments to Siberia," https://www.komisija.lt/wp-content/uploads/2016/06/A.-Anu%C5%A1auskas-%E2%80%9E1941-...-tr%C4%97mimai%E2%80%9C.-Patvirtintos-i%C5%A1vados.pdf.

Chapter Twenty-Six: Exile

1. Kestutis Pūkelis, *Leiskitį Tėvyne: Tremtinių Atsiminimai* [Let Us into the Fatherland: Memories of the Exiled], (Kaunas, Lithuania: Šviesa, 1989).

2. See this entry at Lithuanian-language Wikipedia for a photograph showing one such mountain passage: "Altajaus rezervatas," Vikipedija, https://lt.wikipedia.org/wiki/Altajaus_rezervatas.

3. Arimantas Dumčius, "Tautos Sovietinis Genocidas—Kasmetinis Altajaus Krašto ir Šiaurės Jakutijos Tremtinių Susitikimas" [The Nation's Soviet Genocide—Annual Meeting of the Altajaus Region and Northern Jakutijos Exiled] (brochure), December 23, 2011.

4. Joseph Melamed, "The Malicious Face and Criminal Acts of the 'Provisional Government' of Lithuania. June 23–August 5, 1941," in *Lithuania: Crime & Punishment* (Tel Aviv: Association of the Lithuanian Jews in Israel, January 1999), pp. 36–41.

5. Virginija Rudiene, ed., *Lietuvos gyventojai lageriuose ir tremtyje, 2 knyga —1944–1953* [Lithuania's Residents in the Camps and in Exile, Second Book—1944–1953] (Lithuanian National Museum, 2018) contains the following statistics: 14,000 deported in 1941 and another 118,000 deported between 1945 and 1953 (none were deported during the Nazi occupation), resulting in a total of 132,000. Of these, 28,000 (21 percent) perished. A further 50,000 (comprising nearly 40 percent) did not return to Lithuania, or did not do so until much later. Thus, roughly 54,000 people (40 percent) returned to Lithuania as soon as they were able to do so; see also https://

www.delfi.lt/news/daily/lithuania/jei-ne-okupacijos-lietuva-turetu-
5-mln-gyventoju.d?id=13516063.

Chapter Twenty-Seven: Playing for Power

1. Alfonsas Eidintas, *Jews, Lithuanians and the Holocaust* (Vilnius, Lithuania: Institute of International Relations and Political Science, Vilnius University, 2012).
2. Ilona Limantienė, personal interview, July 2013.
3. The Lithuanian Activist Front declared independence and selected the ministers who composed the Provisional Government of Lithuania (*Laikinoji Vyriausybė*), which then appointed Noreika and others.
4. In fact, the Provisional Government suspended its activity and disbanded on August 5, 1941, believing that it was pointless to continue after the introduction of the German civil administration of the occupation. Noreika replaced Ignas Urbaitis, who had stepped down.
5. Viktoras Ašmenskas, *Generolas Vėtra* [General Storm] (Vilnius, Lithuania: Lietuvos Gyventojų Genocido ir Rezistencijos Tyrimo Centras [Lithuanian Genocide and Resistance Research Centre], 1997).
6. A page dated July 27 explicitly advocates ethnic cleansing. The nominal editor, Vladas Pauža, was in Kaunas at the time. The actual editor was Algirdas Julius Greimas, who became a renowned semiotician.
7. Josifas Levinsonas, *ŠOA Hokokaustas Lietuvoje: Skaitiniai I dalis* [Shoah Holocaust in Lithuania: Essays Part I] (Vilnius, Lithuania: Valstybinis Vilniaus Gaono Žydu Muziejus [Vilna Gaon Jewish State Museum], 2001.)
8. Ibid.
9. Josef Rosin, "Šiauliai," in *Encyclopedia of Jewish Communities in Lithuania* (Jerusalem: Yad Vashem, 1996).
10. G. Erslavaite, *Masinės Žudynės Lietuvoje 1941–1944* [Mass Slaughter in Lithuania 1941–1944] (Vilnius, Lithuania: Mintis, 1973).
11. Evaldas Balčiūnas, "The Posthumous Remaking of a Holocaust Perpetrator in Lithuania: Why is Jonas Noreika a National Hero?" Defending History, June 13, 2014, https://defendinghistory.com/posthumous-remaking-of-a-holocaust-perpetrator-in-lithuania-why-is-jonas-noreika-a-national-hero-by-evaldas-balciunas/31531.
12. Erslavaite, *Masinės Žudynės.*
13. Jewish and "Bolshevik" property was inventoried and assessed as being worth 5.8 million rubles (equivalent to $18.3 million today). The official Soviet exchange rate was: 1 ruble = $0.19. Consequently, 5.8 million rubles were equal to nearly 1.1 million dollars. Today, those dollars would be

worth $16.67 each. See "Value of $100 from 1941 to 2017," CPI Inflation Calculator, http://www.in2013dollars.com/1941-dollars-in-2017.

14. Šiauliai archives on Jonas Noreika, 1941.

15. Ibid.

16. "Kryžių Kalno Naikinimai" [Hill of Crosses destruction], Kryžių Kalnas [Hill of Crosses], Catholic Internet Council, 2008, http://www.kryziukalnas.lt/apie/sovietmeciu/naikinimai/.

17. Vanda Sruogiene, "Lietuvos Ikaitai Stutthofe ir Ju Likimas" [Lithuania's Hostages in Stutthof and Their Destiny], *Draugas*, January 10, 1981, part 2, front page.

18. Jonas Noreika interrogation, Case #9792, KGB transcripts, March 16, 1946– February 1947, Lithuanian Special Archives, vol. 1, p. 128.

Chapter Twenty-Eight: Germany's Fifth Column

1. Viktoras Ašmenskas, *Generolas Vėtra* [General Storm] (Vilnius, Lithuania: Lietuvos Gyventojų Genocido ir Rezistencijos Tyrimo Centras [Lithuanian Genocide and Resistance Research Centre], 1997).

2. The Lithuanian Activist Front was active in 1940 and 1941, until the Nazis shut it down. Subsequently, some of its members—mostly Catholic Democrats—started the Lithuanian Front (Lietuvių frontas), which was part of the anti-Nazi underground.

3. Arunas Bubnys, "Kiek žinau, vienintelis toks kartas buvo 1944 m. vasarą kažkur prie Platelių ežero Žemaitijoje, kai LLA susidūrė su vokiečiais, bet aukų, berods, tuomęt nebuvo. Lietuvių antinacinė rezistencija vokiečių atžvilgiu laikėsi neginkluotos kovos taktikos" [To my knowledge, the only time was in the summer of 1944, somewhere by Plateliu lake in Zemaitija, when the LLA (Lithuanian Freedom Army) met with the Germans, but it seems that there were no deaths at the time. The Lithuanian anti-Nazi resistance did not involve any weapons against the Germans], personal letter dated October 22, 2018, to Andrius Kulikauskas. Bubnys was a historian at the Genocide Centre.

4. Josifas Levinsonas, *ŠOA Holokaustas Lietuvoje: Skaitiniai I dalis* [Shoah Holocaust in Lithuania: Essays, Part I] (Vilnius, Lithuania: Valstybinis Vilniaus Gaono Žydu Muziejus [Vilna Gaon Jewish State Museum], 2001).

5. The Žemaičių Legionas appears to have been related to the Lithuanian Freedom Army. See "Lla Žemaičių Legionas. A. Kubiliaus Grupė," Partizanai: Istorija ir dabartis [Partisans: History and the Present] website, http://www.partizanai.org/

laisves-kovu-archyvas-14-t-1995-m/3515-lla-zemaiciu-legionas-a-kubiliaus-grupe. The Vanagai were part of the Lithuanian Freedom Army. See "Lietuvos laisvės armija" [Lithuania's Freedom Army], Vikipedija [Lithuanian-language Wikipedia], https://lt.wikipedia.org/wiki/Lietuvos_laisv%C4%97s_armija.

6. Lietuvos Gyventojų Genocido ir Rezistencijos Tyrimo Centras [Lithuanian Genocide and Resistance Research Centre], December 14, 2013.

7. Damijonas Riauka, *Pasakojimai apie Generola Vėtra, Lietuvos Radijo ir Televizijos Laidos* [Stories about General Vėtra, Lithuanian Radio and TV Broadcasts] (Kaunas, Lithuania: Atmintis, 1994); Damijonas Riauka, *Iškilmės Žemaitijoje Minint Jonas Noreikos—Generolo Vėtros 85-ąjį Gimtadienį 1995: Jis Taip Mylėjo Lietuvą* [Celebrations in Žemaitija Remembering Jonas Noreika—General Storm on His 85th Birthday 1995: He So Loved Lithuania] (Kaunas, Lithuania: Atmintis, 1995).

8. Quoted in the diary of Zenonas Blynas, general secretary of the Lithuanian Nationalist Party (LNP), LYA, F. 3377, Ap. 55, b. 235, l. 150–52.

9. Gediminas Rudis, *Zenonas Blynas Karo Metų Dienoraštis 1941–1944* [Zenonas Blynas Wartime Diary 1941–1944] (Vilnius, Lithuania: Lietuvos Istorijos Institutas, 2007).

10. A. Kalnis, *Teviškės Žiburiai* (1982). Gurevičius, who worked for Jonas Noreika, claims that my grandfather supported this foster home and thus—presumably unwittingly—was saving the Jews hiding there. The fact that this was the best example that Gurevičius could provide of Noreika's helping Jews speaks for itself; there was no evidence of his ever having done so knowingly. Burauskaitė herself removed this purported example from her revision of Gurevičius's lists.

11. Although a newspaper states that he assumed his post on August 4, 1941, other documents declare that Noreika was appointed by Jonas Šlepetys on August 3 in the name of the provisional government and that Noreika succeeded Ignas Urbaitis.

12. Arūnas Bubnys, "Holocaust in Lithuania: An Outline of the Major Stages and Their Results," in Stefan Schreiner and Leonidas Donskis, *The Vanished World of Lithuanian Jews* (Amsterdam; New York: Rodopi, 2004), pp. 218–19; Dina Parat, "The Holocaust in Lithuania: Some Unique Aspects" in David Cesarani, *The Final Solution: Origins and Implementation* (London: Routledge, 2002), pp. 161–62.

13. Ašmenskas, *Generolas Vėtra*.

14. Damijonas Riauka, personal interview, June 2013.

15. Riauka, *Pasakojimai apie*; Riauka, *Iškilmės*.

Chapter Twenty-Nine: The Death of Denial

1. Evaldas Balčiūnas, "The Posthumous Remaking of a Holocaust Perpetrator in Lithuania: Why is Jonas Noreika a National Hero?" Defending History, March 1, 2012, https://defendinghistory.com/ posthumous-remaking-of-a-holocaust-perpetrator-in-lithuania-why-is- jonas-noreika-a-national-hero-by-evaldas-balciunas/31531.

Chapter Thirty: A Holocaust Map

1. Jonas Noreika interrogation, Case #9792, KGB transcripts, March 16, 1946– February 1947, Lithuanian Special Archives, vol. 1, p. 128, translated from Russian to Lithuanian by Damijonas Riauka in 1997 and from Lithuanian to English by the author.

2. "Holocaust Exposition," Vilniaus Gaono žydų istorijos muziejus [Vilna Gaon Jewish State Museum], http://www.jmuseum.lt/en/ holocaust-exhibition/.

3. For instance, the Germans had recommended that Lithuanians use the following euphemistic terms: *siunčiama*: "sent away"; *išvedama*: "sent away"; *sutvarkyti*: "arrange." Alex Faitelson, *The Truth and Nothing but the Truth: Jewish Resistance in Lithuania* (Jerusalem: Gefen Publishing House, 2006), 165.

4. The Jäger Report appears to misspell the name "Hamann" as "Hamman." Every other available source gives his name as "Hamann," including Yitzhak Arad, *The Holocaust in the Soviet Union* (Lincoln, Nebraska: University of Nebraska Press, 2009): "In his Report, Karl Jäger wrote, 'The goal of clearing Lithuania of Jews could only be achieved through the establishment of a specially mobile unit, under the command of Obersturmführer Hamann who...was also able to ensure the cooperation of the Lithuanian partisans and the relevant civil authorities.'"

5. Karl Jäger, "The Jäger Report," A Teacher's Guide to the Holocaust, 2005, https://fcit.usf.edu/holocaust/resource/document/DocJager.htm.

6. Before the mass murder of Plungė's 1,800 Jews on July 12–13, 1941, roughly 2,500 Jewish men had been killed at Kauen Fort VII (Kaunas Fortress). Other mass murders of hundreds of Jewish men, by the Tilsit (Tilžė) Einsatzkommando, had taken place in Lithuania's border towns, such as Gargždai, Palanga, and Kretinga.

7. As Simon points out, the Jäger Report notes that 4,000 Jews were killed before the EK 3 commenced its *Akcijas*. To account for the deaths of the other 2,000 Jews included in that figure, I have assumed that the number of

Jews killed in Telšiai before the EK 3 *Akcijas* also was around 2,000.
According to several online sources, in 1940 Telšiai's Jewish population was
2,800, comprising 48 percent of the city's entire population. See, for
example, Yad Vashem, "Telšiai," The Untold Stories, https://www.
yadvashem.org/untoldstories/database/index.asp?cid=555.

8. Vincas Bartusevičius, Joachim Tauber, and Wolfram Wette, *Jägers Karriere in der SS 1936–1941: Holocaust in Litauen: Krieg, Judenmorde und Kollaboration im Jahre 1941* (Cologne, Germany: Böhlau Verlag, 2003), pp. 80–82.

9. "Karl Jaeger," Yad Vashem website, https://www.yadvashem.org/untoldstories/hyperlinks/karl_jaeger.html.

10. Ibid.

11. Peisachas Freidhamas, *Lietuva Antrajame Pasauliniame Kare 1935–1945* [Lithuania in the Second World War 1935–1945] (Vilnius, Lithuania: Politika, 2008).

12. This fact may be accounted for as follows: At the top of the report, it is stated: "The Wilna [Vilnius] area was taken over by EK 3 on 9 Aug. 1941, the Schaulen area on 2 Oct. 1941. Up until these dates EK 9 operated in Wilna and EK 2 in Schaulen." Thus, it was EK 2 that was in charge of Plungė and Telšiai.

13. Viktoras Ašmenskas, *Generolas Vėtra* [General Storm] (Vilnius, Lithuania: Lietuvos Gyventojų Genocido ir Rezistencijos Tyrimo Centras [Lithuanian Genocide and Resistance Research Centre], 1997).

14. Vrublevskių is best known as the founder of the library. See "Istorija" [History], Lietuvos Mosklu Adademijos Vrublevskių Biblioteka [Lithuanian Academy of Sciences Wroblewski Library], http://www.mab.lt/lt/apie-biblioteka/istorija.

15. Zigmas Laukaitis interrogation, KGB transcripts, March 16, 1946–February 1947, Lithuanian Special Archives, vol. 4, pp. 200–222, translated from Russian to Lithuanian by Damijonas Riauka in 1997 and from Lithuanian to English by the author.

16. Noreika interrogation, Case #9792, vol. 1, p. 17.

17. Gediminas Rudis, *Zenonas Blynas Karo Metų Dienoraštis 1941–1944* [Zenonas Blynas Wartime Diary 1941–1944] (Vilnius, Lithuania: Lietuvos Istorijos Institutas, 2007).

18. Yosef Rosin, "Telz (Telšiai)," Jewishgen.org, https://kehilalinks.jewishgen.org/telz/telz3.html.

19. See the Jäger Report and "Kaunas Massacre of 29 October 1941," VilNews, http://vilnews.com/2012-12-18261.

20. An ironic counterpoint: Kipras Petrauskas, the tenor singer and one of the founders of the National Lithuanian Opera, lived, during the years of the German occupation, in Kaunas, with his wife Elena Žalinkevičaite Petrauskienė, a well-known actress and poet. In the spring of 1942, Petrauskas was asked to provide shelter for a six-month-old Dana Pomeranz, the daughter of violinist Daniel Pomeranz, a famous musician in a pre-war Lithuania. Petrauskas and his wife gave their agreement, and one day a baby girl was smuggled from the ghetto and brought to the Petrauskases' home. Since the Petrauskas family was rather famous in Lithuania and many people were interested in their private life, giving shelter to a Jewish baby was enormously risky for them. So, after a short while they chose to leave the city. Together with the Jewish infant and their own three children, the Petrauskases moved first to a village, then, in 1944, to Austria and later to Germany. Throughout all these moves, the Petrauskases treated little Dana with warmth and devotion. In 1947, when they returned to Lithuania, the Petrauskases located Dana's parents and returned their daughter to them safe and sound. Dana remained in close touch with her rescuers, regarding them as a second set of parents. Like her biological father, Dana Pomeranz-Mazurkevich became a violinist. "Kipras Petrauskas and Elena Žalinkevičaite-Petrauskienė," Yad Vashem, https://www.yadvashem.org/righteous/stories/petrauskas-zalinkevicaite.html.

Chapter Thirty-One: Interview at the Museum of Genocide Victims

1. G. Erslavaitė, E. Rozauskas, Kazys Rukšnas, and Boleslovas Baranauskas, *Masinės Žudynės Lietuvoje 1941–1944* [Mass Slaughter in Lithuania, 1941–1944)] (Vilnius, Lithuania: Mintis, 1973).

2. Teresė Birutė Burauskaitė, director general of the Genocide and Resistance Research Centre of Lithuania, at the Museum of Genocide Victims, "Lithuania Renames Museum of Genocide Victims," Baltic Course, April 19, 2018, http://www.baltic-course.com/eng/baltic_news/?doc=19321&output=d; "Lithuania to Rename Museum of Genocide Victims after Lengthy Discussions," Defli.en, September 8, 2017, http://defendinghistory.com/wp-content/uploads/2017/03/Lithuania-to-rename-Museum-of-Genocide-Victims-after-lengthy-discussions-EN.pdf; "The Museum of Genocide Victims, Situated in the Former KGB Building in Vilnius, Has Been Renamed the Museum of Occupation and Freedom

Fighters," Delfi.en, April 19, 2018, https://en.delfi.lt/culture/
lithuania-renames-museum-of-genocide-victims.d?id=77759729.

Chapter Thirty-Two: The Mud Pits

1. Aleksandras Pakalniškis Jr., *Praeities Atgarsiai* [Echoes from the Past]
   (Chicago, Illinois: M. Morkūno spaustuvė, 1988).
2. Julius Norwilla, "The Twelve Holocaust Mass Murder Sites in the Vilnius
   Region," Defending History, September 18, 2016, http://defendinghistory.
   com/the-twelve-holocaust-mass-murder-sites-in-the-vilnius-region/83863.
3. While the plaque cites the number 1,800, Jakovas Bunka claims—as we
   shall see later in this chapter—that 2,234 Jews from Plungė were murdered.
   Adam B. Ellick, "The Last Jew in the Lithuanian Village of Plunge Has
   Made It His Life's Work to Commemorate the Jews Killed There in War
   World II—and to Remind Locals of Their Past Deeds," Jakovo Bunkas,
   http://jbfund.lt/the-last-jew-in-the-lithuanian-
   village-of-plunge-has-made-it-his-lifes-work-to-commemorate-the-jews-
   killed-there-in-war-world-ii-and-to-remind-locals-of-their-past-deeds/.
4. Bunka says in his memoir that there were 138 Jews in Plungė in 1938.
   Twenty years later, there were 45 Jews. He was the last survivor. Jacob
   Bunka, "Plungyan," United States Holocaust Memorial Museum, accession
   number 2004.417, https://collections.ushmm.org/search/catalog/irn522008.
5. Jakovas Bunka, *Jakovas Bunka* (Plungė, Lithuania: Viešoji Įstaiga
   Tautodailininkų Sąjungos Fondas [Public Institution Fund of Folk Artists
   Union], 2013).
6. Bunka served in the Sixteenth Division of the Soviet army, fighting the
   Nazis. Nominally the Lithuanian division, it was composed predominantly
   of Jews and Russians.
7. Ellick, "The Last Jew."
8. Rūta Budrytė, personal interview, July 2013.
9. Bronislovas Pocius, personal interview, July 2013; Bronislovas Pocius,
   "Plungės Žydų Bendruomenė," *Plungės Žinios*, July 12, 2013.
10. Bunka, *Jakovas Bunka.*
11. Ibid.
12. Ibid.
13. Ibid.
14. Ibid.
15. Aleksandras Pakalniškis, *Plungė* (Chicago, Illinois: M. Morkūno
    spaustuvė, 1980); Pakalniškis, *Praeities Atgarsiai.*
16. Pakalniškis, *Plungė.*

17. Bunka, *Jakovas Bunka*.

18. Ibid.

19. Ibid.

20. This scene was reconstructed from several sources: Interview with
     Monika Lučinskienė, United States Holocaust Memorial Museum,
     RG-50.473*0123; Interview with Konstancija Bidviene, United States
     Holocaust Memorial Museum, RG-50.473.0069; Julija Kiškienė,
     "Kausenai: An Interview with Konstancija Kardinskaite-Bidviene,"
     Teviškė, April 22, 1998, United States Holocaust Memorial Museum;
     Bunka, *Plungyan*. A memorial plaque for these seventy-six maidens was
     placed at the entrance of the Kaušėnai site in Plungė on June 18, 2019.

21. Pakalniškis published several memoirs, at least four of which describe
     these events in detail. The most detailed is Aleksandar Pakalniškis,
     Septintoji Knyga [The Seventh Book].

Chapter Thirty-Three: Killing Ground

1.   Josef Rosin, "'Siauliai'–Encyclopedia of Jewish Communities in Lithuania,"
     Translation of the "Siauliai" chapter from *Pinkas Hakehillot Lita*,
     JewishGen, https://www.jewishgen.org/yizkor/pinkas_lita/lit_00658c.
     html; "Šiaulių getas: Kalinių sąrašai 1941" [The Šiaulių Ghetto: List of
     Prisoners 1941] (Vilnius, Lithuania: Valstybinės Vilniaus Gaono žydų
     muziejus [Vilna Gaon Jewish State Museum], 2002), pp. 52–70; The Shavli
     Ghetto, Association of Lithuanian Jews in Israel, November 27, 2013.

2.   Rosin, "'Šiauliai'"; "Šiaulių getas"; The Shavli Ghetto.

3.   Ibid.

4.   Ibid.

5.   Ibid.

6.   G. Erslavaite, *Masinės Žudynės Lietuvoje 1941–1944* [Mass Slaughter in
     Lithuania 1941–1944] (Vilnius, Lithuania: Mintis, 1973).

7.   Josifas Levinsonas, *ŠOA Hokokaustas Lietuvoje: Skaitiniai I dalis* [Shoah
     Holocaust in Lithuania: Essays Part I] (Vilnius, Lithuania: Valstybinis
     Vilniaus Gaono Žydu Muziejus [Vilna Gaon Jewish State Museum], 2001.)

8.   Rose Zwi, *Last Walk in Naryshkin Park* (North Melbourne, Australia:
     Spinifex Press, 1997).

9.   Ibid.

10. Ibid.

11. Levinsonas, *ŠOA Holokaustas Lietuvoje*.

12. Vaidas Reivytis, *Saulėleidis Lietuvoje* [Sunset in Lithuania] (film), 2000.

Chapter Thirty-Four: A Stolen House

1. The house's address has remained the same: Vaižganto g. 11 (although in the Google image the street name appears as J. Tumo-Vaižganto g.).

2. Aliza Cohen-Mushlin et al. *Synagogues in Lithuania, A Catalogue* (Vilnius, Lithuania: Academy of Arts Press, 2012).

3. In the Google image, taken in 2012, the house is flanked by a patch of grass and trees on one side and by a small parking lot on the other. About the black and white photo above, researcher Andrius Kulikauskas told me, "I spoke by phone with Zita and then [with] Bronislavas just now. They both confirmed that the Noreikas lived in the rightmost house. Zita said the photo was from Bronislavas. He said the photo was taken in the 1950s. He says that the reason no window can be seen in the photo on the side of the house that faces the Kromas is because he thinks the window was boarded up after the war. Which is to say, there was a window before the war and in 1941. Later, the window got boarded up, and then it was fixed again. The Kromas is a bit uphill. But you can see the window in this link https://google/maps/v1sAmvtAN5N2."

Chapter Thirty-Five: Acts of Remembrance

1. The monument pictured here lists the victims' names: http://alkas.lt/wp-content/uploads/2014/06/BZN_Rainiai_chapel_back_board.jpg. A seventy-fifth victim, Georgijus Kiriličevas, is included in the Genocide Centre's list of seventy-five bodies found at Rainiai. Apparently, he was not included in the list on the monument because of his Russian name. See "Versija spausdinimui Žudynės Rainių miškelyje," Lietuvos gyventojų genocido ir rezistencijos tyrimo centras, http://genocid.lt/centras/lt/1378/a/. Three Red Army soldiers were found not far away, evidently executed. Additionally, three Lithuanians who had escaped from prison that night were caught and killed near the village of Džiuginėnų. Consequently, tallies of the number of victims vary. See *Pamirštas SSRS karo nusikaltimas Rainiai 1941 06 24–25* [Forgotten USSR War Crime in Rainiai], 2nd ed. (Vilnius, Lithuania: 2007), available at http://www.partizanai.org/failai/html/rainiai-1941-06-24-25.htm. Some of the men were alleged to have been in possession of guns or dynamite. The decision as to which were "political" prisoners (who then were killed) and which were not (and who therefore were not killed) was made immediately before the executions. One family offered an account that is available online. See Antanas Baužys, "Plungės Gimnasistai Laisvės Kovoje: 1941 M. Sukilimas," Partizanai: Istorija ir dabartis, http://www.partizanai.org/

laisves-kovu-archyvas-25-t-1999/3711-plunges-gimnazistai-laisves-kovoje. A newspaper account states that the victims' bodies were discovered the following day, June 25, while the Genocide Centre asserts that they were found on June 28. A Dr. Plechavičius recorded the results of their exhumation. See J. Padaubietis, *Telšių Kankinai 1941* [Martyrs from Telšiai], first published in Pittsburgh in 1949 and available online at http://www. partizanai.org/failai/html/telsiu-kankiniai.htm. Many of the victims were found to have been mutilated, apparently subsequent to their deaths. For more information about Rainiai, please see *Rainių Tragedija: 1941 M Birželio 24 25 D.*, available at http://www.partizanai.org/failai/html/rainiu-tragedija. htm.

2. They also claimed that the gruesome murders were evidence of the Soviet Communist regime's pathological nature. Such narratives were intended to incite local hatred against Communists and Jews and to provide Lithuanians with a pretext for rounding them up. Later, these "explanations" served, nationally, both to disguise and to legitimize the mass murder of Jews. After the war, they were useful in blaming the Jews and in vilifying the Soviet regime.

3. "Rainiai Massacre," Wikipedia, https://en.wikipedia.org/wiki/ Rainiai_massacre.

4. A letter in the Lithuanian Genocide and Resistance Research Centre's archives indicates that he had arrived on June 24, 1941. Kazys Šilgalis writes that Jonas Noreika left for Telšiai on June 24. LGGRTC 12.17.Š-135. In any case, it is a short ride from Plungė to Telšiai.

5. A report of the funeral in the local newspaper, *Žemaičių žemė*, is available online at http://www.partizanai.org/failai/html/rainiai-1941-06-24-25.htm.

6. All the Jews of Telšiai had been forced to leave their homes on June 27, 1941. Their houses were robbed. The women and children were permitted to return to stay overnight; the men were marched to Rainiai. On the following day, LAF (Lithuanian Activist Front) members assembled the women and children, forcing them to walk to Rainiai. There, the men were murdered on July 15–17. A week later, the women and children were forced from Rainiai to Geruliai. From there, about five young Jewish women were sent to the Telšiai ghetto and then to the forest, where they were shot. The 1,600–4,000 women and children remaining in Geruliai were murdered two days later, on August 30. See Aleksandras Vitkus and Chaimas Bargmanas, "The Fate of the Jews in the Small Ghetto of Telsiai," *Genocide and Resistance* 2, no. 34 (2013), p. 10.

7. The inscription is in both Yiddish and Lithuanian: "Įrašas, Čia buvo pralietas apie 7000 žydų—vyrų, moterų ir vaikų kraujas. Juos 1941 metais žiauriai žudė nacistinia ibudeliai ir jų vietiniai talkininkai jidiš ir lietuvių kalbomis." Roughly translated, it says, "Here, about 7,000 Jews—men, women and children—were brutally murdered in the year 1941 by Nazi bullets and by local assistants." Vitkus and Bargmanas, "The Fate of the Jews," 100.

8. According to the website Yad Vashem, "From June 1941 until July 1944, over 75,000 people were murdered in Ponary [Paneriai], most of whom were Jewish[;] the others were Soviet prisoners of war and local opponents to the Nazi regime. The victims were brought to the murder site on foot, by motor vehicles and by train; in groups of tens, hundreds and thousands. There, they were shot and buried." "Vilan during the Holocaust: German Occupation—June 1941," Yad Vashem, https://www.yadvashem.org/yv/en/exhibitions/vilna/during/ponary.asp.

9. "On the Vilnius Massacres," Holocaust Encyclopedia, United States Holocaust Memorial Museum, https://encyclopedia.ushmm.org/content/en/article/vilna.

Chapter Thirty-Six: Storm in the Fatherland

1. See Evaldas Balčiūnas, "My Seven Long Years with Jonas Noreika ('General Storm')," Defending History, January 13, 2019, http://defendinghistory.com/my-seven-years-in-lithuania-with-jonas-noreika-general-storm/97329.

2. Grant Arthur Gochin, "About Jonas Noreika," Letter to the Genocide and Resistance Centre, July 23, 2015, https://www.grantgochin.com/wp-content/uploads/2020/11/04_Kreipimasis-inteligentu-grupes-i-Vilniaus-mera.pdf.

INDEX